Modernisation of Social Work Education

Modernisation of Social Work Education

Pradeep Kotwal

ADHYAYAN

ADHYAYAN PUBLISHERS & DISTRIBUTORS

NEW DELHI (INDIA)

Published by

ADHYAYAN PUBLISHERS & DISTRIBUTORS
4378/4B, 105, J.M.D. House, Murari Lal Street
Ansari Road Darya Ganj, New Delhi - 110002
Ph.: 011-23263018, 011-23277156, Fax: 011-23280028
Email: adhyayanpublishers@yahoo.com

Modernisation of Social Work Education

Edition 2011
ISBN 978-81-8435-230-6

Printed in India

Published by Harish Chandra Yadav for Adhyayan Publishers & Distributors, Laser Typeseting at A.V. Rao and Printed at Tarun Offset Printers, Delhi

Preface

Social work has always been characterised by multiple roles and identities. The directions for where these roles are enacted, which knowledges are utilised, how power and authority are distributed and what meanings are accorded social justice are, at this point in time, both anxiety-producing and deeply contestable. Of itself, this is healthy and is paralleled in education. In education, however, the contest is not out on the table. Until the issues are debated, social work educators cannot claim a powerful collective voice for their constituencies.

In light of the extensive theoretical and professional diversity in a context of economic markets and political conservatism, where social work is flighting to consolidate new roles, to create new opportunities, to appreciate the implications for practice of new theories and what are increasingly accepted as new global processes, we would argue that the idea of an essential curriculum must give way to innovation, experimentation and acceptance of these diversities. This may mean rethinking the goals, structures and outcomes of professional education.

This book explores contemporary issues in social work education. It examines formative influences on the structures and content of education, specifically the ways over time in which demographic, political, economic and social forces have influenced the composition, demand and domain of social work education and practice. It describes the current political context of social work and social work education. It will be an excellent resource for social work educators seeking to become knowledgeable about the international dimensions of their profession.

Pradeep Kotwal

Contents

1

Status of Social Work Education

Social work has always been international. Recently it has become more so; a trend that continues.

Social work education is an important focus in international social work. We have given it considerable attention for this reason. We have done so also because it is a significate context in which knowledge is developed for social work and because education is an important social structure in which social work becomes part of a globalized international market.

Social work is a product of modernism in Western states as industrialized economies developed in the late 19th century. That is, it emerged from an idealist belief that the state could overcome social problems, using science and knowledge to resolve social problems. In most countries, therefore, it is part of state services and claims a rational evidence as the basis of its practice. In rich Western countries social work is substantially part of the state: it is organized public welfare provision. This is so even where services are offered by profit or not-for-profit organizations, because they are mainly funded by states. Its commitment to science means that social work as a profession and as a way of intervening in people's lives relies on the assumption that it can develop universal knowledge. Such knowledge seeks to provide explanation and understanding about human beings, their behaviour and their society. The idea is that universal knowledge will apply to everyone, in whatever culture or society they live. Therefore, it can provide firm evidence for deciding how best to act when intervening with any human beings. Relying on a claim to universal knowledge assumes, uncritically, that such knowledge may be transferred from Western societies in which most of it is developed to societies in the South with markedly different cultures and access to resources.

In the 21st century, globalization leads to changes that challenge social work practice and education, and the idea of postmodernism challenges the validity of a universal knowledge base. This is because where societies are built on different cultural and social assumptions postmodernism raises questions about the dominance of any particular set of ideas, both generally and in social work.

Postmodernism proposes that social phenomena such as social work vary according to the social and historical context in which they operate. An international social work, therefore, raises questions about whether Western models of social work practice and organization are universal in their application.

Among the most important consequences of the development of postmodern, globalized social works is inequality within and across societies. This is important because inequalities create social strains between different groups and psychological stresses for individuals. Social work has a commitment to social justice. Our experience as social workers dealing with individuals and small groups leads us to concern about the impact of the social on the personal. Social work that deals only with psychological problems fails to handle the consequences of unfairness and inequality and with social factors that lead to the problems. Social processes that create inequality and injustice constantly change. This means that practice and education need to be aware of inequalities created by new social trends, to understand them and how they affect individuals and communities.

1.1. International Social Work

Most social work students, educators and practitioners do not cross national borders in their work, so can we say that they work internationally? International social work refers to a number of different activities:

i) *Working in development agencies in the South*: Examples of development agencies might be non-governmental organizations (NGOs) like Save the Children, Caritas, and Médicin Sans

Frontiéres. Many people make careers in international agencies working in the South, or commit parts of their lives when they are young, as 'time out' or in retirement to such work. In some countries, development work in the South would not be considered social work, while elsewhere it would.

ii) *Working for official international agencies*: Examples of international agencies might include a range of United Nations agencies, the European Commission or aid departments of national governments. As with development agencies, there would be similar differences in how such work is viewed; in the United Kingdom of Great Britain and Northern Ireland (UK) and some other countries, work in such agencies would not be viewed as social work.

iii) *Working for agencies dealing with cross-national issues*: Examples might be agencies dealing with international adoption or family matters such as abduction of a child from one legal jurisdiction in family disputes. Some service user organizations, for example for disabled and mentally ill people, have staff working on international links.

iv) *Working for international social work organizations:* Examples might be the International Federation of Social Workers (IFSW) and the International Association of School of Social Work (IASSW) or people employed in countries on projects for or linking with such organizations.

v) Participating in international conferences, educational or professional visits, exchanges and placements and research;

vi) Working as a social worker in a country that is foreign to them;

vii) Working with refugees and immigrants in their own country.

In the South, social workers will often experience directly poverty, inequalities and social and personal problems that arise from the impact of globalization in their societies. Even though the average Western practitioner does not work internationally, daily practice may lead them to experience some of the local consequences of globalization: international migration, asylum seeking, and refugees. They may also experience concern about forced marriage, cultural conflicts and terrorism that are a product of the social trends of globalization. The uncertainty about how to evaluate and respond to them emerges from the impact of postmodern ideas in Western societies.

Our analysis starts from experiences in Western countries, where social work originated and developed most strongly, and where it is most firmly established. However, it is developing fast in a diverse range of other countries in Africa, China, Eastern European countries that have little connection with and reliance on Western culture and social structures. Inevitably, those developments in other countries and cultures challenge dominant Western ways of thinking about social work.

We argue for seeing this interaction in these ways:

i) Western social work is not necessarily relevant to non:Western countries and its relevance should always be challenged.

ii) Western social work should be influenced by non:Western social work, which will inevitably have different values and practices. Nevertheless, Western cultural and economic power means that we have to establish ways for it to achieve that influence.

iii) Non-Western countries should and do create their own social works, and may, but should not need to, compare them with or justify them against Western values and practices.

A worldwide view of social work might be richer if it included ideas from and perceptions in non-Western countries. For example, Graham's work on African worldviews suggests alternative perspectives on family and community that might lead Western social workers to value shared experience and collective spiritual, family and community engagement in resolving social and personal problems. Western cultural, economic and social power has given social work ideas from the West too much influences in other countries and cultures.

The fact that there are international social work organizations suggests that there is an international social work. This has been promoted over the years by an 'internationalist view' held by activists in the international social work organizations, particularly IFSW and IASSW. It may be seen, for example, in the successive reports about social work education across the world by Alice Salomon, Eileen Younghusband, and Katherine Kendall. The international view proposes that there is one diverse social work, with local variations, rather than local social works that share some common elements.

Around the millennium, the international associations began to pursue these projects by devising and promoting an international definition of social work, and international standards for education and training in social work, a significant figure in the education project, accepts that postmodernism challenges such endeavours towards a 'grand narrative' of social work. Gray suggests that there is a risk that promoting global standards for social work education may lead to Western models of practice being seen as universal ideals to be reached. She notes that it may be possible to consider an international model of practice or education as a touchstone for comparisons, without trying to gain international agreement to definition or standards.

There is evidence that alternative forms of social work are available for adoption or adaptation. This questions the internationalist view, because it says that there are different forms of social work with different cultural roots, rather than variations on a common social work. Walton and el Nasr suggested that two parallel processes of interaction between international and local forms of social work may occur:

i) *Indigenization* of non-local social work practice, by adapting imported ideas to make them relevant to local practice;

ii) *Authentization* of local practices to form a new locally-relevant structure of ideas.

Gray argues that indigenization is a cross-cultural practice. However, it may be an outgrowth of the history of colonialism, since it works from a largely Western conception of practice.

Gray and Fook propose that in considering international social work, we should think about four tensions, between:

i) *Globalization and localization:* the tendency for globalizing and localizing tendencies to occur together

ii) *Westernization and indigenization:* the balance between Western and alternative conceptions of practice

iii) *multiculturalism and universalization:* the implication and response to inbuilt cultural biases

iv) *universal-local standards:* the incorporation of both universal and localized conceptualizations of social work within our thinking.

It is important to examine the issues represented in these tensions. Some argue that they are not necessarily oppositions. Sewpaul for example, sees a universal definition of social work and a universal standard for social work education as assisting the integration of social work into countries where it is underdeveloped or insecure. In this way, universal and local standards can support each other. Similarly, Western approaches may become a touchstone against which local practices may be authentized. Nimmagadda and Cowger's study of authentization and indigenization in Indian social work agencies is an example of such a process. They look at how Western practices such as giving advice, family intervention, confrontation and reassurance are adapted by Indian social expectations and concepts of Dharma and Karma. For example, mainly female workers, who were not expected to act assertively, were not always able to confront the behaviour of mainly male alcoholics, as Western social workers would. Advice-giving, which was contrary to Western social work values of self-determination and non-directiveness, was accepted because Indian values acknowledge the duty of workers to take authority in particular situations.

In summary, we argue that social workers need an understanding of international social work as part of their profession. Even if they are not international social workers themselves, their daily practice and the needs and problems that users of their services face will be affected by international social trends. Students and educators will also be aware that the international element in the literature and practice that they study questions universal validity of knowledge and practice.

1.2. Social Work Education at the Crossroads

Social work has been a player in the international arena since 1928 when the International Association of Schools of Social Work (IASSW) was founded alongside its sister organisations, the International Federation of Social Workers (IFSW) and the International Council for Social Welfare (ICSW). These divided their remit into education, practice and policy respectively. Their development has been an interesting one, but the details of it need not detain us here.

This aim has been thwarted by a range of factors that those acting in this domain had to address, namely, the contradictory position of the profession in negotiating its idealistic ambitions within the realities of the messy politics of practice as altruistic motives clashed with proselytising values and imperialistic adventures. For in the world of national aggrandisement embedded in the belief in the superiority of one particular people or 'race' and its culture excluding those outside its boundaries and 'doing good' to them were unquestioned assumptions that created great wrongs as languages, peoples and cultures disappeared under messianic and imperialistic rule. Consequently, some of social work's international initiatives have been successful in promoting egalitarian relations, others have not.

1.3. Whither International Social Work

That social work educators and practitioners become involved in international social work because they are and remain interested in egalitarian relationships does not mean that this has been achieved in practice either within the nation-state or internationally. Nor does the history of activity in the international domain suggest that national policymakers and governments have not set other objectives for such endeavours, independent of educators and practitioners. Indeed, a crucial myth of state nationalism is that there is only one voice, the hegemonic one that represents the nation, and social work as its handmaiden has been expected to comply with that. Those challenging this discourse have had to struggle to be heard above its cacophonous din. The view that there is one hegemonic version of truth can be sustained only at the expense of ignoring other voices, particularly those that are suppressed or considered inferior or irrelevant. In these constructs, the dominant discourse does not have to be specified as dominant, it is assumed to be so through its normalisation, i.e., being treated as 'normal' or 'natural' and therefore beyond question. Thus, for example, in racist discourses on skin color in the West, 'white' is the color of privilege and so does not have to be referred to as such in referring to white people, only 'black' is explicitly seen and treated as a color in reference to people and an inferior one at that.

The global hegemony of particular nation states in 1928 as now has drawn strength from the (mis)use of education, its theoretical concepts, knowledge and experiences to promote the notion that some ideas are superior to others, and that those that are developed by Westerners are best of all. Sewpaul outlines the pernicious effects of such approaches to other people and provides a moving account of how people in South Africa have resisted this blatant breach of their agency. Resistance against these colonising practices has given rise to the theoretical constructs of 'subjugated knowledges' and 'dominating knowledges'. The framing of knowledge in these terms supports dichotomous thinking that other or exclude and treat as inferior those who are socially constructed as having 'subjugated knowledges'. Dichotomous conceptualisations of reality promote either/or thinking and constitute the dominant paradigm used to define, explain and change (or not) the world. Dichotomous thought can be found within social work and the geographical locales in which it is practised, between nation-states at national level and within regions and the broader world in which they are situated. This dualistic construction of knowledge establishes hierarchies of knowing in the international arena that privilege the voices of 'experts', usually Western ones, over those of service users and lay people locally and internationally. In the process, marginalised discourses exist outside the mainstream, a feature that can be found in both the West and other countries. Razak provides an interesting example of how 'black' people from the South who have lived and trained in the North can return to the South and be marginalised as local people defer to white Westerners and their experiences and knowledges. Thus, the issues embedded within international social work are extremely complicated and require a more sophisticated level of analysis than is currently evident in much of the literature.

Discourses become signifiers of how particular individuals or groups view the world and theirs and other peoples' place(s) in it. From their location within the nation-state, individual social workers have both reproduced hegemonic ways of viewing the world and at times challenged them, depending on their own personal and political values and what it was that they were trying to achieve through their work. As a profession with Western origins, social work has been allied to the discourses of liberal democracy where helping the underdog occurs under contradictory conditions aimed at supporting those in need, but in terms associated with the punitive welfarism of the New Poor Law which blames those in need for their plight. At the same time, social work within the nation-state, particularly that part of it linked to the welfare-state, has also existed as a profession that has operated both within and outside the mainstream. In these conditions, its outsider status has been particularly important in challenging dominant discourses that have denied vulnerable people assistance and social justice. In this sense, social work has played a key role in initiating alternative discourses that stand in opposition to those that dominate a particular society, despite the pressure to conform to the hegemonic ones as signified in the discourses that prevail in what Davies called the 'maintenance' school of social work.

In Britain, those associated with antioppressive practice exemplify oppositional discourses. These have challenged the absence of issues relating to equality and social justice in traditional paradigms for practice. Over time, elements of antioppressive practice have been incorporated by being partially mainstreamed although there is considerable suspicion of their capacity to reshape practice is evident amongst its opponents. In other words, alternative discourses can also generate resistance to them from those endorsing dominant discourses. International social work has to decide whether it will support the further privileging of those with power and resources or ally itself with those who have been excluded from participation in the social, political and economic development whether in the country in which they live or more broadly. The answer to the direction it takes or where (whither) it will go in the long-run will determine whether international social work withers or flourishes. In the fluid world of globalisation, support for colonising other people's minds or their practices is diminishing and in the struggle to ensure people's well-being throughout the world, it is important that international social work allies itself to the emancipatory projects produced by those holding 'subjugated knowledges'.

Making this a reality will be a considerable challenge for social work educators and practitioners, particularly those who fail to see the relevance of becoming involved in international issues. Additionally, there is a legacy of opportunistic and shameful experiences in the international domain that the profession has to acknowledge, rectify and move beyond. Social work has been both a propagator of imperialist discourses and a dismantler of them. For example, the former took place through the use of Western clinical models of social work in South Africa when what was needed was a social development approach that dealt with poverty and other structural inequalities. Other negative instances involved the destruction of the caring and cultural heritages of indigenous peoples as occurred in countries such as Canada, Australia and New Zealand.

However, the appropriation and negation of these knowledges has begun to shift in favor of their retention. Moreover, indigenous knowledge is penetrating the structures of Western social work thinking and doing and is contributing towards reshaping practice in the West. The example of the Family Group Conference (FGC) model which was developed by the Maori peoples in New Zealand to give them a greater say in the welfare of Maori children has been adopted in countries as diverse as England, Canada and Sweden with their different histories and traditions, but facing a common problem in how to best support children and families when things go wrong.

Movements to indigenise the social work curriculum testify to the continued controversy about what international social work is and what it stands for. Thus, international social work has to address several competing ontological and epistemological claims in establishing the validity of particular local knowledges while remaining cognisant of the contested terrain of practice at the local, national and international levels. Although there may be a dominant or mainstreamed 'expert' knowledge which is accepted without challenge within a particular nation-state, this may not necessarily follow through at the local level. Here, people's life experiences may encourage them to question 'expert' opinion. This has been the case in the redevelopment of First Nations forms of practice at the local level in Canada, for example. These have challenged the dominant Anglocentric models that provide the dominant paradigms for social work at the national level, and by changing local discourses, First Nations' initiatives have led to changes in national discourses. Additionally, layered within these local and national knowledges are the discourses which occur in the international domain. These are primarily taken to be those emanating from the West, particularly the English-speaking world located primarily in the United States and the

United Kingdom. Resistance to their continued dominance has facilitated the indigenisation of social work in various regions of the world, e.g., South East Asia, where the Asia Pacific Journal of Social Work has highlighted this matter as of key concern for the whole region.

However, this West-non-West approach to the local-global issue continues the dualistic thinking that is an essential feature of discourses of dominance and casts those owning 'subjugated knowledges' as passive consumers of knowledge that has been appropriated by or is described as belonging to the dominant group, rather than featuring them as creators of knowledge who both shape and are shaped by hegemonic forms of knowledge. Additionally, a dualistic framing of the matter underplays the interactive nature of these encounters and the ways in which 'subjugated knowledges' already engage with dominant knowledges to challenge and reshape them even in the international domain. People do not just passively sit on the floor of knowledge waiting to have their thinking taken over by others. They engage with them in and have a range of options with which to respond acceptance, accommodation and resistance. These can lead to the formation of new knowledge paradigms and shifts in ways of knowing which can be owned by all those involved.

The interactive nature of the knowledge acquisition, creation and recreation processes is evident in struggles against colonialism. And, it is evidenced in the way that migrants have already been 'Westernised' to a significant degree before leaving their country of origins by having already participated in Western systems of education, language, culture and expectations prior to departure. Tasse carefully plots this trend in his analysis of Ethiopian migrants living in the United States and France. Moreover, the interpermeability of these domains is being intensified as globalisation brings different parts of the world closer together and promotes faster and deeper levels of interaction between them in exchanges to which all the participants contribute, albeit in different ways and from different positions. Yet, we cannot ignore the continued importance of the nation-state. It does not seem to be disappearing. Indeed, in some areas, new nation-states are coming into being, for example, in parts of the former Soviet Union. Besides, the nation-state provides the locale within which most people live and it regulates most of their day-to-day lives and routines. Additionally, some nation-states are only just beginning to assert their power. China is a case in point. Containing one-sixth of the world's population, its increasing economic power can bring it to the stage where it begins to dominate what happens in other economies. Its political role in the international arena, particularly in the United Nations cannot be ignored either. This may develop in new directions once it secures a strong economic position.

1.4. Re-theorising Social Work

The further development of International social work is currently at the crossroads and needs to consider its future growth in terms of the directions in which it wishes to proceed. Those interested in promoting international social work will have to decide whether they will follow the international definition of social work which has been adopted by IASSW and IFSW. The full version of this definition is available from the IASSW website, but the key part is:

> The social work profession promotes social change, problem solving in human relationships and the empowerment and liberation of people to enhance well-being. Utilising theories of human behavior and social systems, social work intervenes at the points where people interact with their environments. Principles of human rights and social justice are fundamental to social work.

This affirms social work's commitment to human rights and social justice, but their pursuit may place the profession at odds with national governments that are not committed to these principles including the rejection of the idea of the redistribution of the earth's resources in ways that ensure the well-being of all its inhabitants. If international social work is to endorse upholding human rights, citizenship and social justice, it will have to take a stand against the use of education as a neoliberal arm of imperialist ventures. And, it has to enhance principled development within its own theoretical and practice frameworks. As this growth will occur within the context of globalisation, the profession has a number of difficult challenges to address. These are:

— (Re)theorising social work in an interdependent world;

— Retaining diversity and richness in human encounters;

— Acting collectively within the international domain to advocate for the profession's desire to promote human well-being within a human rights and social justice framework and gain support for policies and practices that further these aims; and

— Changing the social work curricula in the academy and the field to address the international dimensions of social problems.

These four points are interrelated, but we will consider each one in turn.

Social work has tended to be thought about and theorised primarily within the context of modernity and the nation-state. Even the majority of texts on international social work perpetrate the myth that international social work merely involves the crossing of borders. The journal, International Social Work, is also dominated by articles that cover discrete countries and there is little truly comparative work evident within its pages. Social work educators and practitioners need to retheorise social work in ways that situate practice in a locality within the global context within which it is embedded and begin to unpack the connections that exist between different levels of activity.

Retheorsing international social work also requires those involved in thinking how the diversity and richness of human encounters can be retained to reveal what we hold in common as well as what is different between us. This will not be easy given the significant number of different factors that interact with each other and that have to be taken into account. Given the links between the social and physical environment of which we are becoming increasingly aware, as is evident for instance in the case of pollution and global warming, social workers' retheorisation of the profession has to include both these two dimensions of people's reality alongside that of the spiritual domain wnich has already been highlighted by several forms of indigenous knowledge.

Acting collectively within the international domain will continue to be a major challenge in a profession that is marked by division and fragmentation even within the confines of the nation-state. The profession has to develop a strong and coherent voice in which different players can make significant contributions to the overall effort. IASSW, IFSW and ICSW have been active in international fora such as the United Nations. IASSW has been involved at this level since 1948. However, their capacities and resources for such activities are limited. Consequently, so is their influence. Ways of expanding these in more egalitarian and inclusive directions must be found if the reorientation of the profession beyond its Western origins to reflect the whole of humanity is to be realised.

Although these organisations also have a tradition of working together, their achievements in this endeavour have been modest, as the initiatives described below demonstrate. The question of what values or principles social workers hold in common across the globe and how far these can enhance intercollegial solidarity and joint actions is one that remains to be answered. The relationship between individual and collective or group rights is a further contentious issue. And there are other key concerns that have to be addressed. Amongst these are: What is it that holds the profession together in the international domain? Is there even a global profession? How can this be developed and by whom?

IASSW and IFSW began a recent round of work on this never ending project in the late 1990s and have developed a Joint Collaboration Committee to assist them in this process. In June 2001, these two organisations declared the definition of social work that they had both worked on over the previous four years with IFSW taking the lead as a joint one for the first time in their history as 'sister organisations'. These two bodies are currently working on a joint Code of Ethics (under the leadership of IFSW) and Global Qualifying Standards (under the leadership of IASSW). Meanwhile, they are both working in defence of human rights through a Joint Human Rights Commission in which there is a Chair and Co-Chair from each institution. The Chair is intended to rotate between the two bodies, and IFSW has taken this role to begin with. Discussions amongst IASSW, IFSW and ICSW have been less structured than those between IASSW and IFSW, but discussions around the journal, International Social Work, which is jointly owned by these three organisations are promising.

Looking at the failure of social workers to deal effectively with many internationalising social problems including the sex trade in children or trafficking in people, asylum seekers and refugees, HIV/AIDS, and armed conflict, current approaches to and definitions of international social work seem to offer limited hope of producing the innovations necessary for effective practice in this regard. Even in more established international endeavours such as international adoptions, the regulatory frameworks controlling the movement of adopted children remain problematic and many poor parents lose their children to richer ones where the children's identity and cultural heritage can be easily ignored and/or obliterated. The rise in global poverty and the failure of international initiatives to contribute effectively to its elimination also call for a rethinking of how theory and practice in this area come together to change people's lives for the better. The profession has to acquire a prominent voice in this endeavour.

Looking at the international dimensions of social problems highlights how poorly the modernist project in which social work has been embedded has served those in need when even basic commodities such as food, shelter and water remain denied to them. Social workers, acting through the organisations of civil society have been unable to make significant inroads upon the elimination of poverty and other forms of structural inequalities despite a number of attempts at doing so. The reasons for this failure require examination and the lessons for the future learnt. These are likely to reveal the importance of forming partnerships that encompass all stakeholders ranging from policymakers to service users but also expose the importance of different ways of involving people in making decisions that affect their lives. In other words, inputs, processes and outcomes will have to be considered as an integrated whole to change governance structures and forms of participation in more empowering directions. At the same time, the power of civil society organisations has grown so that some of the larger ones have more financial resources at their disposal than many of the low-income countries that they seek to serve. This gives them enormous political leverage and the potential to abuse their powers as they are not held accountable by any particular constituency.

Ultimately, developments in the theoretical and practice domains have to be carried through to what is taught in the classroom, what happens in practice, what policies are promulgated and what is done in and through research. This will mean reformulating the social work curriculum and making it more relevant to practising in a world in which many social problems have become internationalised and the crossing of borders is an integral part of both the problem and what needs to be done to resolve it locally, nationally or internationally, rather than treating its international dimension as a tangential add-on or afterthought. Fortunately for those committed to this endeavour, there are a few texts that have attempted the retheorisation of international social work in new directions, Lyons and Healy providing two of these texts.

There is much work to be done in responding to the agenda of developing international social work within a globalising world, and because knowledge is contested, there will be many disagreements as the profession progresses on this journey—assuming that it sees this endeavour as an important one to pursue. Moreover, the process is a constantly changing one because just as we alter one element in a particular situation, the others are rearranged or transformed and so the process begins anew.

1.5. Evidence-Based Practice in Social Work Education

The words "evidence-based practice" (EBP) are currently permeating the delivery of health care, education and human services. This is affecting teaching and scholarship within the disciplines that educate micro and macro-level practitioners for the broad array of services encompassed within these systems and it is also impacting policy and funding decisions and how services are delivered. The focus for Thyer and Corcoran as well as this symposium hosted by the School of Social Work at the University of Texas, Austin is on improving the teaching of evidence-based practice in social work. And the questions that need to be addressed are how? For what purpose? What are the expected outcomes? And can we and should we come to agreement on what we mean by evidence-based practice. For Corcoran teaching evidence-based practice includes teaching about the history of science and social work and he covered three key areas: An historical perspective on how innovations slowly wend their way into practice; an attempt to discern the many levels and varying qualities of what is considered 'evidence;' and a congratulatory note to the young social work profession in adapting to an evidence-based practice approach so early in its history. Corcoran also asserts that evidence-based practice should be taught throughout the curriculum, and most certainly in research classes.

Thyer focuses more on the question of evidence-based macro-practice—do we teach it? Do we research it and if so how? Are evidence-based government-funded services possible? Does the government use evidence in making decisions? ls social work adequately and appropriately involved in the national discussions about practice guidelines and the establishment of lists of evidence-based programs, treatments and/or interventions? Thyer's point that much of the discussion about evidence based practice focuses on clinical interventions is valid. To some extent, evidence-based practice in social work morphed from the evidence-based medicine movement. With a focus on outcomes for individuals, the Institute of Medicine (IOM) defines "evidence-based medicine" as the integration of best researched evidence and clinical expertise with patient values".

While this may be the origins, the current environment has taken the words "evidence-based" and applied them to policy, program, research, and interventions suggesting that we need to consider the empirical base and think critically about the services provided to social work clients from every perspective. Thyer also raises concerns about the definition of EBP, noting that the Social Work Dictionary's definition is very narrow, defining EBP as practices emerging from "evidence derived from randomised controlled outcome studies and meta-analysis of outcomes studies........" This definition might be welcomed by the Coalition for Evidence-based Policy of the Council on Excellence in Government that advocates for the government to support evidence-based practices and policies. The high powered Coalition with a prestigious advisory board views randomised controlled studies as the gold standard and has several working papers recommending that policy and funding decisions be based on the findings of randomised controlled trials (RCTs).

The Coalitionhelped develop guidance for the Office of Management and Budget entitled What Constitutes Strong Evidence of a Program's Effectiveness? This memo "points to the randomised controlled trial (RCT) as an example of the best type of evaluation to demonstrate actual program impact." The memo includes several examples where an RCT finds different outcomes than a program evaluation. However those agencies that fund evaluations of programs do not have the funding resources to actually carry-out RCTs. More on this later in discussion of policy. In regard to types of evidence, Thyer asserts that forms of evidence besides RCTs are not only useful, but are more prevalent and might even be more appropriate. This includes all of the sources of evidence as cited by Thyer citing Strauss, Richardson, Glasziour & Haynes, including qualitative research. There are many areas of practice and policy where there have been no RCTs nor would an RCT be appropriate. In fact there is concern about RCTs in health, mental health and social services when the 'usual' treatment is known to be inferior services. There are also concerns that new treatments that are tried in an RCT might be harmful. At a recent meeting at the National Institutes of Health (NIH), that was touting the outcomes of several large scale clinical trials, it was mentioned that if there was a clear finding that something was not working during a trial it would be stopped so that participants would not be subject to a clearly inferior outcome. Even if one does consider RCTs the 'ultimate' evidence, RCTs also have shortcomings.

McCall & Green suggest that other research methods should complement experimental designs because although RCTs have strong internal validitythey may have limited generalisablity to real world situations. And one of the reasons they have strong internal validity is that they encompass a narrow scope and usually exclude participants who have co-morbidities—a common attribute of social work clients. "Research Designs for Complex, Multi-Level Health and Program Interventions" a symposium convened jointly by the National Institutes of Health (NIH), the Centers for Disease Control and Prevention (CDC) and the Agency for Healthcare Research and Quality (AHRQ) tried to address this issue of RCTs in the real world. The convening examined research strategies beyond individual random assignment in RCTs—including those that use random assignment at the group or community level, community-based participatory research strategies and methodical systematic research reviews in order to develop more generalisable findings.

In regard to strengths of evidence, Corcoran wants to make sure that his students are able to be able to discern the value of different types of evidence. With the internet, blogs and personal websites, students today have access to so much information, thus they need to have excellent skills to be able to understand the differences between reliable and unreliable sources of input to a particular problem. The role of librarians and information specialists in social work education programs is increasingly important. Students also need to develop a clear understanding of the difference between a review of the literature and a review of research. Perhaps learning how to do a search for research findings, clinical guidelines, evidence-based clearinghouses, etc. should be part of each student's orientation. Also important is to develop skills to analyse research findings so as to be able to carefully examine the quality and the strength (effect) of the research. Unfortunately in many areas we have not developed a strong 'evidence' base because we have done small studies, often with convenience populations, or program evaluations of varying quality. Perhaps lack of funded support for research, high teaching loads and lack of research resources has kept many in academia away from large scale studies that use common and validated measures and that can be replicated in multiple sites.

IASWR's systematic review of research on retention of child welfare workers found little consistency across studies, even among retention studies of CalSWEC students in different regions of California, making it difficult to report that there is "strong" evidenc. Social workers may also be less involved, thus far in RCTs because many RCTs have had very defined samples and social workers' clients often have complex and multiple problems that exclude them from eligibility. As NIH and the Substance Abuse and Mental Health Services Administration (SAMHSA) say that they are moving toward translational research from the bedside to the community and research moves beyond efficacy and effectiveness to implementation research, social work research opportunities should increase.

The NIH Program Announcement to examine "Social Work Practice and Concepts in Health" (RO1) provides such a potential opportunity. The growing number of clinical trials attempting to involve real world complexities and increased support for community-based participatory research strategies provide opportunities to use a social work perspective in growing the evidence base. Both Corcoran and Thyer touch on the relevance of evidence-based practice for policy and for teaching policy. They also distinguish the evidence based practice processes defined by Gibbs and others, and evidence-based practices (or empirically supported interventions) that are deemed evidence-based practices through various websites and clearinghouse. Many health and human service practices, programs and interventions have not been the subject of RCTs, and as stated previously, testing of many social interventions may not lend themselves to RCTs. However, there is increasing support by the government to create clearinghouses and registries of effective programs and practices that have been developed indicating that policy decision-makers are also engaged in dialogue about the value of evidence-based practices. A note of caution is however necessary.

Table 1: California Evidence-Based Clearinghouse for Child Welfare Scientific Rating Scale

---

1. Well Supported—Effective Practice

- There is no clinical or empirical evidence or theoretical basis indicating that the practice constitutes a substantial risk of harm to those receiving it, compared to its likely benefits.
- The practice has a book, manual, and/or other available writings that specify components of the service and describes how to administer it.
- Multiple Site Replication: At least two rigorous randomised controlled trials (RCTs) in different usual care or practice settings have found the practice to be superior to an appropriate comparison practice. The RCTs have been reported in published, peer-reviewed literature.
- In at least two of the RCT's meeting criteria for "C" above, the practice has shown to have a sustained effect at least one year beyond the end of treatment, with no evidence that the effect is lost after this time.
- Outcome measures must be reliable and valid, and administered consistently and accurately across all subjects.
- If multiple outcome studies have been conducted, the overall weight of the evidence supports the effectiveness of the practice.

2. Supported—Efficacious Practice

- There is no clinical or empirical evidence or theoretical basis indicating that the practice constitutes a substantial risk of harm to those receiving it, compared to its likely benefits.
- The practice has a book, manual, and/or other available writings that specifies the components of the practice protocol and describes how to administer it.
- At least two rigorous randomised controlled trials (RCTs) in highly controlled settings (e.g., university laboratory) have found the practice to be superior to an appropriate comparison practice. The RCTs have been reported in published, peer-reviewed literature.

- In at least two of the RCT's meeting criteria for "C" above, the practice has shown to have a sustained effect at least one year beyond the end of treatment, with no evidence that the effect is lost after this time.
- Outcome measures must be reliable and valid, and administered consistently and accurately across all subjects.
- If multiple outcome studies have been conducted, the overall weight of evidence supports the efficacy of the practice.

3. Promising Practice

- There is no clinical or empirical evidence or theoretical basis indicating that the practice constitutes a substantial risk of harm to those receiving it, compared to its likely benefits.
- The practice has a book, manual, and/or other available writings that specifies the components of the practice protocol and describe how to administer it.
- At least one study utilising some form of control (e.g., untreated group, placebo group, matched wait list) has established the practice's efficacy over the placebo, or found it to be comparable to or better than an appropriate comparison practice. The study has been reported in published, peer-reviewed literature.
- If multiple outcome studies have been conducted, the overall weight of evidence supports the efficacy of the practice.

4. Acceptable/Emerging Practice—Effectiveness is Unknown

- There is no clinical or empirical evidence or theoretical basis indicating that the practice constitutes a substantial risk of harm to those receiving it, compared to its likely benefits.
- The practice has a book, manual, and/or other available writings that specifies the components of the practice protocol and describes how to administer it.
- The practice is generally accepted in clinical practice as appropriate for use with children receiving services from child welfare or related systems and their parents/caregivers.
- The practice lacks adequate research to empirically determine efficacy.

5. Evidence Fails to Demonstrate Effect

- Two or more randomised controlled trials (RCT's) have found the practice has not resulted in improved outcomes, when compared to usual care.
- If multiple outcome studies have been conducted, the overall weight of evidence does not support the efficacy of the practice.

6. Concerning Practice

- If multiple outcome studies have been conducted, the overall weight of evidence suggests the intervention has a negative effect upon clients served; and/or

- There is a reasonable theoretical, clinical, empirical, or legal basis suggesting that the practice constitutes a risk of harm to those receiving it, compared to its likely benefits.

There is some concern that all of the discussions in Washington, DC and state capitols about EBP and some of the policy documents that tout the value of RCT evidence over other levels of evidence may have negative impact on funding and support for social programs. One concern is that even when there is a well documented EBP to fit a certain situation it may not be used because of insufficient funding to support the service, the lack of adequate training of staff or the conflict that the intervention might have with other treatments. Another concern is that in tight fiscal times, policy makers might decide to defund valuable programs because there is no RCT that has proved the programs effectiveness. A third concern is that the distinction between a program having no effect on a particular outcome is often confused with a program having a negative effect. These are all important issues to take into consideration when thinking about "evidence-based policy-making. "

References

Dominelli, L. 2000. 'International Comparisons in Social Work', in: Pierce, R and Weinstein, J (eds.): *Innovative Education and Training for Care Professionals.* London, Jessica Kingsley.

Dominelli, L. 2002. *Anti-Oppressive Social Work Theory and Practice.* London, Palgrave.

Lyons, K. 1999. *International Social Work.* Aldershot, Ashgate.

Razak, N. 2003. *Perils and Possibilities: Complicating the Understandings of Racism, Imperialism and Nationalism in International Social Work.* PhD-Thesis. Adelaide, Australia, Flinders University.

2

Importance of Social Work Education

The process of developing global standards for the education and training of the social work profession is as important as the product; the actual standards that have been developed. In undertaking such an initiative it was also vital that minority opinions were considered and reflected in the development of the document.

2.1. International Definition of Social Work

In July 2001, both the IASSW and the IFSW reached agreement on adopting the following international definition of social work:

> The social work profession promotes social change, problem solving in human relationships and the empowerment and liberation of people to enhance well-being. Utilising theories of human behavior and social systems, social work intervenes at the points where people interact with their environments. Principles of human rights and social justice are fundamental to social work.

Both the definition and the commentaries that follow are set within the parameters of broad ethical principles that cannot be refuted on an ideological level. However, the fact that social work is operationalised differently both within nation states and regional boundaries, and across the world, with its control and status-quo maintaining functions being dominant in some contexts, cannot be disputed. Lorenz considered the ambiguities, tensions and contradictions of the social work profession, which have to be constantly negotiated and re-negotiated, rather than resolved, to constitute its success and challenge. It is, perhaps, these very tensions that lend to the richness of the local-global dialectic, and provide legitimacy for the development of global standards. According to Lorenz: "It is its paradigmatic openness that gives this profession the chance to engage with very specific (and constantly changing) historical and political contexts while at the same time striving for a degree of universality, scientific reliability, professional autonomy and moral accountability."

2.2. Purposes of the Social Work Profession

Social work, in various parts of the world, is targeted at interventions for social support and for developmental, protective, preventive and/or therapeutic purposes. Drawing on available literature, the feedback from colleagues during consultations and the commentary on the international definition of social work, the following core purposes of social work have been identified:

— Facilitate the inclusion of marginalised, socially excluded, dispossessed, vulnerable and at-risk groups of people.

— Address and challenge barriers, inequalities and injustices that exist in society.

— Form short and longer-term working relationships with and mobilise individuals, families, groups, organisations and communities to enhance their well-being and their problem-solving capacities.

— Assist and educate people to obtain services and resources in their communities.

— Formulate and implement policies and programes that enhance people's well-being, promote development and human rights, and promote collective social harmony and social stability, insofar as such stability does not violate human rights.

— Encourage people to engage in advocacy with regard to pertinent local, national, regional and/or international concerns.

— Act with and/or for people to advocate the formulation and targeted implementation of policies that are consistent with the ethical principles of the profession.

— Act with and/or for people to advocate changes in those policies and structural conditions that maintain people in marginalised, dispossessed and vulnerable positions, and those that infringe the collective social harmony and stability of various ethnic groups, insofar as such stability does not violate human rights.

— Work towards the protection of people who are not in a position to do so themselves, for example children and youth in need of care and persons experiencing mental illness or mental retardation, within the parameters of accepted and ethically sound legislation.

— Engage in social and political action to impact social policy and economic development, and to effect change by critiquing and eliminating inequalities.

— Enhance stable, harmonious and mutually respectful societies that do not violate people's human rights.

— Promote respect for traditions, cultures, ideologies, beliefs and religions amongst different ethnic groups and societies, insofar as these do not conflict with the fundamental human rights of people.

— Plan, organise, administer and manage programes and organisations dedicated to any of the purposes delineated above.

2.3. Standards for Eduction in Social Work

2.3.1. School's Core Purpose or Mission Statement

All schools should aspire toward the development of a core purpose statement or a mission statement which:

1. Is clearly articulated so those major stakeholders who have an investment in such a core purpose or mission understand it.
2. Reflects the values and the ethical principles of social work.
3. Reflects aspiration towards equity with regard to the demographic profile of the institution's locality. The core purpose or mission statement should thus incorporate such issues as ethnic and gender representation on the faculty, as well as in recruitment and admission procedures for students.
4. Respects the rights and interests of service users and their participation in all aspects of delivery of programes.

2.3.2. Programme Objectives and Outcomes

In respect of programme objectives and expected outcomes, schools should endeavour to reach the following:

1. A specification of its programe objectives and expected higher education outcomes.
2. A reflection of the values and ethical principles of the profession in its programe design and implementation.
3. Identification of the programe's instructional methods, to ensure they support the achievement of the cognitive and affective development of social work students.
4. An indication of how the programe reflects the core knowledge, processes, values and skills of the social work profession, as applied in context-specific realities.
5. An indication of how an initial level of proficiency with regard to self-reflective use of social work values, knowledge and skills is to be attained by social work students.
6. An indication of how the programe meets the requirements of nationally and/or regionally/internationally defined professional goals, and how the programe addresses local, national and/or regional/international developmental needs and priorities.
7. As social work does not operate in a vacuum, the programe should take account of the impact of interacting cultural, economic, communication, social, political and psychological global factors.
8. Provision of an educational preparation that is relevant to beginning social work professional practice with individuals, families, groups and/or communities in any given context.
9. Self-evaluation to assess the extent to which its programe objectives and expected outcomes are being achieved.
10. External peer evaluation as far as is reasonable and financially viable. This may be in the form of external peer moderation of assignments and/or written examinations and dissertations, and external peer review and assessment of curricula.
11. The conferring of a distinctive social work qualification at the certificate, diploma, first degree or postgraduate level as

approved by national and/or regional qualification authorities, where such authorities exist.

2.3.3. Programme Curricula including Field Education

With regard to standards regarding programe curricula, schools should consistently aspire towards the following:

1. The curricula and methods of instruction being consistent with the school's programe objectives, its expected outcomes and its mission statement.
2. Clear plans for the organisation, implementation and evaluation of the theory and field education components of the programe.
3. Involvement of service users in the planning and delivery of programes.
4. Recognition and development of indigenous or locally specific social work education and practice from the traditions and cultures of different ethnic groups and societies, insofar that such traditions and cultures do not violate human rights.
5. Specific attention to the constant review and development of the curricula.
6. Ensuring that the curricula help social work students to develop skills of critical thinking and scholarly attitudes of reasoning, openness to new experiences and paradigms, and commitment to life-long learning.
7. Field education should be sufficient in duration and complexity of tasks and learning opportunities to ensure that students are prepared for professional practice.
8. Planned co-ordination and links between the school and the agency/field placement setting.
9. Provision of orientation for fieldwork supervisors or instructors.
10. Appointment of field supervisors or instructors who are qualified and experienced, as determined by the development status of the social work profession in any given country, and provision of orientation for fieldwork supervisors or instructors.
11. Provision for the inclusion and participation of field instructors in curriculum development.

12. A partnership between the educational institution and the agency (where applicable) and service users in decision-making regarding field education and the evaluation of student's fieldwork performance.
13. Making available, to fieldwork instructors or supervisors, a field instruction manual that details its fieldwork standards, procedures, assessment standards/criteria and expectations.
14. Ensuring that adequate and appropriate resources, to meet the needs of the fieldwork component of the programe, are made available.

2.3.4. Core Curricula

In respect core curricula, schools should aspire toward the following:

1. An identification of and selection for inclusion in the programe curricula, as determined by local, national and/or regional/ international needs and priorities.
2. Notwithstanding the provision of 4.1 there are certain core curricula that may be seen to be universally applicable. Thus the school should ensure that social work students, by the end of their first Social Work professional qualification, have had exposure to the following core curricula which are organised into four conceptual components:

2.3.5. Domain of the Social Work Profession

— A critical understanding of how socio-structural inadequacies, discrimination, oppression, and social, political and economic injustices impact human functioning and development at all levels, including the global.

— Knowledge of human behavior and development and of the social environment, with particular emphasis on the person-in-environment transaction, life-span development and the interaction among biological, psychological, socio-structural, economic, political, cultural and spiritual factors in shaping human development and behavior.

— Knowledge of how traditions, culture, beliefs, religions and customs influence human functioning and development at all levels, including how these might constitute resources and/or obstacles to growth and development.

— A critical understanding of social work's origins and purposes.

— Understanding of country specific social work origins and development.

— Sufficient knowledge of related occupations and professions to facilitate inter-professional collaboration and teamwork.

— Knowledge of social welfare policies (or lack thereof), services and laws at local, national and/or regional/international levels, and the roles of social work in policy planning, implementation, evaluation and in social change processes.

— A critical understanding of how social stability, harmony, mutual respect and collective solidarity impact human functioning and development at all levels, including the global, insofar as that stability, harmony and solidarity are not used to maintain a status quo with regard to infringement of human rights.

2.3.6. Domain of the Social Work Professional

— The development of the critically self-reflective practitioner, who is able to practice within the value perspective of the social work profession, and shares responsibility with the employer for their well being and professional development, including the avoidance of 'burn-out'.

— The recognition of the relationship between personal life experiences and personal value systems and social work practice.

— The appraisal of national, regional and/or international social work codes of ethics and their applicability to context specific realities.

— Preparation of social workers within a holistic framework, with skills to enable practice in a range of contexts with diverse ethnic, cultural, 'racial' and gender groups, and other forms of diversities.

— The development of the social worker who is able to conceptualise social work wisdom derived from different cultures, traditions and customs in various ethnic groups, insofar that culture, tradition, custom and ethnicity are not used to violate human rights.

— The development of the social worker who is able to deal with the complexities, subtleties, multi-dimensional, ethical, legal and dialogical aspects of power.

2.3.7. Methods of Social Work Practice

— Sufficient practice skills in, and knowledge of, assessment, relationship building and helping processes to achieve the identified goals of the programe for the purposes of social support, and developmental, protective, preventive and/or therapeutic intervention depending on the particular focus of the programe or professional practice orientation.

— The application of social work values, ethical principles, knowledge and skills to confront inequality, and social, political and economic injustices.

— Knowledge of social work research and skills in the use of research methods, including ethical use of relevant research paradigms, and critical appreciation of the use of research and different sources of knowledge about social work practice.

— The application of social work values, ethical principles, knowledge and skills to promote care, mutual respect and mutual responsibility amongst members of a society.

— Supervised fieldwork education, with due consideration to the provisions of Item 3 above.

2.3.8. Paradigm of the Social Work Profession

Of particular current salience to professional social work education, training and practice are the following epistemological paradigms (which are not mutually exclusive), that should inform the core curricula:

— An acknowledgement and recognition of the dignity, worth and the uniqueness of all human beings.

— Recognition of the interconnectedness that exists within and across all systems at micro, mezzo and macro levels.

— An emphasis on the importance of advocacy and changes in socio-structural, political and economic conditions that disempower, marginalise and exclude people.

— A focus on capacity-building and empowerment of individuals, families, groups, organisations and communities through a human-centred developmental approach.

— Knowledge about and respect for the rights of service users.

— Problem-solving and anticipatory socialisation through an understanding of the normative developmental life cycle, and expected life tasks and crises in relation to age-related influences, with due consideration to socio-cultural expectations.

— The assumption, identification and recognition of strengths and potential of all human beings.

— An appreciation and respect for diversity in relation to 'race', culture, religion, ethnicity, linguistic origin, gender, sexual orientation and differential abilities.

2.3.9. Standards Regard to Professional Staff

With regard to professional staff, schools should aspire towards:

1. The provision of professional staff, adequate in number and range of expertise, who have appropriate qualifications as determined by the development status of the social work profession in any given country. As far as possible a Masters level qualification in social work, or a related discipline (in countries where social work is an emerging discipline), should be required.
2. The provision of opportunities for staff participation in the development of its core purpose or mission, in the formulation of the objectives and expected outcomes of the programe, and in any other initiative that the school might be involved in.
3. Provision for the continuing professional development of its staff, particularly in areas of emerging knowledge.
4. A clear statement, where possible, of its equity-based policies or preferences, with regard to considerations of gender, ethnicity, 'race' or any other form of diversity in its recruitment and appointment of staff.

5. Sensitivity to languages relevant to the practice of social work in that context.
6. In its allocation of teaching, fieldwork instruction, supervision and administrative workloads, making provision for research and publications.
7. Making provision for professional staff, as far as is reasonable and possible, to be involved in the formulation, analysis and the evaluation of the impact of social policies, and in community outreach initiatives.

2.3.10. Standards with Regard to Social Work Students

In respect of social work students, schools should endeavor to reach the following:

1. Clear articulation of its admission criteria and procedures.
2. Student recruitment, admission and retention policies that reflect the demographic profile of the locality that the institution is based in with active involvement of practitioners and service users in relevant processes. Due recognition should be given to minority groups that are under-represented and/or under-served. Relevant criminal convictions, involving abuse of others or human rights violations, must be taken into account given the primary responsibility of protecting and empowering service users.
3. Provision for student advising that is directed toward student orientation, assessment of the student's aptitude and motivation for a career in social work, regular evaluation of the student's performance and guidance in the selection of courses/modules.
4. Ensuring high quality of the educational programe whatever the mode of delivery. In the case of distance, mixed-mode, decentralised and/or internet-based teaching, mechanisms for locally-based instruction and supervision should be put in place, especially with regard to the fieldwork component of the programe.
5. Explicit criteria for the evaluation of student's academic and fieldwork performance.
6. Non-discrimination against any student on the basis of 'race', color, culture, ethnicity, linguistic origin, religion, political

orientation, gender, sexual orientation, age, marital status, physical status and socio-economic status.

7. Grievance and appeals procedures which are accessible, clearly explained to all students and operated without prejudice to the assessment of students.

2.3.11. Standards with Regard to School Administration

With regard to structure, administration, governance and resources, the school and/or the educational institution should aspire towards the following:

1. Social work programes are implemented through a distinct unit known as a Faculty, School, Department, Centre or Division, which has a clear identity within the educational institution. The school has a designated Head or Director who has demonstrated administrative, scholarly and professional competence, preferably in the profession of social work.
2. The Head or Director has primary responsibility for the coordination and professional leadership of the school, with sufficient time and resources to fulfil these responsibilities.
3. The school's budgetary allocation is sufficient to achieve its core purpose or mission and the programe objectives.
4. The budgetary allocation is stable enough to ensure programe planning and sustainability.
5. There are adequate physical facilities, including classroom space, offices for professional and administrative staff and space for student, faculty and field-liaison meetings, and the equipment necessary for the achievement of the school's core purpose or mission and the programe objectives.
6. Library and, where possible, internet resources, necessary to achieve the programe objectives, are made available.
7. The necessary clerical and administrative staff are made available for the achievement of the programe objectives.
8. Where the school offers distance, mixed-mode, decentralised and/or internet-based education there is provision of adequate infrastructure, including classroom space, computers, texts, audio-visual equipment, community resources for fieldwork

education, and on-site instruction and supervision to facilitate the achievement of its core purpose or mission, programe objectives and expected outcomes.

9. The school plays a key role with regard to the recruitment, appointment and promotion of staff.
10. The school strives toward gender equity in its recruitment, appointment, promotion and tenure policies and practices.
11. In its recruitment, appointment, promotion and tenure principles and procedures, the school reflects the diversities of the population that it interacts with and serves.
12. The decision-making processes of the school reflect participatory principles and procedures.
13. The school promotes the development of a cooperative, supportive and productive working environment to facilitate the achievement of programe objectives.
14. The school develops and maintains linkages within the institution, with external organisations, and with service users relevant to its core purpose or mission and its objectives.

2.3.12. Standards with Regard to Cultural Diversity

With regard to cultural and ethnic diversity schools should aspire towards the following:

1. Making concerted and continuous efforts to ensure the enrichment of the educational experience by reflecting cultural and ethnic diversity, and gender analysis in its programe.
2. Ensuring that the programe, either through mainstreaming into all courses/modules and/or through a separate course/module, has clearly articulated objectives in respect of cultural and ethnic diversity, and gender analysis.
3. Indicating that issues regarding gender analysis and cultural and ethnic diversity, are represented in the fieldwork component of the programe.
4. Ensuring that social work students are provided with opportunities to develop self-awareness regarding their personal and cultural values, beliefs, traditions and biases and how these

might influence the ability to develop relationships with people, and to work with diverse population groups.

5. Promoting sensitivity to, and increasing knowledge about, cultural and ethnic diversity, and gender analysis.
6. Minimising group stereotypes and prejudices and ensuring that racist behaviors, policies and structures are not reproduced through social work practice.
7. Ensuring that social work students are able to form relationships with, and treat all persons with respect and dignity irrespective of such persons' cultural and ethnic beliefs and orientations.
8. Ensuring that social work students are schooled in a basic human rights approach, as reflected in international instruments such as the Universal Declaration on Human Rights, the United Nations Convention on the Rights of the Child and the UN Vienna Declaration.
9. Ensuring that the programe makes provision for social work students to know themselves both as individuals and as members of collective socio-cultural groups in terms of strengths and areas for further development.

2.3.13. Standards with Regard to Values

In view of the recognition that social work values, ethics and principles are the core components of the profession, schools should consistently aspire towards:

1. Focused and meticulous attention to this aspect of the programe in curricula design and implementation.
2. Clearly articulated objectives with regard to social work values, principles and ethical conduct.
3. Registration of professional staff and social work students (insofar as social work students develop working relationships with people via fieldwork placements) with national and/or regional regulatory (whether statutory or non-statutory) bodies, with defined codes of ethics. Members of such bodies are generally bound to the provisions of those codes.
4. Ensuring that every social work student involved in fieldwork education, and every professional staff member, is aware of the

boundaries of professional practice and what might constitute unprofessional conduct in terms of the code of ethics. Where students violate the code of ethics, programe staff may take necessary and acceptable remedial and/or initial disciplinary measures, or counsel the student out of the programe.

5. Taking appropriate action in relation to those social work students and professional staff who fail to comply with the code of ethics, either through an established regulatory social work body, established procedures of the educational institution, and/or through legal mechanisms.
6. Ensuring that regulatory social work bodies are broadly representative of the social work profession, including, where applicable, social workers from both the public and private sector, and of the community that it serves, including the direct participation of service users.
7. Upholding, as far as is reasonable and possible, the principles of restorative rather than retributive justice in disciplining either social work students or professional staff who violate the code of ethics.

2.4. Developing Global Standards for Social Work Education

The Global Minimum Qualifying Standards Committee was formally established as a joint initiative of the International Association of Schools of Social Work (IASSW) and the International Federation of Social Workers (IFSW) at the joint IASSW/IFSW Conference in Montreal, Canada in July 2000. This discussion document was put together with the input of various Committee members, a review of relevant documents, e-mail consultations, and personal consultations with colleagues wherever possible.

On the whole there was a favorable response to IASSW and IFSW developing a standards setting document that elucidates what social work represents on a global level. This document that identifies certain universals, may be used as a guideline to develop national standards with regard to social work education and training. Such a document should reflect some consensus around key issues, roles and purposes of social work. However, given the profession's historically fragmented strands; the contemporary debates around social work's intra-professional identity; its identity vis-à-vis other categories of personnel in the welfare sector such as development workers, child care workers, probation officers, community workers and youth workers (where such categories of personnel are differentiated from social work); and the enormous diversities across nations and regions, there was some scepticism about the possibility of identifying any such 'universal'. The suggestion was that such a document must be sufficiently flexible to be applicable to any context. Such flexibility should allow for interpretations of locally specific social work education and practice, and take into account each country's or region's socio-political, cultural, economic and historical contexts while adhering to international standards.

The main reasons for the development of global standards were to (stated in no particular order of priority):

— Protect the 'consumers', 'clients' or 'service users' of social work services;
— Take account of the impact of globalisation on social work curricula and social work practice;
— Facilitate articulation across universities on a global level;
— Facilitate the movement of social workers from one country to another;
— Draw a distinction between social workers and non-social workers;
— Benchmark national standards against international standards;
— Facilitate partnerships and international student and staff exchange programes;
— Enable IASSW and IFSW, in developing such guidelines, to play a facilitative role in helping those faculties, centres, departments or schools of social work that lack resources to meet such guidelines.
— Give practical expression to the aim of IASSW as some saw the formulation of international guidelines for social work education and training to be the core business of IASSW.

Clearly not all of the above expressed purposes are feasible, e.g. it is not feasible via such an endeavour to draw a clear distinction between social workers and non-social workers, neither might we be able to realise the objective of protecting 'clients' through the standards. Facilitating the movement of social workers from one country to another is a contentious issue in view of the direct recruitment of social workers from some countries to others, e.g. from South Africa and the Caribbean to the United Kingdom to the disadvantage of South Africa and the Caribbean. However, from an ethical point of view the migration of those social workers that wish to practice in another country should be enabled and not blocked. The retention of social work skills within countries is dependent on such factors as service conditions, salaries and validation of the profession which need to be addressed on national levels.

A few participants expressed the view that the document should go further to include more practical guidelines. These practical guidelines should include: a multi-tiered classification for the basic qualification, e.g. with a range from the number of years of basic schooling, plus at least one year of full time social work education to a degree with 3 or 4 years of social work education (the minimum period of practical training should be specified in such a classification); the acknowledgement and recognition of prior learning experiences; and the identification of core competencies, knowledge and skills as applied to context-specific realities. A very small minority went as far as asking for the global standards to prescribe texts and minimum number of hours that students need to spend on reading. This was clearly an impossible request to include at the global level as it would entail a complete denial of context-specific realities. Indeed, it would perhaps be impossible to entertain such a request even at local or national levels, as it would contribute to the curtailment of academic freedom, restrict knowledge development and constrain the development of critical thinking. Other participants expressed concern that the proposed multi-tiered system may appear to be far too elitist, with perhaps social workers from the Two-Thirds World being more likely to be categorised into the lower ranks. Prescribing the duration of training or the number of course credits is problematic, given the variations of the academic year across countries and regions, and the diversities in crediting courses in different contexts. Also, for example, a six to twelve month intensive social work programe, with careful selection of mature students with appropriate prior learning experiences and/or related qualifications, might prove to be as valuable as a first degree social work programe with school leaving students. It is the *quality* of the educational programe that must not be compromised. From available information, it would appear that the academisation of social work is becoming the norm, with many countries opting for either a three or four-year Bachelors degree in Social Work, with a few countries, like Chile, being an exception with a five-year Bachelors degree.

A minority view was that IFSW and IASSW begin with no document; that a grassroots approach be used in encouraging national bodies to formulate their own standards. These national standards, formulated for example via a five-year action plan, could then be processed into global standards. However, one does not have to adopt an either/or approach to the development of global standards. If we accept the premise that such standards do not represent a finite or static product, but a dynamic process through which we continue building a framework that we aspire towards, then we accept that such an endeavour would involve a global-regional-national-local dialectical interaction. This must involve cross-national and cross-regional dialogue.

In developing global standards, care needed to be taken that we did not further fragment and de-professionalise social work, as so clearly elucidated by Dominelli in her discussion on the impact of the competencies-based approach to social work education and practice. This view was supported by Lorenz, who, while not invalidating the need for quality control by having some benchmark criteria, warned that it might "trivialise social work skills even further". To circumvent this possibility we made concerted efforts to transcend the kind of reductionist language used within many national/regional contexts in their development of unit standards, designed to meet criteria for the competencies-based approach that fragments social work skills and roles into minute, constituent parts. We acknowledge that there might be merits to the competencies-based approach on national/regional levels. However, this is seen to be far too specific to be applied to the global level.

During consultations questions were raised regarding 'minimum' by whose or what standards? Is it possible that 'minimum standards' could decrease rather than enhance the profession's standards? An alternative argument was that as 'standards' represent an ideal, they could, in effect, come to be 'maximum standards' that all schools of social work in all countries and regions are put under pressure to attain. The experience of South Africa in the early 1990s is a case in point. The then Council for Social Work, which was actually a State apparatus designed to uphold the ideology of apartheid, proposed what it called 'minimum standards'. However, the document actually reflected superior standards and proposed control mechanisms, which, if accepted, would have jeopardised the position and, perhaps, the very existence of schools of social work at the historically disadvantaged black institutions, which were poorly resourced compared with the white universities. Fortunately there was sufficient solidarity among social work educators who rejected the document, so it did not become part of the statutory requirement.

Some colleagues who engaged in the consultation process also expressed concern about the possibility of a western domination. Given the western hegemony in social work education and practice, and that "Western European countries and the USA perhaps have fairly settled views of what social work is and what it means to provide good social work education', such fears are not merely speculative. We acknowledge that the claim to what constitutes good social work education in Western Europe and the USA may be based on ill-founded premises. Australia and Canada also seem to have made a great deal of progress in the development of national standards. In order to prevent such a western domination, the following were considered, and must continue to be considered in relation to the global standards:

— Ensuring representation from different regions of the world on the Committee in the formulation of the standards.

— Facilitating as much consultation and inclusion in the process as possible.

— Ensuring that the global standards take into account a country's unique historical, political, cultural, social and economic contexts.

— Ensuring that the unique developmental needs of countries are considered in relation to the global standards.
— Ensuring that the profession's developmental status and needs in any given country are considered.
— While encouraging schools to secure adequate resources to the extent possible, that we ensure that there is no assumption that schools with lesser resources provide poorer quality programes.
— Facilitating open dialogue across national and regional boundaries.

Amongst those who participated during consultations, there was overwhelming concern that context-specific realities, and the resources available to individual institutions to meet the global standards, are taken into consideration. In the development of global standards we should not create unintended consequences by disadvantaging some educational institutions. As much as global standards may be used to benchmark national norms and standards, as far as possible, national and regional experiences and practices (even where formal standards do not exist) were incorporated into the formulation of the global standards. Where national or regional standards do not exist, IASSW and IFSW should collaborate to facilitate the development of such standards. The circular, interactive and discursive processes in developing national and global standards can, in these ways, become and remain continuous and dynamic. The process-product dialectic, in the formulation of the global standards, has been vital. While we had necessary predetermined time frames, we tried, as far as possible, not to compromise consultation processes.

Two participants during consultations recommended a two-phased process; the first would involve consultations to "get everyone on board" that might span a two to six year period. The second phase would consist of submissions by each region/ national body to IASSW to ensure compliance. The recommendations ranged from bi-annual submissions to submissions once in five years. The majority believed that, beyond the formulation of a standards document, IASSW/IFSW could play no role, and that these bodies could not really effect any mechanisms to "ensure compliance". Monitoring, conforming to the global standards and the possibility of downgrading or up grading of educational institutions were not seen as the tasks of IASSW/IFSW.

The roles of IASSW and IFSW should be facilitative and supportive. Payne pointed out that by virtue of membership with IASSW, educational institutions had to uphold at least the following minimum criteria:

— That social work education takes place after a school leaving certificate has been obtained; and that

— Social work education takes place at the tertiary level.

References

Bruyere, G. 2001. 'Making Circles: Renewing First Nations Ways of Helping', in: Dominelli, L, Lorenz, W, and Soydan, H (eds) *Beyond Racial Divides: Ethnicities in Social Work.* Aldershot, Ashgate.

Davies, M. 1985. *The Essential Social Worker.* Aldershot, Gower.

Deacon, B., Stubbs, P. and Hulse, M. 1997: *Global Social Policy: International Organisations and the Future of Welfare.* London, Sage.

Dominelli, L. 1998. Culturally Competent International Social Work in the 21st Century: An Analysis and Critique. Paper presented at the CSWE Conference on Culturally Competent Social Work, held at the University of Michigan, Ann Arbour, 8 December.

3

Dilemmas of International Social Work

International social work is on the horns of a three-pronged dilemma. The dilemma arises from the paradoxical directions or contradictory processes surrounding indigenisation, universalism and imperialism in social work. Cross-cultural dialogue and exchange is moulding and shaping new forms of social work (indigenisation) while social work is, at the same time, trying to hold onto some form of common identity (universalism). This is taking place at the same time as efforts toward internationalising social work raise the spectre of Westernisation and imperialism. Put another way, indigenisation raises challenges for universalisation and the challenges are compounded by international efforts which can quickly become imperialistic depending on what is proposed as 'universal' in social work. Culture can play an important role in enabling indigenisation and retaining universals while avoiding imperialism. The dilemmas raised by Tsang and Yan in relation to the development of social work in China provide an example of the way in which considerations about culture can promote universality in social work while avoiding imperialistic applications of Western notions of social work.

Indigenisation essentially refers to the extent to which social work practice fits local contexts. Social work practice is, in turn, shaped by the extent to which local social, political, economic, historical and cultural factors, as well as local voices, mould and shape social work responses. Universalism refers to trends within social work to find commonalities across divergent contexts such that it is possible to talk about a profession of social work with shared values and goals wherever it is practised. Imperialism refers to trends within social work promoting the dominance of Western world-views over diverse local and indigenous cultural perspectives. International social work is about the spread of social work across the globe to extend the reach of the profession as widely as possible. It also refers to the practice of, and education for, social work by members of one context, say North America, in another context, such as China or Eastern Europe. Parallels can be drawn with international agencies offering aid such that they become known as 'international aid agencies' and people working within them are said to be 'international aid workers'. To begin the discussion of the 'dilemmas of international social work encapsulated in the paradoxical processes of indigenisation, universalism and imperialism', the author's understanding of the inter-relationship between indigenising, universalising and imperialising forces within international social work is outlined.

3.1. Indigenisation

Universalising processes within the International Federation of Social Workers (IFSW) and the International Association of Schools of Social Work (IASSW) to find a global definition of social work and global standards for social work education are once again raising questions about indigenisation and imperialising forces within international social work. Indigenisation challenges universal knowledge and the cultural hegemony of dominant discourses globally and locally. As such, it is an effort to bring out multiple voices and ways of knowing situated in particular socio-historical and cultural locations so as to establish a solid foundation for meaningful cross-cultural communication in international encounters. There is no doubt that it is a postmodern notion wherein monolithic, static definitions of local culture, and of Western social work for that matter, are being deconstructed to make way for the fluid and shifting nature of culture and knowledge processes intensified by globalising forces and international exchanges. In such a world there is no such thing as a pure culture. Indigenisation is also conceived not only as a professional concern with the relevance and socio-cultural appropriateness of imported knowledge, but also as 'a political position that asserts the intellectual and professional autonomy of... social work academics and practitioners' in particular contexts.

Gray proposed that indigenisation was essentially about culture, whether it be articulating local cultures and the way in which they differed from Western cultures or reclaiming culture and possibly also tradition. In this sense indigenisation can be seen as cross-cultural practice. Given the international social work literature on cultural diversity and culturally sensitive social work practice that privileges local cultures, universalising trends might seem out of place in social work for 'indigenisation refers to the idea that the theories, values and philosophies that underlie practice must be influenced by local factors including local cultures' (Osei-Hwedie,, emphasis added). Social work is so context bound that Tsang and Ya n stated that 'any universal claim regarding the nature, purpose and method of the profession must be regarded with caution'. Hessle proposes that acceptance of the context-bound nature of social work is a universal. Hence, definitions of social work might vary at different times in history and in various regions since the form and shape that social work takes is shaped by sociocultural contexts. Thus, he notes that the international definition of social work formulated by the IFSW and IASSW could be considered as a framework guiding practice for differences across diverse contexts that are, in part, moulded by variations in the relationship of welfare policy and social work to state welfare programes. For example, Hessle notes that when the state takes full responsibility for the welfare of its citizens, as is the case in Sweden, then social work has a recognised role in social reform and in ensuring that citizens' rights are fulfilled. However, where the state does not want to intrude on the privacy of citizens, as in the USA, then the role of social work becomes one of diagnosing the vulnerability of those unable to adjust to social norms. One might add that in neo-liberal systems, such as Australia and the UK, social work becomes inter alia a contracted arm of government to deliver state-determined and sanctioned welfare programes.

Certainly there are many countries where social work has been moulded and shaped by colonial influences, such as most countries where social work is practised in post-colonial Africa and Asia. For social workers in post-colonial situations, universalisation (and possibly globalisation) is seen as a new form of colonisation and indigenisation as a reactivation of tradition. Could it be that indigenisation is itself an international movement taking shape in different parts of the world as a reaction against globalisation? As such, might it be a reaction, within social work, against colonisation now in the guise of globalisation and universalisation?

3.2. UNIVERSALISATION

Gray and Fook suggested possible approaches to finding a flexible framework for universal social work that allowed for differences yet provided for accountability, responsiveness and connectivity. In so doing, they articulated the dilemmas surrounding the notion of universal social work as follows:

1. The globalisation–localisation debate grapples with the dilemma that, alongside the process of globalisation, there is a counter tendency towards the development of locally based solutions and the privileging of local cultures.
2. The Westernisation–indigenisation debate concerns the relevance of Western social work to Third World or developing contexts, such as Africa, Eastern Europe and Asia.
3. The multicultural–universalisation debate concerns the 'implications of built-in cultural biases' within social work's multicultural or culturally sensitive perspective. The notion that its values are universalisable creates potential conflict with non-Western and traditional cultures with collectivist values based inter alia on kinship, community networks and the extended family system.
4. The universal–local standards debate may or may not be relevant to the notion of 'universal social work' since it might be acceptable to think philosophically about an international orientation without necessarily attempting to attain universal agreement on definitions of, or standards for, professional social work education and practice.

What then are the universals in social work and why do we need them? Gray and Fook take 'universal social work' to mean those elements that transcend national boundaries and which give 'social work a global face such that there are commonalities in theory and practice across widely divergent contexts'. As well as increasing our knowledge and understanding of human problems, strengthening practice and raising the profession's profile, an 'emphasis on shared social work aims and activities can serve political ends in raising standards and expectations of good service, especially in countries less inclined to value social services'. However, professional preservation and universalising values aside, we need to find ways to 'best achieve the goals of social justice and of making the world a better place for those who suffer as a result of widespread injustice and poverty'. Gray and Fook see the issues involved as being 'less about imposing a unified conception of social work, and more about a ground up collaborative process for finding and developing commonalities to fight a common cause'. Lorenz draws attention to the tensions inherent in professionalised social work trying to commandeer areas of activity which have long been the realm of volunteers or paraprofessionals and self-help groups. Hessle thus questions whether 'social work can claim the status of a proper profession' when it carries out activities long fulfilled by volunteers.

For Hessle, and for Gray and Fook, the essential question is 'how can we become more accountable and responsive to our different contexts, and at the same time become more connected with one another's work, so that together we can develop ways in which our practice becomes more transferable across contexts?' Gray and Fook suggest a grounded approach where we celebrate and recognise commonalities while at the same time valuing and including differences; an expansive approach to professional definition rather than a self-protective stance; the relevance of a social development response to poverty and injustice; social work as contextual practice, i.e. not only working with people in contexts but also working with whole contexts; and valuing dialogical processes within local contexts that does not exclude honouring existing social work knowledge.

Hessle proposed acceptance of social work as context-bound; as dependent on external influences, like natural disasters, globalisation and migration; as directing attention towards marginalised people in society, such as the poor and vulnerable; as multidisciplinary; as practice-oriented; and as focusing on at least three levels of analysis, namely, the structural, organisational or group, and family and individual levels. Likewise, Gray proposed, first, that social workers, at the very least, agreed on an ecological approach wherein the constant interplay of the person-in-environment remained the focus, and the achievement of social justice was an overriding goal. Within this holistic, ecological perspective there was place for a multiplicity of goals and levels of activity in social work in its quest for social justice. Coates proposed a social ecology model as best suited to a holistic understanding of the interrelatedness and connectedness of all life forms, human and non-human. Second, Gray also agreed that social workers promoted the welfare and interests of people in society and third, that social workers were committed to the achievement of social justice and hence took human rights seriously. Gray believed that an egalitarian, humanistic and democratic conception of social justice prevailed to give expression to social work's central values of self-determination, respect for persons, equality and the recognition of basic human rights. Fourth, Gray maintained that there was acceptance that social workers adopted a critically, reflective approach to practice.

Gray and Fook might well ask whether these are 'shared areas of understanding and... commonalities in social work education, practice and research... which provide common ground for discussion and debate' . Historically, we have been united by the notion of our shared humanity and our 'common human needs' and problems. There is some agreement that we are 'united by shared human rights and social justice goals'. Of necessity, the 'universals' in social work can only refer to generalities since the form social work's mission takes will vary greatly in different countries given diverse social, economic, political, historical and cultural circumstances.

3.3. Imperialisation

Given its central focus of privileging, *the local* indigenisation seeks to resist 'universalising forces' and the 'cultural imperialism' of Western social work. No one puts this better than Tsang and Ya n writing about the struggle in China 'to find a balance between importing social work knowledge and methods and the need to develop indigenous conceptual frameworks and structures for organising social work principles and practices'. They illustrate the paradoxes giving rise to the dilemmas in international social work. Since culture is central to the solutions herein proposed, it is also necessary to review current understanding of culture and of international social work.

Upon reviewing the literature on indigenisation (and cultural imperialism), it became increasingly apparent that there was a need to review related literature on the connection between indigenous social work and ecology, spirituality, religion, cross-cultural social work and culturally sensitive social work practice as well as international social work. For the most part it seemed that many authors were saying that indigenous voices had been silenced by Western social work. However, in this related literature there is evidence that indigenous cultures are enriching and adding to new discourses in social work beyond the conventional, radical and postmodern; they are opening up new ways of thinking about social work in tune with indigenous ways. Perhaps the extent to which these discourses influence social work discourse might reflect the extent of interaction between Western and indigenous cultures. The literature on ecology and spirituality seemed to reflect indigenous voices. They appeared not as knowledges for particular contexts but as knowledges with wider application, and in this they seemed to differ from the social work literature on cross-cultural and culturally sensitive practice.

Gray and Allegritti stressed the importance of cross-cultural or intercultural understanding within indigenising processes, and noted current definitions of culture as relating to, *inter alia*, a system of beliefs and practices that is articulated at several levels wherein art, morals, rules and norms constitute 'societal culture'. They noted that cultural identities were continually changing and evolving, and the internal variations existed even within specific cultures. They drew attention to the political dimension of culture, which was seen to be constituted through contested practices, and was also often used as a synonym for 'a nation' or 'a people'. Thus, while there might be such a thing as a dominant Australian, African, European and North American culture, in truth these comprise a host of minority cultures that may or may not conform to the dominant culture or, if they do, there are varying degrees of conformity and harmony between cultures. The reality is that most of us live in multi-cultural, multi-ethnic, multi-racial and multi-class societies.

Given that culture is central to indigenising, universalisation and imperialising processes, we need to examine the definition of culture we are using in the context of these paradoxical processes. Are we seeing culture as a context-specific and 'historically created system of meanings and significance' relating to basic activities and social relationships that remain fairly static, such as 'how one mourns and disposes of the dead and how one treats one's parents, children, wife, neighbours and strangers'? Or are we seeing it in postmodern terms as 'continually changing and evolving'? Do we agree that 'every culture is internally varied, speaks in several voices, and its range of interpretive possibilities is often indeterminate'? Do we share Tully's idea that cultures 'are continuously contested, imagined, reimagined, transformed, and negotiated both by their members and through their interaction with others' or are we using culture to refer to 'a nation' or 'a people' and do we agree that most nations have a dominant culture and 'a relatively small number of minority cultures'? Do we agree that there are injustices within cultures and that 'political movements... concern themselves with... the pre-servation of culture... [and in this sense that culture is] about trying to implement and/or maintain a set of power relationships in a contemporary context'? Clearly, our understanding of culture affects the way in which we view universalising trends within social work. This tension is ably demonstrated by Tsang and Ya n when they raise the perplexing question of 'which type of social work do we want to adopt in China?' However, before taking a closer look at the dilemmas they raise, a note on the nature of international social work is needed in order to outline the complexities of the paradoxes under discussion fully.

3.4. International Social Work

International social work has long been defined as collaborative, comparative, exchange or dialogue. Barker, in the Social Work Dictionary, defines international social work as 'the transfer between countries of methods or knowledge about social work' and Midgley asserts that 'the most frequently identified sources of ideas and innovations are Great Britain and the United States'. An important aspect of this international social work exchange is its focus on professional practice in different parts of the world and the development of social work 'as a profession is a primary objective of international social work'. Since 'social work remains a profession with a largely local orientation', it is surprising that despite its 'growing involvement in international activities, no systematic attempt has been made to examine the common characteristics and diverse forms of the profession, and the challenges it faces from an international perspective'.

International social work is also described as a direct practice activity that takes place through international humanitarian organisations. Through the efforts of these 'international development agencies aided by private organisations and western schools of social work' social work education based on the Western professional and scientific model of social work with academic training of several years' duration spread from Britain and North America to widely divergent social, political, historical, economic and cultural contexts in Asia, Africa and Latin America. The United Nations (UN), with 'its many commissions and allied agencies', has played a key role in the transfer of Western social work to so-called developing countries 'through seminars, technical assistance, and exchange schemes'.

Critiques of this neutral transfer perspective on international social work are found in the indigenisation literature. Thus a balanced study of international social work also requires an examination of the indigenous social work literature. Healy describes an 'era of indigenisation' in the 1970s when 'intense... consultation, transplantation, and borrowing' of Western models was met with resistance and appeals for 'an indigenous form of social work'. She attributes this to 'strong anti-(North) American feelings developed along with a rejection of the process of borrowing and using models from the industrialised countries'. However, as Kendall noted, 'there was no one to gainsay (Western social workers)... in countries where social work, if it existed at all, was the prerogative of a leisure class intent on performing what it regarded as its moral obligations to the poor'. Thus, driven by altruistic intentions, social work was promoted with a kind of missionary seal in colonial and post-colonial situations where inherent power imbalances and the relevance of Western models went unquestioned. As a consequence, UN surveys of social work training repeatedly revealed the 'limited applicability of the US model', suggesting 'the need to promote indigenous methods, curricula and study material'. Despite findings of this nature, most 'UN publications and personnel... tacitly assumed... that the US social work philosophy (was) somewhat superior' to that of the developing context concerned, and that the principles and methods of North American social work had 'universal applicability'.

Underpinning this 'professional imperialism' was the implicit assumption that developing countries were incapable of finding their own models. Thus, diverse, indigenous forms of social care, which were unique to their specific cultural contexts, were 'silenced, devalued, displaced, ignored, made invisible, and disqualified' as inferior to Western social work knowledge and practice. Concerns about the relevance of and the search for indigenous models persist today with valid reason despite Dominelli's dislike of the term 'indigenous'. In many countries, indigenous people self-identify as such and are proud of their indigenous heritage. The cross-cultural and indigenous social work literature is giving rise to constructive dialogue about the way in which indigenous and local solutions can inform global perspectives on social work. As Midgley argued, 'it is time to challenge the one-way international flow of ideas and practices and to learn from the Third World'.

Despite greater awareness of the need for an understanding of international social work in this globalising era, 'most social workers have limited, if any, exposure to programs or practice beyond the boundaries of their own countries'. Hokenstad and Midgley noted that it was 'essential for social workers to have an international perspective and understanding to be effective practitioners in today's world' where the cross-cultural nature of international exchanges is increasingly recognised. Thus, Midgley notes that the term 'international social work' is now widely (although imprecisely) used to denote the exchanges that take place between social workers from different societies and cultures. Rather than a static body of knowledge, international social work should be seen as an emerging discourse—a moveable feast with Eastern, Western and Indigenous cuisine to which new flavours might be added and in which new combinations might be made to produce deliciously edible and highly desirable new dishes! Harris referred to it as a 'moving target', as something that was changing even as we were attempting to understand it. As we embark on international changes, not only do we change our ideas and perspectives but we add to understanding of the complex issues inherent in cross-cultural contexts. Thus, learning about international social work is not just preparation for social work academics and students to study or practice abroad. International practice enables social workers to develop a critical understanding of the way in which international development works. It is not a neutral process and even though the Grameen Bank might have done a lot of good, it has yet to be proven that it has succeeded in substantially altering the position of women in the societies in which it operates. Development, like social work, is not a neutral activity. Unless we have the insight and ability to step outside of our Western paradigms and to view international situations through a cultural lens and to approach them with humility, we run the danger of perpetuating professional imperialism.

Thus, given the paradox of diversity and commonality across contexts, 'social work should be aware of the dangers of overstandardisation... The tendency toward standardisation can inhibit the profession's ability to respond effectively to local needs and impede the goals of professional development'. Instead, cross-cultural exchange and dialogue, networking or working through or with international organisations are means through which we might express solidarity with global or local causes, make connections and work to transform and reshape the world. As Lyons points out, internationalising social work is not just about the mobility of professionals but also 'a way of viewing and understanding individual societies and the global environment in order to develop practices which are responsive to identified and emerging needs, and which include (exchanging) comparative perspectives or cross-national (or cross-cultural) activity, or which contribute to international policy change, as appropriate'.

Thus, international social work is not just about the spread of professional social work across the globe, it is also about the development of practices that are relevant in local contexts. As such, different forms of social work emerge and take hold, moulded and shaped by the social, political, economic circumstances, the history and culture of particular contexts, as well as prevailing social work knowledge and values. It might be more useful to think about 'social works' rather than a single monolithic entity given the vast diversity of the world in which we live and the countries within it. There is much of value in Western thinking about social work, but this must not stifle the wisdom and experience of local cultures. However, in light of the 'universals' proposed above, social work clearly has a goal to change unjust cultural practices that do not value human rights.

International social work is not just about inter-nationalising social work if that means spreading a single type of social work as conceived in the West. Universalising trends such as global educational standards and international definitions can only serve as guides and would smack of cultural imperialism if used mainly to promote Western social work for, even within and across Western regions, different types of social work are practised. There is diversity even within Western social work and the social, political, economic and cultural contexts within many of these regions are driving social work towards what Australians call an 'economic rationalist' or managerial model of social work which is overly obsessed with standards and definitions because of the demands being placed on social work to prove its worth in economic terms, i.e. its efficiency and effectiveness. It is within this context that notions of evidence-based practice have arisen. This is often a vastly different context from that found in countries where social work is only now being introduced, such as in Eastern Europe and China, for example. In other countries, such as South Africa, where social work has a history almost as long as that in the UK and USA, social work is being transformed to meet a changed social, political and economic situation where issues of culture, expressed in calls for indigenous social work practice, have called into question Western social work models like casework. What is evolving is something akin to a 'development practitioner' as social work has embraced a developmental focus so as to respond to widespread poverty, unemployment, crime and HIV/AIDS occurring on a scale, especially in rural areas, which is incomprehensible in a developed world.

International social work, in being responsive to diverse contexts and sensitive to local cultures, must, of necessity, be a flexible entity, open to new forms of social work evolving as it responds to local problems and needs in culturally appropriate and sensitive ways. This requires a different type of seeing and responding when social workers from the West enter into new terrain to advise on the type of social work needed. It requires us to pay attention to local cultures. We need to find ways of appealing to common human needs and values in countries and local communities divided by seemingly irreconcilable differences. What answers do we have for people who have suffered years of victimisation and oppression at the hands of their oppressors? How can we expel deep-seated fear and hatred in a world which is becoming increasingly fearful and divided? We need to tread lightly, to learn to listen and to tune into culture lest we too quickly impose our culture on others and hence stand guilty of imperialism.

Furthermore, we need to internationalise the curricula in Western schools of social work and read international literature so that we learn about cultures and contexts other than our own. At a recent gathering of North American social workers, most of whose work was well-published and familiar to me, it was surprising to learn that none of them read the international literature. While there are many social workers across the globe engaged in international exchanges, their work is not widely read and would appear to be known by a minority interested in, engaging in and writing about social work in contexts other than their own.

We also need to engage in debates about internationalising trends in social work, such as global education standards and international definitions. Too few schools of social work belong to international social work organisations and most faculty members are totally unaware of them or the work they are doing. As noted by Tsang, Ya n and Shera, the social work education agenda cannot be dictated by foreign or domestic experts, but must be 'grounded in the realities of the practitioners and educators coming from diverse geographical and social locations'. Writing about a China– Canada collaborative project, they note that the 'models of social work practice and education that emerge... may not, and need not, be totally compatible with the established standards and conventions of Western social work'.

3.5. Paradoxical Processes in Social Work

In China, indigenisation is seen as a 'political position' to assert 'the intellectual and professional autonomy of Chinese social work academics and practitioners'. It is interesting to note that issues surrounding the development of social work in China in the 2000s relate very much to those that faced social work as it spread across the Western world in the early decades of the 1900s. In both cases social work was closely tied to government welfare provision and thus 'most social work functions are (were) directly operated and monitored by the state'. For example, in South Africa the development of social work was inextricably linked with service provision along racial lines within the apartheid system. It is one of the few countries where a professional regulatory body was written into welfare legislation such that social workers could not practice if they were not registered with the Council for Social Work. Perhaps there are parallels between the authoritarian nature of South Africa under apartheid and the emergent modern Chinese state.

Interestingly, Tsang and Ya n grapple with 'what type of social work' China should import, showing quite clearly that Western social work is definitely 'not a monolithic entity with a coherent set of ideologies, teleologies, epistemologies and technologies'. They note how debates on cultural pluralism raise questions about the universality of social work values. Surely, this drives a stake into the very heart of Western thinking on social work values. Furthermore, they note the extent to which 'the ideology of social work is anchored to a belief in the welfare state' which has a strong tie with democratic socialism when 'western welfare states have never had a coherent set of ideologies that nurtures the humanistic values embraced by the social work profession'. Is the social work profession out of step with reality? Its values cannot be universal, yet it says they should be. It strives for the ideal of the welfare state which no longer exists in the 'Beveridgian' sense anywhere in the world. Even the core concept of the person-in-environment is open to dispute between those who see the purpose of social work as primarily to help people to adjust to their environment and those who see it as being to change the environment to eliminate the structural causes of human suffering. The former is complicated by social control functions within individual helping for social work is surely 'an effective social apparatus to control the poor', especially given the way governments exploit the expertise of professionals.

Similar critiques have been made about development and the way in which national governments and international aid agencies control the poor. What then of the therapeutic model? 'China has not gone through a period of psychologisation and widespread adoption of the language of mental health and therapy as the West has', so this model won't fit either. Nor will empowerment or social action approaches for, 'In China, the government has stated clearly that the major social assignment for the social work profession is to remedy any social problems caused by economic reform and modernisation'. In other words, the Chinese government wants social work to go back to its roots! It seems then that Chinese social work might favor a technocratic approach which 'assumes that through professional education and training social workers can acquire the expert knowledge needed to solve individual and community problems'. Tsang and Ya n note the massive opportunity for creativity and innovation in designing Chinese social work and the potential benefit of this for everyone. There is no clear, unquestioned type of social work worth importing, but there are ideas worth considering. If the stimulus might be Western, the response will definitely be Chinese!

References

Burlington, VT, Ashgate. Dominelli L, Bernard WT, eds. 2003. *Broadening horizons: international exchanges in social work.* Burlington, VT, Ashgate.

Dean R . 2001. The myth of cross cultural competence. *Families in Society* 82(6): 623–630.

Dominelli L, Bernard WT, eds. *Broadening horisons: international exchanges in social work.*

Goldstein H. 1986. Education for social work practice: a cognitive, cross-cultural approach. *International Social Work* 29(2): 149–164.

Healy LM. 2001. *International social work: professional action in an interdependent world.* New York, Oxford University Press.

NASW Press. Coates J. 2003. *Ecology and social work: toward a new paradigm.* Halifax, Fernwood Press.

4

Professionalism in Social Work

Professional distance, professional boundaries and objectivity have been key concepts in education for many social and health professions. 'Professional objectivity was valued as the quality that allowed the helper to divorce him or herself from subjective feeling, attitudes and beliefs'. However, radical, postmodern, feminist and rural social work approaches suggest that practice based on the 'expert' role is not only inappropriate, but can create unnecessary boundaries and unrealistic expectations. The professional expert role entailed workers distancing themselves from their clients in order to remain professionally objective.

Maintaining professional distance may even be counterproductive to good practice in some situations. Postmodern approaches to this dilemma seem more akin to the notion of partnership between social worker and client. Our explorations in this area led us to consider the ideas of professional distance and objectivity, the essential understanding of professional behavior and how we might move along a continuum of self-disclosure/exposure according to the particular context. Professional distance and professional boundaries, we believe, can be flexible and elastic, while still ensuring competent and appropriate practice. It may be useful to picture boundaries as a 'stretchy piece of elastic' or a continuum between the 'professional, objective expert' and the 'helpful friend' rather than the dichotomy of professional and nonprofessional that is often presented.

In the present chapter, radical, postmodern, feminist and rural social work literature and research are used to explore this practice issue. There are strategies and supports to enable social workers to practice ethically and appropriately without the constraints of maintaining strict professional distance. Adopting a continuum model allows that it is possible for social workers to move along the spectrum, depending on their particular role and using conscious judgement as to their place and how elastic the boundaries should be at any given time.

In many contexts, the elasticity of such boundaries can facilitate effective and empowering relationships with the people with whom we come into contact, improving practice rather than detracting from it. However, 'stretching' of the boundary or any movement along the continuum should stem from a conscious decision of the appropriateness of self-disclosure/exposure, the protection of oneself and good practice principles. It is also linked to concepts of self-reflection and reflexivity, but is perhaps an addition or extension to these skills and attributes.

4.1. Professional Objectivity

Understanding the notion of professionalism is a prelude to a discussion about professional objectivity and professional distance. Social work has struggled to identify with traditional forms of professionalism. Social work is unusual among aspirant professions in that a substantial section of the social work workforce has actively sought to develop an anti-professional stance. A desire to close the social distance between social worker and 'client', for example when taking a radical egalitarian stance, is at the core of this perspective, along with an inherent mistrust of the way the relationship between the two is conceptualised.

There has been a long-standing debate in social work about the benefits and disadvantages of pursuing a model of elite professionalism and being equated with traditional professions such as medicine and law. A glance at a recently published Australian undergraduate social work text provides some insight into current thinking about professionalism.

Social work has considered itself a profession in that it has codes of practice, regulation and accreditation of social work courses to maintain specialised knowledge and skills and ensure that principles of professional conduct are taught. The recognised benefits of professional status include a shared commitment to high practice standards and ethical behavior, as well as the status to influence public policy and social change. Camilleri argues that 'Professionals are necessary. Consumers of services recognise the value and expertise of the professional'.

Professionalism, it has been argued, implies the acquisition of some form of specialism: knowledge and skills that are not possessed by untrained workers. Professionalism has been portrayed as emphasising technical proficiency, impartiality and, therefore, an apolitical approach. It has been claimed that professionalism encourages the introduction of business-like career structures where 'correct' and 'professional' behavior are highly prised. In this scenario, correct behavior, including detachment and controlled emotional involvement, is rewarded. Professionalism has also been seen to support and reinforce the unequal distribution of power within traditional client/professional relationships.

The role of professional expert is well documented in individual work and clinical practice. The expert role relates to a positivist philosophy, which holds that human behavior can be understood and studied objectively. It can be argued that social work can never be objective or value-neutral and that it is always morally and politically charged. Indeed, Clark argues that social workers, like teachers and other human service professionals, cannot pretend to be neutral because of the nature of the contact, and the issues for work, with service users.

Furthermore, proponents of this belief contend that the expert approach follows certain laws and rules that enable the qualified social worker to 'prescribe' the suitable treatment or intervention. In this approach, the social worker '... becomes a skilled technician, who, understanding the 'laws' can 'intervene' appropriately to bring about change'.

The continuing debate about regulation and registration of the profession in Australia attests to the concern held by some social workers about protecting their status and reinforcing their professional niche. Social work jargon acts to reinforce this 'specialism' and to create divisions between trained and untrained workers, as well as between social workers and service users. The language of the profession, using terms such as 'caseload', 'case notes', 'home visits', 'office interviews' and work with 'clients' or 'cases', has been seen to serve as a linguistic device to distance workers from citizens who are service users. In this environment, it is claimed, '... face-to-face contacts between human beings begin to take on the appearance of contact between things; terminology and language place a shield between worker and client'. It has also been argued that the development of professionalism has neutered the political aspects of the profession. In Mullaly's view:

> '... professionalism emphasises technical aspects of helping, such as impartiality, emotional neutrality, and apolitical service. Thus, it masks the political component of social work practice and perpetuates the notion that capitalist social relations are natural and normal functions of an industrialised society'.

Proponents of the radical practice tradition mounted a critique of the expert model of social work practice and the move to professionalise social work. In their view, these developments were linked with:

> '... a growing sense of distance between the worker and the client. This is expressed in several ways, e.g. the growth of jargon in the language of social workers; the restriction of access to clients in department buildings; the increasing importance of professional qualifications as a condition of employment and promotion in agencies; the development of a code of ethics to regulate practice. All of this, it is claimed, has driven a wedge between the worker and the client... Moreover, by creating the basis for the monopolisation of power over standards of practice and control over entry into the profession, it can act as a drawbridge shutting out all new ideas and innovations which run counter to it'.

The structural analysis of personal problems inherent in the radical approach included a critique of the social control functions of the social work profession and welfare arrangements. Similarly, Leonard has argued:

> 'Where there is welfare... there is expertise directed to the organisation and control (in their own interests) of those who are subject to its gase'.

This approach also adopted earlier ideas from the anti-psychiatry movement, including rejection of the medical model of mental health practice and the professional distancing it implied. In a discussion of 'objectivity' and 'self-determination', Fook states:

> 'The rationale for professional objectivity may be the belief that clients are best helped by someone they see as a respected authority who is not emotionally involved with them. Like many functional myths, this has true and false components'.

The effect, it Professional Distance and Social Workis argued, may be that service users uncritically accept the views of the social worker, both because that is what they believe is expected of them and because of the inherent power imbalance. A belief in self-determination ignores the fact that the professional usually has the power in the relationship, and that many service users are involuntary.

Models of practice have developed to address the perceived problems arising from the expert-professional tradition. These problems include the distancing of people using services, the unequal power relationships between workers and service users, divisions between qualified and unqualified workers and the reinforcement of inequality in society resulting from an apolitical stance. Approaches based on citizenship and partnership, for example, work towards developing democratic relationships between workers and service users. Anti-oppressive and anti-discriminatory practice models also act to affirm a person's subjective experience and overcome professional distancing. They work to create equal relationships and demystify processes involved in helping.

The impact of postmodern thinking on social work has contributed to these debates. Whereas the radical critique of professionalism focused on inequalities between professionals and service users, postmodern critiques strive to understand '... how professionalism maintains power relations through many levels of discourse'. In discussing empowerment and social work practice, Parker *et al.* argue that in a postmodern approach, clients are truly at the centre of decision making about practice because they 'supply the interpretive framework' suited to a particular context. This approach directly challenges the positivist, truth-based tradition of expert professional knowledge. Postmodernists argue that the consequence of this new way of thinking about professionalism is not to simply discard the traditional ideas of professionalism but, rather, to reconfigure them to suit today's contexts. As Fook argues, professionalism '... must be reconceptualised as the ability to produce knowledge in ways which are applicable to specific settings'. This includes recognition of the ability to handle uncertainty and change, in situations where generalisation and prediction are less valid. In her approach to this challenge, Osmond discusses how individuals make sense of knowledge '... according to the specific situation, circumstance, place and time in which they act'. Others refer to the way social workers act creatively and with flexibility to meet the context they face.

For our purposes, a key message from these practice approaches concerns the reduction of professional distance by increasing the use of self-disclosure and of seeing the relationship as a 'partnership'. Appropriate self-disclosure of positive and negative experiences, and sharing some aspects of one's own experience, enables the worker to be seen as a 'normal' person rather than a remote professional. Judicious sharing of personal experience is connected to the concept of 'professional use of self', described as the use of the worker's personal manner and skills, including presence, to effect the best outcome for the client. The use of self-knowledge and self-awareness '... involves the conscious employment of social work skills, knowledge, values and personal experience in ways that are illuminating to the work at hand'. Some researchers have been interested in how practitioners integrate professional knowledge and values with personal experience and emotions. Osmond includes personalised and historical knowledge, as well as practice wisdom, in her conceptualisation of how workers use knowledge in a particular practice situation. Findings reported from a study of clinicians indicated that:

> '... the clinicians we interviewed did not appear to sacrifice rationality and objectivity in practicing compassionate care, but were able to balance 'the head and the heart''.

The professional relationship, it is argued, is disciplined and the self is used to help the service user. Brill explores the use of self in the professional relationship, where mutual trust and respect are key ingredients. She argues that the conscious use of self does not mean that interactions will be stiff or formal, but rather that '... the best ones are warm and safe although not always comfortable'. Trevithick argues that there are two aspects of this 'use of self' idea: (1) appropriate self-disclosure; and (2) the maintenance of professional boundaries. Echoing our earlier reference to a continuum, she explains:

> 'In personal terms, it is where we take up an appropriate position of separateness while also maintaining a clear connection to service users, so that we are not too distant or inflexible on the one hand, nor too merged or inappropriately accommodating on the other'.

Intuition is a related concept and Trevithick recommends that further research is needed on the place of intuition in social work. In a contribution to this emerging field, an Australian study of the development of professional expertise found that expert practitioners made practice decisions intuitively, in accordance with the context and the situation. These ideas of self-knowledge, self-disclosure and intuition shed light on how social workers' thoughts and feelings interact with and complement their professional practice skills: the intersection of heart and head.

4.2. Feminist Approach

Feminist practice in social work is underpinned by a feminist analysis of social arrangements, emphasising the recognition, acknowledgement and naming of women's experiences. This approach connects the personal and the political, it works to change oppressive social, economic and legal structures and it challenges traditional ways of delivering services. In a feminist approach, attention to detail such as furniture, color and comfort in interview settings, reception areas and waiting rooms can lessen the distance between workers and service users, encourage maximum sharing and help demystify the helping process. In feminist practice, the power imbalance between worker and service user may be acknowledged and discussed. This achieves a more equal and non-authoritarian style, as well as being open with service users about possible interpretations of their situation. Feminist practitioners stress that feminist therapy is, first and foremost, a relationship between two women:

> 'It is a relationship between two women who have come together for a clearly defined purpose and, when that purpose has been fulfilled, the

> relationship, as such, will be over. The roles are clear. The difference in power is clear, though not an issue'.

Feminist services in Australia developed in the 1970s in response to women's dissatisfaction with traditional service models, including the dominance of the medical model, sexist attitudes towards women and other concerns, such as the prevalence of mother-blaming in family welfare practice. The feminist critique included the negative impact on women of a professional belief in objectivity and neutrality, as Weeks outlined:

> 'The hierarchical service or helping model supports a model of professionalism in which 'experts' believe they should divorce their personal experiences, and certainly their lives, from the service users with whom they work. They should aim to be neutral, objective helpers-not noticing that their race, ethnicity, gender and personal experience must have an enormous impact on what they see and hear, how they think, what they consider evidence and what are the range of possible solutions they might propose'.

In a feminist approach, personal problems are redefined using an analysis of oppression and understanding of power. This has helped women who have experienced abuse and oppression use their agency as women to develop a public voice to talk about their oppression and influence the way services are provided. This political and public aspect of feminist practice faces resistance from policy makers, funding bodies and service managers, as well as professional bodies. Individual client throughput, for example, is more likely to be rewarded with funding, than public advocacy activities by workers in women's services.

The continuing feminist critique of professionalism includes recognition of the vested interest of professionals in controlling expert discourses and knowledge. In the area of violence against women, for example, the control of knowledge '... has relied on the suppression of the voice of the victim and a privileging of professional knowledge that mostly supports the cultural status quo and professional self-interest'. In a reaction to this suppression, victim/survivors are asking service providers to '... make more than cursory room for them at the table, to resist the urge to speak on their behalf and to dominate the space through which we carve our future agendas for change'.

4.3. Rural Approach

Similarities to the feminist approach of breaking down professional barriers can be found in the rural social work literature. The reality of living in a small community means that all members perform multiple roles. Such role multiplicity in the rural practice context means a fusion of personal and professional lives. Major challenges for rural social workers include managing professional and personal role boundaries, as well as dual and multiple roles. Boundaries blur and roles overlap when professionals live and work in small communities. According to Mellow, professionalism is an urban concept and '... rural life problematises the notion of professionalism'.

One Australian text has developed a different construction of social welfare practice by Aboriginal and Torres Strait Islander people, where the authors discuss deprofessionalisation, the 'Murri way' and the role of everyday helping of neighbours and 'resourceful friends' as follows:

> 'In a deprofessional approach, friendship, yarning, recognition of your common humanity with the client, sharing of stories, sharing of self, including spirituality and humour, are recognised and valued techniques. A relationship characterised in this form works with power and equality in a more complex way than the present approaches within social and welfare work'.

The rural social worker is a neighbour and 'citizen in the community' and belongs to community groups and organisations, both in her role as a social worker and in her own right as a citizen. Because rural communities feature dense social networks, professional and personal contacts are not necessarily discrete and separate. In addition, role blurring occurs in rural practice owing to a variety of contextual factors. In small organisations, positions are often multidimensional and generalist and flexibility of staff is required. There is an expectation that 'if it needs doing... do it', often meaning that social workers extend their roles into areas not formally recognised in their position descriptions or, indeed, covered by agency funding agreements. Sometimes other staff extend their boundaries into the province of what would usually be the 'territory' of the social worker. This blurring can have positive outcomes, where staff work with their strengths and acknowledge each other's specific expertise, but it can create additional stresses.

Role blurring and the experience of dual and multiple roles is not necessarily a 'bad thing', but can be constructed as both a challenge and as a positive experience for the worker and community members. It is maintained that '... rural contexts pose unique challenges for practitioners in constructing professional identity and the need for active negotiation with clients about roles in small communities'. Active negotiation is a useful construct and appears to be commonly practised in rural social work:

> 'In fact when [rural social workers] are working with clients they often have to share information of how they can act if their clients see them in public at places like Woolworths, the hotel, or many other venues. The general rule is social workers will not acknowledge their clients until they are acknowledged'.

Rural workers negotiate availability and privacy on a daily basis. Rural communities can have different expectations from urban communities of what is considered private or semi-private and where these boundaries, social and psychological, are drawn. The rural social worker is identified as both a professional with expertise and a member of the community (individual, partner, parent, group member etc.). The resultant high levels of visibility in the community are perceived by some authors as an asset that may lead to increased confidence of community members and by others as problematic. Although some workers struggle with lack of privacy, others enjoy the recognition and respect. It appears that the high visibility of the rural social worker, socially and professionally, leads to greater informality in their professional persona and this can often improve outcomes for service users, but it can also be problematic.

In rural areas, there is both an expectation that some personal information will be publicly known (and that this may be much more information than would be known in an urban environment) and caution about exposing too much because it will have ramifications for a long period, particularly in small, relatively stable populations. Living, working, raising a family and being highly visible in one's work role can create some concerns for rural social workers around safety and security. Anecdotally, rural workers have commented, in conversation variously with the authors, that feelings of acceptance, alienation, visibility, scrutiny and belonging change over time, depending on the circumstances, the relationships involved and the length of time in the community. Lonne also noted that changes over time were experienced by workers, which he conceptualised as stages of adjustment to rural practice.

REFERENCES

Bailey R & Brake M (eds). 1975. *Radical Social Work,* Edward Arnold, London.

Brill N. 1995. *Working with People: The Helping Process,* 5th edn, Longman, White Plains.

Camilleri P. 1999. Social work and its search for meaning: Theories, narratives and practices, In Pease B & Fook J (eds), *Transforming Social Work Practice,* Allen & Unwin, Sydney, pp. 25-39.

Rojek C, Peacock G & Collins S. 1998, *Social Work and Received Ideas,* Routledge, London.

Rosenthal H. 2005, The deprofessionalisation of social workers, *AASW National Bulletin,* 16 (1), 15.

Schon D. 1983, *The Reflective Practitioner: How Professionals Think in Action,* Basic Books, New York.

5

Teaching for Social Justice

The increasing ethnic, cultural, language, and religious diversity in nation-states throughout the world has raised new questions and possibilities about educating students for effective citizenship. Since World War II, nation-states throughout the Western world have become more diversified because of immigration and other factors. Ethnic and cultural diversity in the Western European nations such as the United Kingdom, France, Germany, and the Netherlands increased greatly after World War II. Groups from the former colonies of these nations in Asia, Africa, and the West Indies immigrated to Europe to satisfy labor needs and to improve their economic status.

Although the United States has been diverse since its founding, the ethnic texture of the nation has changed dramatically since the Immigration Reform Act was enacted in 1965. Most of the immigrants to the United States came from nations in Europe between 1901 and 1910. Between 1991 and 1998, however, the majority of immigrants to the United States came from nations in Latin America and Asia. The U.S. Census Bureau projects that ethnic groups of color will make up 47 percent of the U.S. population in 2050. Students of color now make up 40 percent of the students in the nation's public schools.

5.1. Assimilationist Notion of Citizenship

An assimilationist conception of citizenship education existed in most of the Western democratic nation-states prior to the rise of the ethnic revitalisation movements of the 1960s and 1970s. A major goal of citizenship education in these nations was to create nation-states in which all groups shared one dominant mainstream culture. It was assumed that ethnic and immigrant groups had to forsake their original cultures to fully participate in the nation-state.

The ethnic revitalisation movements of the 1960s and 1970s strongly challenged the assimilationist conception of citizenship education. These movements, triggered by the Civil Rights Movement in the United States, echoed throughout the world. French and Indians in Canada, West Indians and Asians in Britain, Indonesians and Surinamese in the Netherlands, and Aborigines in Australia joined the series of ethnic movements, expressed their feelings of marginalisation, and worked to make the institutions within their nation-states responsive to their economic, political, and cultural needs.

Indigenous peoples and ethnic groups within the various Western nations—such as American Indians in the United States, Aborigines in Australia, Maori in New Zealand, African Caribbeans in the United Kingdom, and Moluccans in the Netherlands—wanted their histories and cultures to be reflected in their national cultures and in school, college, and university curricula. Multicultural education was developed, in part, to respond to the concerns of ethnic, racial, and cultural groups that felt marginalised within their nation-states.

The right of ethnic and cultural minorities to maintain important aspects of their cultures and languages has been supported by philosophers and educators since the first decades of the 1900s. Julius Drachsler and Horace M. Kallen—of immigrant backgrounds themselves—argued that the southern, central, and eastern European immigrants who were entering the United States in large numbers had a right to retain parts of their cultures and languages while enjoying full citizenship rights. Cultural democracy, argued Drachsler, is an essential component of a political democracy.

In the first decades of the 1900s, Rachel Davis DuBois established school ethnic heritage programs for European immigrant groups. Leonard Covello was the principal of a community school that incorporated the culture of Italian-American students. More recently, Will Kymlicka, a Canadian political theorist, maintained that ethnic and immigrant groups should have the right to maintain their ethnic cultures and languages as well as participate fully in the civic cultures of democratic nation-states.

5.2. Balancing Unity and Diversity

Cultural, ethnic, racial, language, and religious diversity exists in most nations in the world. One of the challenges to diverse democratic nation-states is to provide opportunities for different groups to maintain aspects of their community cultures while building a nation in which these groups are structurally included and to which they feel allegiance. A delicate balance of diversity and unity should be an essential goal of democratic nation-states and of teaching and learning in democratic societies. Unity must be an important aim when nation-states are responding to diversity within their populations. They can protect the rights of minorities and enable diverse groups to participate only when they are unified around a set of democratic values such as justice and equality.

Citizenship education must be transformed in the 21st century because of the deepening racial, ethnic, cultural, language, and religious diversity in nation-states throughout the world. Citizens in a diverse democratic society should be able to maintain attachments to their cultural communities as well as participate effectively in the shared national culture. Unity without diversity results in cultural repression and hegemony. Diversity without unity leads to Balkanisation and the fracturing of the nation-state. Diversity and unity should coexist in a delicate balance in democratic, multicultural nation-states.

5.3. Social Justice and Citizenship Education

Literacy as defined and codified in the high-stakes tests that are being implemented in most states in the United States is often interpreted as basic skills in reading, writing, and mathematics. Although it is essential that all students acquire basic skills in literacy, basic skills are necessary but not sufficient in our diverse and troubled world. Literate citizens in a diverse democratic society should be reflective, moral, and active citizens in an interconnected global world. They should have the knowledge, skills, and commitment needed to change the world to make it more just and democratic. The world's greatest problems do not result from people being unable to read and write. They result from people in the world—from different cultures, races, religions, and nations—being unable to get along and to work together to solve the world's intractable problems such as global warming, the HIV/AIDS epidemic, poverty, racism, sexism, and war. Examples are the conflicts between the United States and Iraq, North Korea and its neighbors, and the Israelis and Palestinians.

In addition to mastering basic reading and writing skills, literate citizens in democratic multicultural societies such as the United States, Canada, and the United Kingdom should develop multicultural literacy. Multicultural literacy consists of the skills and abilities to identify the creators of knowledge and their interests, to uncover the assumptions of knowledge, to view knowledge from diverse ethnic and cultural perspectives, and to use knowledge to guide action that will create a humane and just world. When we teach students how to critique the injustice in the world, we should help them to formulate possibilities for action to change the world to make it more democratic and just. Critique without hope may leave students disillusioned and without agency.

5.4. Citizenship Education Project

Citizenship education needs to be changed in significant ways because of the increasing diversity within nation-states throughout the world and the quests by racial, ethnic, cultural, and religious groups for cultural recognition and rights. The Center for Multicultural Education at the University of Washington has implemented a project to reform citizenship education so that it will advance democracy as well as be responsive to the needs of cultural, racial, ethnic, religious, and immigrant groups within multicultural nation-states. The first part of this project consisted of a conference, "Ethnic Diversity and Citizenship Education in Multicultural Nation-States," held at the Rockefeller Foundation's Study and Conference Center in Bellagio, Italy, June 17–21, 2002 (Bellagio Conference). The conference, which was supported by the Spencer and Rockefeller Foundations, included participants from 12 nations: Brasil, Canada, China, Germany, India, Israel, Japan, Palestine, Russia, South Africa, the United Kingdom, and the United States. The papers from this conference are published in Diversity and Citizenship Education: Global Perspectives.

One of the conclusions of the conference was that world migration and the political and economic aspects of globalisation are challenging nation-states and national borders. At the same time, national borders remain tenacious; the number of nations in the world is increasing rather than decreasing. The number of United Nations member-states increased from 80 in 1950 to 191 in 2002. Globalisation and nationalism are contradictory but coexisting trends and forces in the world today. Consequently, educators throughout the world should rethink and redesign citizenship education courses and programs. Citizenship education should help students acquire the knowledge, attitudes, and skills needed to function in their nation-states as well as in a diverse world society that is experiencing rapid globalisation and quests by ethnic, cultural, language, and religious groups for recognition and inclusion. It should also help them to develop a commitment to act to change the world to make it more just.

Another conclusion of the Bellagio Conference was that citizenship and citizenship education are defined and implemented differently in various nations and in different social, economic, and political contexts. It is also a contested idea in nation-states throughout the world. However, there are shared problems, concepts, and issues, such as the need to prepare students in various nations to function within, as well as across, national borders. An international group should identify these shared issues and problems and formulate guidelines for dealing with them. In response to this Bellagio Conference recommendation, the Center for Multicultural Education at the University of Washington created an international consensus panel that is developing principles and identifying concepts for educating citizens for democracy and diversity in a global age.

5.5. Global Citizenship Education

Citizens in this century need the knowledge, attitudes, and skills to function in their cultural communities and beyond their cultural borders. They also should be able and willing to participate in the construction of a national civic culture that is a moral and just community. The national community should embody democratic ideals and values, such as those articulated in the Universal Declaration of Human Rights, the Declaration of Independence, the Constitution, and the Bill of Rights. Students also need to acquire the knowledge and skills required to become effective citizens in the global community. The community cultures and languages of students from diverse groups were to be eradicated in the assimilationist conception of citizenship education that existed in the United States prior to the Civil Rights Movement of the 1960s and 1970s. One consequence of assimilationist citizenship education was that many students lost their original cultures, languages, and ethnic identities. Some students also became alienated from family and community. Another consequence was that many students became socially and politically alienated within the national civic culture. Members of identifiable racial groups often became marginalised in both their community cultures and in the national civic culture because they could function effectively in neither. When they acquired the language and culture of the Anglo mainstream, they often were denied structural inclusion and full participation into the civic culture because of their racial characteristics.

5.6. Development of Global Identifications

Assimilationist notions of citizenship are ineffective in this century because of the deepening diversity throughout the world and the quests by marginalised groups for cultural recognition and rights. Multicultural citizenship is essential for today's global age. It recognises and legitimises the rights and needs of citizens to maintain commitments both to their cultural communities and to the national civic culture. Only when the national civic culture is transformed in ways that reflect and give voice to the diverse ethnic, racial, language, and religious communities that constitute it will it be viewed as legitimate by all of its citizens. Only then can citizens develop clarified commitments to the nation-state and its ideals.

Citizenship education should help students to develop thoughtful and clarified identifications with their cultural communities and their nation-states. It also should help them to develop clarified global identifications and deep understandings of their roles in the world community. Students need to understand how life in their cultural communities and nations influences other nations and the cogent influence that international events have on their daily lives. Global education's major goals should be to help students understand the interdependence among nations in the world today, to clarify attitudes toward other nations, and to develop reflective identifications with the world community.

Nonreflective and unexamined cultural attachments may prevent the development of a cohesive nation with clearly defined national goals and policies. Although we need to help students develop reflective and clarified cultural identifications, they also must be helped to clarify their identifications with their nation-states. Blind nationalism, however, will prevent students from developing reflective and positive global identifications. Nationalism and national attachments in most nations are strong and tenacious. An important aim of citizenship education should be to help students develop global identifications. They also must develop a deep understanding of the need to take action as citizens of the global community to help solve the world's difficult global problems. Cultural, national, and global experiences and identifications are interactive and interrelated in a dynamic way.

Students should develop a delicate balance of cultural, national, and global identifications. A nation-state that alienates and does not structurally include all cultural groups into the national culture runs the risk of creating alienation and causing groups to focus on specific concerns and issues rather than on the overarching goals and policies of the nation-state. To develop reflective cultural, national, and global identifications, students must acquire the knowledge, attitudes, and skills needed to function within and across diverse racial, ethnic, cultural, language, and religious groups.

5.7. Stages of Cultural Identity

Self-acceptance is a prerequisite to the acceptance and valuing of others. Students from racial, cultural, and language minority groups that have historically experienced institutionalised discrimination, racism, or other forms of marginalisation often have a difficult time accepting and valuing their own ethnic and cultural heritages. Teachers should be aware of and sensitive to the stages of cultural development that all of their students—including mainstream students, students of color, and other marginalised groups of students—may be experiencing and facilitate their identity development.

Using these Stages of Cultural Development Typology, teachers can help students attain higher stages of cultural development and develop clarified cultural, national, and global identifications. Students need to reach Stage 3 of this typology, "Cultural Identity Clarification," before we can expect them to embrace other cultural groups or attain thoughtful and clarified national or global identifications. The typology is an ideal-type concept. Consequently, it does not describe the actual identity development of any particular individual. Rather, it is a framework for thinking about and facilitating the identity development of students who approximate one of the stages.

During Stage 1, "Cultural Psychology Captivity," individuals internalise the negative stereotypes and beliefs about their cultural groups that are institutionalised within the larger society and may exemplify cultural self-rejection and low self-esteem. Cultural encapsulation and cultural exclusiveness, and the belief that their ethnic group is superior to others, characterise Stage 2, "Cultural Encapsulation." Individuals within this stage often have newly discovered their cultural consciousness and try to limit participation to their cultural group. They have ambivalent feelings about their cultural group and try to confirm, for themselves, that they are proud of it. In Stage 3, "Cultural Identity Clarification," individuals are able to clarify their personal attitudes and cultural identity and to develop clarified positive attitudes toward their cultural group. In this stage, cultural pride is genuine rather than contrived. Individuals within Stage 4, "Biculturalism," have a healthy sense of cultural identity and the psychological characteristics to participate successfully in their own cultural community as well as in another cultural community. They also have a strong desire to function effectively in two cultures.

Individuals in Stage 5, "Multiculturalism and Reflective Nationalism," have clarified, reflective, and positive personal, cultural, and national identifications and positive attitudes toward other racial, cultural, and ethnic groups. At Stage 6, "Globalism and Global Competency," individuals have reflective and clarified national and global identifications. They have the knowledge, skills, and attitudes needed to function effectively within their own cultural communities, within other cultures within their nation-state, in the civic culture of their nation, and in the global community. Individuals within Stage 6 exemplify cosmopolitanism and have a commitment to all human beings in the world community. Gutmann argued that the primary commitment of these individuals is to justice, not to any human community.

Strong, positive, and clarified cultural identifications and attachments are a prerequisite to cosmopolitan beliefs, attitudes, and behaviors. It is not realistic to expect Puerto Rican students in New York City to have a strong allegiance to U.S. national values or deep feelings for dying people in Afghanistan if they feel marginalised and rejected within their community, their school, and in their nation-state. We must nurture, support, and affirm the identities of students from marginalised cultural, ethnic, and language groups if we expect them to endorse national values, become cosmopolitans, and work to make their local communities, the nation, and the world more just and humane.

References

Alba, R. D., and V. Nee. 2003. *Remaking the American mainstream: Assimilation and contemporary immigration*. Cambridge, Mass.: Harvard University Press.

Banks, C. A. M. 2004. *Improving multicultural education: Lessons from the intergroup education movement*. New York: Teachers College Press.

Center for Multicultural Education, University of Washington. Castles, S. 2004. Migration, citizenship, and education. In *Diversity and citizenship education: Global perspectives*, ed. J. A.

Gillborn, D. 1990. *Race, ethnicity, and education: Teaching and learning in multi-ethnic schools*. London: Unwin Hyman/Routledge.

Gordon, M. M. 1964. *Assimilation in American life: The role of race, religion, and national origins*. New York: Oxford University Press.

Gutmann, A. 1987. *Democratic education*. Princeton, N.J.: Princeton University Press.

Zeitlinger. Freire, P. 1997. *Pedagogy of the oppressed*, 20th anniv. ed., trans. M. B. Ramos. New York: Continuum..

6

Social Work Education in Europe

All European states with the exception of the small principalities offer training for the social professions. This training follows various models: from a system of basic training to university study. The process of graduate education and professionalisation has been particularly marked during the last three decades of the twentieth century. With regard to the orientation of content, social pedagogic, social work and social policy are dominant. Generally social work has become so differentiated that it can be called an independent discipline, which encompasses and intersects with material provision, care, control, education, forms of leisure, as well as health and psychosocial care. There is thus a variegated measure of inter–linked activities relating to care, therapy and others such as pedagogy and leisure.

The generally expanded areas of study and professional knowledge and practical and research competencies are equally varied. For example, the proportion of practice based learning can vary from 5% to 50% of time spent in training . Also the forms of regulation and licensing vary considerably. On the one hand there are the centralised politically controlled systems, and on the other hand (as in Switzerland) regulation is undertaken by a union of the training establishments. Moreover, responsibility for the financing of training establishments ranges from the state through local authority to private, voluntary or religious bodies. For a complete picture of the training landscape, one would need a separate handbook. in this general overview of the systems of different countries, those where training systems have been developed over a more lengthy period of time will be described in more detail. The northern, western and southern European countries fall into this category. Whereas in central and eastern Europe, the processes of transformation are not complete, so it will mainly be only the developing trends that will be covered.

6.1. Denmark

The content of Danish social work methods and practice is influenced by the pronounced economic orientation of Danish welfare research. On the other hand, curriculum planning affords only marginal significance to social psychology or legal studies subjects which in other European countries are an integral component of training. This one-sided alignment is in part responsible for the present structure and content of training courses, but also underlies the many reforming endeavours.

6.1.1. Training in a Fachschule Fachschulen

In Denmark belong to the tertiary sector, for which the entry requirement is the *Studentereksamen* (comparable to the *Arbitur*). Study can be undertaken in 32 *Fachschuhlen* (*Socialpaedagogiske Seminarium)* of which four are state run and 28 are independent (although state financed). The number of social pedagogues in training at each school is between 400 and 900. The courses comprise seven semesters within which three practical placements (of three, six and six months) must be completed. There is a prospect of the establishment of a practice placement (of several weeks) in a foreign country in the fifth semester.

6.1.2. Training in a Fachhochschule

Education at a *Fachhochschule* takes place in four vocational training institutes (*Social Hojskole*), the so called 'National Schools of Social Work'. The use of the English term in the education system is on pragmatic grounds, namely the reliance on English language literature and teaching. Graduation follows six semesters of study (of which one is in practice) and leads to the award of the 'Diploma in Social Work'.

6.1.3. Training at a University

The University of Aalborg offers a post-graduate course in social work (without the possibility of a doctorate). Graduates from *Fachhochschulen* with a Diploma in Social Work can obtain an MA in Social Work at Aalborg. The University of Roskilde offers an academic course in social economics. In Greenland (which is part of Denmark) social workers are trained at University (BA in social work).

6.1.4. Developments and Perspectives

The Nordic Committee of Schools of Social Work (NCSSW), a consortium of Scandinavian social work training establishments, is at present concerned with clarifying training standards. It is envisaged that there should be a partial rapprochement between the *Sozialen Hochschulen* and the universities, among other things in such a way as to enable the lecturers in the Sozialen Hochschulen to undertake research.

6.2. Finland

Until very recently, social work, sociology and social policy courses laid emphasis upon a theoretical background in social policy, while the students were overwhelmingly interested in practice. This situation has given rise to numerous demands for reform.

6.2.1. Training in a Fachschule

At the level of the vocational schools, training comprises 100 weeks of study leading to the attainment of basic examinations in social and health services; the professional title sounds comparable to 'assistant social worker'. After this two year basic education, there follows a half-year specialised elective course on a chosen client group (children and young people, handicapped, the elderly). Graduates of this course are qualified for so-called 'non-professional' areas of activity within social work (mainly primary care). The basic examinations in social and health services enable entry to study in social work institutes (*opistoaso*). This 140 week (three year) focused training is well regarded in the fields of social work, social pedagogy and work with handicapped people. However, the institute courses are being discontinued, and there is no immediate prospect that they will be offered in future.

6.2.2. Training in a Fachhochschule

The basic examination in social and health services entitles entry for study at a *Fachhochschule*. A comprehensive 140 week course leads to an 'Expert in Social Work' qualification which has greater flexibility and is suitable for work with a variety of client groups and problem situations. This capability was achieved through the integration of applied research in the curriculum.

6.2.3.Training at Universities

The qualification following the study of social work was initially titled Master of Science (M.Sc.) with an emphasis on social policy and sociology, but after 1981 it became an MA in Social Work. Institutes of Social Work, established in faculties of social science exist in six Finnish universities as well as the Swedish department of the University of Helsinki. A three year period of study leads to a BA in social work and a further two years to an MA; following this there is the possibility of a doctorate. The University of Kupio offers an English language MA course in subjects including criminology, the sociology of minorities, social work in the penal system, the probation and youth justice system. The one sided bias in the theoretical teaching of social work in Finland has lead to discussion and controversy. The communes who provide social services are critical of students' remoteness from practice and limited experience of the living conditions of those in need. It has been suggested, and subsequently acted upon, that there should be non-academic teaching centres to complement university education. Teaching centres are local annexes of the university in which university lecturers work in cooperation with social work practitioners. The University of Jyväskylä, for example, has established an introduction to practice, which, in conjunction with trained social workers involves a year long project, as a way of gaining competence. Underlying this principle is the conviction that it is not possible to gain professional competence in the classroom but only in the field. At the University of Turku, for example, social work students are trained together with psychologists and doctors at the University's advice clinic.

6.2.4. Developments and Perspectives

At present training is in a phase of renewal and reform, and discussion about the future is characterised by intense reflexivity: the object of these discussions is the 'average families' which have not previously been among the clientele of social work. Because an increasing proportion of the population (as in other European countries) are encountering (long term-) unemployment, potential problem areas are beginning to emerge. These changed social conditions confront social work with a new clientele and the need for new ways of working, as they also do at the level of social work education. There is a need for social workers to possess adequate and immediately relevant practical competencies as well as their intellectual and moral qualities.

The results of this discussion are already becoming apparent at the training level: in the teaching centres there is increasing involvement of volunteers and non-statutory organisations.

6.3. ICELAND

Social work in Iceland began in 1957 with one social worker. Today there are more than 100. Up to the beginning of 1980, training took place in the neighbouring Scandinavian countries. With the establishment of a university course, the training of students lies in the hands of just three people the professor and her two colleagues.

6.3.1. Training at the University

Social work training was created at the University of Iceland in 1981 in the Faculty of Social Sciences. This is a four year course: the two year basic study comprises psychology, sociology, research methods and social policy. The third year concentrates on social work, includes a practice placement and leads to a BA in Social Sciences. A further year of 'top-up' study along with a four month practical placement completes the four year study period. A Certificate of Qualification in Social Work is linked to the final examinations.

6.3.2. Developments and Perspectives

Because of its relatively isolated geographical position, Iceland is interested in international cooperation and is an active member of the

Socrates Programme. As a member of the Nordic Committee of Schools of Social Work (NCSSW), Iceland is concerned to adapt its training structure to that of the other Scandinavian countries.

6.4. Norway

While most training still takes place in establishments which structurally resemble *Fachschulen*, university training has, since 1981, played an increasingly significant role.

6.4.1.Training in Fachschulen

Training predominates in the eleven state *Fachschulen* (*Sosialhogskolen*). It lasts for two years (including a seven month practice placement), leads to a Diploma in Social Sciences and the professional title *Sosionom*. The areas of work are, for example, rehabilitation, hospital, family work, work with the elderly, probation.

6.4.2. Training at Universities

The Norwegian State College of Local Government Administration and Social Work in the Child Welfare Department of Oslo College offers a three year training leading to the Diploma in Child Welfare which is approved by the Norwegian Council of Social Work Education. The course includes two practice placements each of 15 weeks. Graduates are employed in work with children, young people and families. Since 1984, the Department of Social Work in the College has offered a three year training (including a six month practice placement) leading to the Diploma in Social Work.

6.4.3. Developments and Perspectives

The Norwegian State College is a member of the Nordic Committee of Schools of Social Work(NCSSW) and is concerned to promote standardisation of social work training in the Scandinavian countries.

6.5. Sweden

The study of social work at Swedish universities is markedly similar to the British and American models of university study.

6.5.1. Training at Fachhochschulen

A three year non-academic course in social work and social care is offered in 28 colleges (*vardhögskol*). These course specialise in a particular client group (e.g. the handicapped or the elderly) or on a specific activity (e.g. pedagogy of leisure - *fritidspedagog*).

6.5.2. Training at Universities

Training of social workers (*socionom*) takes place at six universities. The normal qualification (BA -*kandidatexamen*) is attained after three and a half years (seven semesters). The curriculum predominantly involves academic study, but does however conclude with two practice semesters. Further academic qualifications such as the MA (*magisterexamen*, a further two years), licentiate (two years) and doctorate (four years) are likewise available: several *Hochschulen* provide opportunities for in service study for these. The entry qualification for a doctorate is a licentiate. The University of Göteborg additionally offers an English language course International Master of Arts in Social Work which is open to foreign students. The content of graduate courses concentrates on social and behavioural sciences, research methods as well as scientific theory.

6.5.3. Developments and Perspectives

No reform of the training system in Sweden is currently envisaged.

6.6. United Kingdom

Training for social work is sited in more than 100 establishments, of which a third are universities and two thirds colleges of higher education. Most students (90%) choose a non-graduate course which lasts two years leading to a Diploma in Higher Education. Validation of such courses by the Central Council for Education and Training in Social Work is necessary for the professional award of the Diploma in Social Work (DipSW). There is current concern about a modification in the training for workers in the justice system and probation, which is being separated from social work training. Already by 1995 the Diploma in Social Work was no longer a necessary qualification for entry into the Probation Service, although it still is in Northern Ireland and Scotland.

6.6.1. Training in Fachschulen

In 1947 the then Labour government set up training for residential social workers, when a lack of qualified staff had caused national alarm. Two separate training routes were established, one in the universities and one at the *Fachschule* level (training centre). The consequence was that graduates from the latter received less recognition (and were less well paid). So increasingly most qualified employees gravitated towards field work or administration (social services are provided by local authorities) with the result that the residential sector had scarcely any additional qualified staff available. Soon only 20% of residential workers were qualified. Thus in 1998 the Training Organisation for the Personal Social Services (TOPPS) was set up, a quasi-governmental organisation which was to restructure and improve training for residential and youth workers. These areas of work were removed from CCETSW's area of responsibility. From 2002 TOPPS will completely replace CCETSW.

6.6.2. Training in Fachhochschulen

Youth and community work can be studied at 25 colleges of Higher Education or Higher Education Institutions (HEI). State recognised courses lead, until 1995, to the award of Certificate of Social Services (CSS). Since 1995 the above mentioned Diploma in Social Work has replaced the Certificate of Qualification in Social Work (CQSW) and the CSS. The course is for a minimum of two years.

6.6.3. Training at Universities

There are a variety of social science courses on offer which lead to a Bachelor level qualification. These can encompass various specialisations: Bachelor of Arts (BA) in Social Work and Sociology; Bachelor of Social Science (B.Soc.Sc); Bachelor in Social Work (BSW) and others. Courses involve two practice placements of three and four months. In some universities (e.g. East London) placements constitute half of the course: a three month placement in the first year and a six month placement in each of the second and third year must be completed. Courses can also follow a second pathway. After the completion of the first foundation year, there is an entrance examination for all students and applicants. Criteria are academic performance, practical and life experience as well as personal aptitude for the profession. The qualification of Diploma in Social Work is awarded by the national validating body, the Central Council for Education and Training in Social Work (CCETSW). This qualification entitles entry to the profession. Since 1992 the University of Portsmouth in conjunction with the Skovtofte Seminarium in Copenhagen has offered a British/Danish BA in European Social Work. The one year post-professional study builds upon the British DipSW, and for Danish social workers follows on from their three year training at the *Fachschule*.

6.6.4. Developments and Perspectives

The National Council for Vocational Qualifications (NCVQ) will revise the requirements and qualification levels for social work training. And CCETSW is advocating that training should be developed and provided jointly by Universities and social work agencies. Also the Open University system with its many faceted provision for continuing education - especially in the areas of social and residential work should be strengthened. In view of the fact that almost all students opt for the two year non-graduate route to the DipHE and DipSW, there is some discussion in the universities whether this ongoing practice oriented form of study can do justice to the complex requirements of social workers.

6.7. Ireland

Training for work with young people, care and residential work takes place in individual establishments of comparable level to the *Fachschulen* and *Fachhochschulen*. Training for health social workers, those working with the handicapped, and probation officers takes place in universities. With all courses it is the case that student demand for university places is substantially on the increase and so restrictive admission criteria prevail. For many courses there is still a set quota of places reserved for students without formal academic qualifications but who have several years experience in a related occupation. 40% of Irish social workers are employed in work with children and young people (regional health and social services). The most significant employer is the Health Ministry with eight regional service centres.

6.7.1. Training in Fachhochschulen

There is a three year course in Youth and Community Work that has been established at St. Patrick's College in Maynouth which leads to a (non-academic) Diploma. There are three year courses in child care at several regional technical colleges and polytechnics. These lead to the Advanced Diploma in Child Protection or in Child Care. The Dublin Institute of Technology offers a two year training in child care work leading to the Certificate in Early Childhood Care and education (CECCE) that is recognised by the National Council for Educational Awards (NCEA).

6.7.2. Training at Universities

The Irish universities (Dublin, Cork, Trinity College Dublin) offer courses in social and community work that are seen as applied social science: the Institute at University College Cork, for example, is called the Department of Applied Social Studies. Study can be at the (non-graduate) level of the Diploma in Social Work and Diploma in Youth and Community Studies as well as at Bachelor, Higher Diploma and Masters level. These last three are recognised by the National Social Work Qualifications Board (NSWQB) as a National Qualification in Social Work (NQSW). The two year Diploma course targets mature students who already have some experience in social work or allied activity (possibly as a volunteer). A three year (at Cork) or four year (at Dublin) course at a University can lead to a Bachelor in Social Studies (BSS), Bachelor of Social Science (B.Soc.Sc) or Bachelor in Social Work (BSW). Four year courses include a one year foundation year. A Bachelor qualification can, on the one hand, be built upon by a further two years study leading to a higher diploma (in Youth and Community Work, Applied Social Studies or Social Work Studies), and on the other hand, the Master of Social Work (MSW) or Master of Social Science (M.Soc.Sc).

6.7.3. Developments and Perspectives

At present there is an observable increase in students on Masters of

Social Work courses, namely those which combine the subjects of child and youth care (research and practice) with social policy and social research. The reform process in the area of education has been buoyant for some time, partly as a result of the receipt of considerable financial aid from the European Union and the current economic boom.

6.8. Austria

The profound changes in social work activity (the spread of crisis situations, long term unemployment, social need, housing problems, migration problems, new poverty) brings in its wake a need in Austria for changes in the content of training. The previous concentration on treatment methods, counselling and therapy, case work and family work has not shown itself to be fully adequate.

6.8.1.Training in Fachschulen

In the secondary sector there are numerous state *Fachschulen*, so called vocational high schools (*Bervfsbildende Höhere Schulen* - BHS), which include Fachschulen for social services (70 training establishments) as well as education establishments (6) and colleges of social pedagogy. The duration of courses is between two and three years.

6.8.2.Training in Fachhochschulen

Training takes place in eight Academies of Social Work, maintained by the state as well as the Catholic Church (Caritas), the professional association and the regions which are also involved. Social work training takes three years (six semesters including a five month practice placement) and leads to a Diploma. The eight schools cater for 1,200 students each year, of whom 320 graduate annually.

6.8.3. Developments and Perspectives

In 1998 a Commission of the Ministries of Education and Culture and Science and Traffic produced recommendations for the future structure of education and training for the social professions. The Commission found fault with the multiplicity of competencies, the lack of coordination, the different qualification levels, incompatibility with international training systems and the lack of networking between the current systems. The multiplicity of those responsible for training reinforced the desire for a new concept of training establishments, which could exist as an academic element of the tertiary sector. At present various suggestions for reform are being discussed: the conversion of the academies in *Fachhochschulen* and the lengthening of the study period to four years (eight semesters) under the umbrella of the discipline of social management. Alternatively, all Austrian academies, including teacher training establishments, pedagogic and denominational academies (included under social work academies) could receive their own statute in the same way as the university-modelled pedagogic *Hochschulen* are; these *Hochschulen* would be organised with like universities with a rector and an academic board and maintained by the Ministry of Education. Finally, one could leave the current system as it is with the state categorising the academies as academic institutions in the sense of the first EU directive. This already happens through a bilateral arrangement with the universities over the recognition of student qualifications. In this way, the Pedagogic Institute of the University of Salzburg recognises a Diploma from the Salzburg Academy as an entrance qualification for study at MA level.

The multiplicity of ways forward, however, carry with them the danger of splitting training even more. So two regional academies are considering converting to *Fachhochschulen*.

6.9. Switzerland

In French-speaking Switzerland, as in France, social work has encompassed a variety of professional activities, while in German-speaking Switzerland, social work has hitherto been differentiated between social work (previously 'care') and social pedagogy (previously 'residential work'). A rapprochement between these concepts is now in prospect, primarily because increasing areas of activity are emerging, which cannot be responded to in a unilateral way by any of the three disciplines of social work, social pedagogy or 'socio-cultural animation'. At present training for the social professions is located in numerous Fachschulen and, for social work and social pedagogy, in *Hochschulen* for social work and *Fachhochschulen*.

6.9.1.Training in Fachschulen

In French and German speaking Switzerland there are numerous courses in the social field which are designed to relate to secondary or tertiary education in different ways. So in the second stage there are various courses on offer which lead to the occupations of, among others, educator, residential worker, carer, worker with the elderly or families.

6.9.2. Training in Fachhochschulen

At 17 *Hochschulen* for social work, there are three types of scientifically based courses of a social nature (albeit with varying structures) which lead to an HFS Diploma: social work (10 schools), social pedagogy (14) and 'socio-cultural animation' (5). This qualifying training extends over four years and includes at least 3,200 lessons of which 1,500 are an introduction to practice. Two to three compulsory practice placements add up to a year's practice. Training organisations are for the most part foundations and associations which derive finance from the cantons (mostly) and the state.

6.9.3. Training at Universities

The University of Friborg offers a course in social work and at the University of Zürich the study of social pedagogy is possible. The universities of Neuenburg and Lausanne, within their social science courses offer specialisation in social work with about 60 graduates a year.

6.9.4. Developments and Perspectives

It is planned that the higher *Fachschulen* should be converted to *Fachhochschulen* in which schools and providers will be amalgamated and financing be largely taken over by the state. The HFS Diploma will henceforth be available in the three disciplines, although attempts are being made to bring all three together in a '*Fachhochschule* for Social Work.'

6.10. The Netherlands

In the Netherlands too, the history of poor relief is associated with the

Church, and when at the end of Spanish rule in the middle of the seventeenth century, the Dutch Reform Church effectively became the State Church, religious and public involvement in care of the poor was almost identical up to the end of the nineteenth century. Only with the 'New Poor Law' of 1912 was the state accorded a complementary role to private welfare. In comparison with neighbouring countries, the social security system was established relatively late in the day: accident insurance 1901, invalidity insurance 1923, sickness insurance came into force in 1930 and statutory unemployment insurance was only introduced in 1952. In the same year the Ministry for Social Work was instituted. The late but rapid industrialisation of the country during the postwar era prompted further social policy developments: in the sixties the *Bijstandswet* ('social help law') and the *Wet op de arbeidsongeschiktheid* ('fitness for work law') were repealed. The establishment of state welfare was accompanied by a diminishing influence of the Church in the welfare system. The first school for social work one of the oldest in the world - was already founded in Amsterdam by Marie Muller–Lulofs in 1896. The number of training institutions grew particularly after the second world war - to 36, mostly religious and ideologically oriented schools (called *Akademien*).

6.10.1. Training in Fachhochschulen

Many of the smaller *Akademien* were integrated with *Hogescholen* (comparable with the German *Hochschulen*) in 1986. These (approximately 60) *Hogescholen,* along with the universities, form the tertiary education sector although vocational training is kept strictly separate from the university education. 23 of these *Hogescholen* offer social work courses (*Hoger Sociaal Agogisch Onderweijs*). To translate this as 'social work' is somewhat imprecise since *Agog* encompasses a broad spectrum of social professions: cultural work, (ergo-)therapy, social work, personnel management, welfare rights advice and social pedagogical work. Since 1986 these fields have been represented six different disciplines in the HSAO-courses. Study is for four years, of which the third is a practice year, and can be undertaken on a full or part time basis. It leads to a BA and is entitlement both to the regulated salary scale for the professional practice of social work and an entrance qualification for post-graduate study at a university (post-professional or MA programme).

6.10.2.Training in Universities

In parallel with the opportunities for social work training in the *Fachhochschulen,* many universities established 'departments of androgogy' in the sixties. Study was oriented towards the European tradition of social pedagogy at the same time as the anglo-saxon concept of social planning and social change. However, most of these departments were closed in the eighties as a consequence of cuts in state funding and the massive neo-liberal critique of the welfare state. Currently it is only possible to obtain a qualification in social work at a university by way of four year study in social sciences (leading to an MA or doctorate). The one exception to this in the Chair in Social Work at the University of Utrecht.

6.10.3. New Developments

Some HSAOs have recently introduced an MA programme, often in conjunction with Anglo-saxon universities in order to be able to offer students an internationally recognised degree. Nonetheless, there is as yet no state recognition of these courses. Aside from this there is an increasing number of fee-paying continuing education courses mostly of one year's duration -postgraduate courses for the social professions. This demand-oriented commercial exploitation of education is also apparent in other European countries is all of a piece with the continuing tendency of 'transformation' of the welfare state through the introduction of market mechanisms and the emphasis upon 'individual responsibility'.

6.11. Belgium

The first 'School for Social Services' was founded in Brussels in 1920 and a second in Antwerp in 1921. Training focused on help for children of poor families. The corresponding self image of social work as a charitable activity only gave way in the fifties, with the development of the welfare state and the care system, and the claims on the social professions changed. The curricula of social work courses broadened to include social, behavioural and legal sciences, and casework became the model for social workers at that time. Schools of social work originating in the post war period were without exception ideologically oriented. So, for example the socialist and Christian workers' movement established their own training establishments such as the 'college for workers' (*École ouvrière supérieure*) or the Christian *Institut Cardijn*.

6.11.1. Training in Fachhochschulen

At present training exists in only 23 *Fachhochschulen*, 12 of which are in the Flemish speaking region and 11 in the Francophone region of the country. Each *Fachhochschule* has relative autonomy and its own traditions and its own particular training orientation within the framework of statutory guidelines and the supervision of the Ministry of Education. *Fachhochschulen* are located under the universities in the tertiary sector and are maintained by private organisations (4 schools), communes, provinces or the state (19 schools). Social work training in the *Fachhochschulen* (*Institut Supérieure de Formation Sociale* and *Hoger Institut voor Maatschappelijk Werk* respectively) involves three years full time study, although there are two courses of four or more years. The practice component varies from school to school. 75% of students are women. Courses lead to a state Diploma in Social Work. Over and above that there are a dozen related qualifications. The national Ministry of Education only recognises the state diploma and, since 1952, the legally protected title of '*assistant social*'.

6.11.2. Training in Universities

Basic social work training courses no longer exist in the universities, but students who have completed study at the *Fachhochschulen* can register for a post-graduate licentiate in social and political science, sociology, criminology, social medicine and hospital administration. In the mid eighties, some universities introduced programmes such as 'Social Work and Social Services' and 'Social Action', but clearly these did not constitute basic training.

6.11.3. New Developments

Fachhochschulen, universities, state institutes, private organisations and professional associations offer a varied range of very different post-graduate courses and further training seminars. These can constitute a danger that the basic state diploma will become devalued which could lead to a 'creeping' shift of social work training away from the *Fachhochschulen* into the universities. On the other hand there is a demand from the *Fachhochschulen* themselves that the universities should set up post-graduate courses so that social workers could become better qualified for a research and management tasks. It is an open question as to whether in future a basic university vocational training can be established alongside the *Fachhochschulen,* as is the case, not only in Belgium's neighbouring countries (with the exception of Luxembourg), but almost everywhere else.

6.12. Luxembourg

Luxembourg is the only country in the EU in which there is no independent training for social work (as it is understood internationally) at *Fachhochschule* or university level. Undoubtedly this is because of the size of the Grand Duchy which only has a population of about 380,000. In the mid eighties, there were only about 140 social workers and since then their number has scarcely increased. Professional social work developed during the twenties when the first foreign-trained professionals came to work in the health and social services. Establishments, and also training, were (and still are) characterised by a marked socio-medical orientation. A law of 1935 regulated the professional titles (*infirmière visiteuse* - since 1967 *assistant d'hygiène social* - and *assistant social*) and the statutory recognition of foreign training courses and entry to the profession. Social work belongs to the 'paramedical professions' and comes under the Ministry of Health. Training opportunities for these professional groups in Luxembourg are limited to a four year *Fachschule* course with a 30% practice component and leading to a state diploma. Social workers who want to train at a *Fachhochschule* or university usually do so in a neighbouring country (Belgium, France or Germany).

6.12.1. New Developments

A law of 11 August 1996 lead to the reorganisation of post-secondary education for, among others, educational and social professions. There are plans for a degree course for educators (*éducateur gradué*) at the Institute for Social and Pedagogical Studies (*Institut d'Études Éducatives et Sociales* -IEES). Aside from this there are (as yet not closely defined) one year short study possibilities at the Luxembourg University Centre which orients and prepares students for study programmes at universities in neighbouring countries.

6.13. France

After the French revolution, support of the needy which had hitherto been the almost exclusive province of the Catholic Church, was replaced in the law of 19 March 1793 by state provision. The concept of solidarity replaced that of charity. Care was no longer a matter of private benevolence, but a task of public and collective involvement. These republican ideas were, however, only materealised later in the wake of industrialisation, beginning in 1898 with mutual insurance as well as other social legislation up to 1913. Modern welfare began in 1896 with the establishment of the first centres for social assistance (*maisons sociales*) in a poor district of Paris and, by 1907 already, the first 'practical school for social education'. In 1908 a 'free school for welfare' was founded. In 1922 a professional diploma for nurses and for health carers was established. From 1930 these occupations began to be termed 'social carers' (*assistantes sociales*) and in 1938, the Social Care Diploma was introduced with a qualification comparable to that of the other two professional groups. After the second world war between 1945 and 1953 the most important provision for prevention and care were assembled under the social security (*Sécurité Sociale*) umbrella. Finally, in 1995, a Ministry of Health, Social Affairs and Local Government (*Ministère de la Santé, des Affaires Sociales et de la Ville*) was instituted at national level. As in Italy, the social professions in France are closely linked to the medical domain both in practice and training. Today there is a broad spectrum of professional specialisms with 160 very varied training institutions, courses and qualifications. The overwhelming majority of training establishments are private, although publicly financed. Only eleven schools have a public or semi-public status, and only 53 have courses classified as social work in the narrowest sense. Moreover, *Travail Social* is not the equivalent of the German conception of social work, but includes the fields of *action sociale* and *aide sociale*, which accounts for why the training options and levels are correspondingly more various.

6.13.1. Training in Fachschulen

The distinction between *Fachschulen* (*École Normale*) and *Fachhochschulen* (*École Supérieure*) is a difficult one. Unambiguous classification is often not possible because of contradictory information in the literature. In principal, 'educators' (*moniteurs-éducateurs, éducateurs, éducateurs de jeunes enfants*) and social pedagogues (*éducateurs spécialisé*) are only trained in *Fachschulen.* Training of social workers (*assistantes de service sociale*) takes place mainly in relatively small state or state recognised *Fachschulen* (47) as well as independent *Fachschulen* (3) and universities (3) and lasts between 8 months (for family workers - *travailleurs familiaux*) and two to three years for the various other professional groups. Within the binding framework of a national curriculum, about a dozen different specialisations are offered, for which the practice component is between 30% and 50%. The requirement for successful completion of the national diploma in social work (*Diplôme d'État d'Assistant de Service Social*) is a three year course of study which includes 14 months of practice. The state diploma is a requirement for entry to professional practice. At present there are about 36,000 social workers in post, of whom 97% are women. An unusual feature is the training for 'home managers' (*directeurs*) - without exception, these are trained on a three year course at the National School for Public Health (ENSP - *École Nationale de la Santé Publique*) in Rennes, the highest state training institution in the social and health fields. Aside from the regular courses there is a confusing number of courses and further training courses on offer from private and public organisations, schools and universities

6.13.2.Training in Universities

At some universities social work can be studied at basic level, as a 'top up' course or additional academic qualification, and with various specialisations and qualifications. Regular social work courses are offered at the IUT (*Institut Universitaire de Technologie*), the University of Grenoble and Paris V and at the IUP (*Institut*

Universitaire Professionalisé) Villetaneuse. The two IUs offer a two year course 'social careers' (*Carrières Sociales*) with a DUT qualification as well as a three year course leading to the state diploma in social work (*Diplôme d'État d'Assistant de Service Social*). As well as these three *Hochschulen*, there is a greater number of universities which have instituted 'top-up' courses and further training for professionals in social welfare leading to a licentiate or masters qualification in social sciences. Finally, for professionals holding the state diploma in social work there are about seven universities which offer further training leading to the Higher Diploma in Social work (DSTS - *Diplôme Supériore de Travail Social*).

6.13.3. Developments and Perspectives

We can observe developments in France that mirror those of other European countries (e.g. Italy). On the one hand, there is the historical tradition of predominantly non-university training for the social professions, and on the other, a trend towards establishing basic social work training (with state diploma) and further training in the universities (as in Germany, primarily in educational science courses). Although it in its beginnings, this process has implications for the future because there will be different demands for qualifications in the social field, and at the same time lead to a competitive situation prompting the defensive reaction that: "University qualifications are for research activities, not so much for practice."

6.14. Spain

In Spain, the development of industrialisation and, with it, social services took place relatively recently (compared with other European countries). This 'lateness' can also be seen in relation to training. Admittedly, by 1849 there was already enacted a general welfare law (*Ley general de beneficencia Social*), however, the founding of the first training establishment only came in the Second Republic with the Schools for Social Studies for Women (*Escuela de Estudios Sociales Para la Mujer*) in Barcelona. This school arose out of the Catalonian Women's and Social movement and was a branch of the Catholic 'School for Social Services' that was established in Brussels. Its object was "The education of the working class and the training of competent professionals who would dedicate themselves to the working class". The second institution, the 'School for Family and Social Education (*Escuela de Formación Familiar y Social*) was founded in 1939 at the end of the Spanish civil war and was linked to the national catholicism and the fascist Falange. Up to the mid-fifties only five further schools were established and only in the wake of intensified industrialisation after 1959 did the number of schools increase, by the end of the sixties, to 42 (29 Church, 9 state, 4 private).

6.14.1. Training in Fachschulen

In 1964 the schools received state recognition as *Fachschulen.* Courses lasted three years, the entry qualification was as for a *Hochschule* and graduates were now called social assistants (*Asistente Social*). The status of this training lead to an expansion in the number of students and schools.

6.14.2. Training in Fachhochschulen / Universities

In 1981 the *Fachschulen* were converted to *Fachhochschulen* (*Escuelas Universitarias*) and affiliated to universities. A decree of April 1983 determined that the study of social work (as the subject was now termed) should be integrated nationwide as a subject in its own right with a practice component of 40%. The three year course is located at the lowest level of the three level Spanish university system and, since 1986, no longer leads to 'social assistant', but the Diploma in Social Work (*Diploma en Trabajo Social*). Since August 1990, 28 university schools have been integrated as independent faculties (*area de conocimento*) in the normal university structure, whereby the status, duration and qualification of the courses remains unchanged. In the mean time it is apparent that (as in Italy and France) an increasing number of universities that were introduced at the October 1991 Rectors' Conference are offering diploma courses in social pedagogy (*Eduacion Social*). This course is classified as a second-level university subject of the science of education and concludes after a total of five years with a licentiate (*licenciado)*.

6.14.3. Developments and Perspectives

If one considers the almost 20 year standstill (connected with international isolation) in the development of the professionalisation of social work up to the end of the dictatorship in 1975, then one has to evaluate the current training for social work and social pedagogy in a different way. On the one hand we find professionalisation 'bogged down' (as it was in Germany in the seventies) characterised by dominance of short courses and the only the beginnings of a scientific approach. On the other hand there is the success within a relatively short period of time of attaching training, ate least structurally, to the universities, and accomplishing a binding curriculum framework. Along with Ireland and Turkey, Spain is the only European country in which social workers are exclusively trained in universities. With the establishment of the complementary course in social pedagogy leading to a licentiate, a dualism has been created which is viewed with some scepticism by the social work subject areas, but could contribute to the establishment of the profession on a more scientific basis, which all would welcome. Finally, it remains to be seen whether a doctorate is a possibility.

6.15. Portugal

The development of social work is more closely bound up with the Catholic Church than in other European countries. On 15 August 1498, the first welfare institution was founded, 'the Holy House of Mercy of Lisbon' (*Santa Casa da Misericórdia de Lisboa* -SCML). This hospital marked the beginning of medieval health and social policy and, over subsequent centuries up until the present day, grew to become the most important welfare organisation, which (particularly during the world economic crisis) annexed numerous smaller private initiatives. Since 1834 the SCML has been a quasi-state institution, whose social, health and cultural activities are financed through various national lotteries (as early as 1783 the crown conferred upon SCML the privilege of managing lotteries). The first public social policy initiatives were taken in the time of the first Republic (1910-1928). During the Salazar dictatorship (1928-1974), there was no further expansion of social services (apart from the foundation of schools). Services were patriarchal in structure and clearly not very efficient. Modernisation of the welfare system only began after the revolution of 1974. Currently there is decentralisation of services and a mix of state and private responsibility. The dominance of the Church is reflected in the training sphere. The first Catholic school for social work (*Instituto de Serviço Social*) was founded in Lisbon in 1935, to be followed in 1937 by a school in the provincial administration in Coimbra (lead by Catholic nuns), and in 1956 by the Catholic school in Porto. In addition, in 1964 a catholic school was set up in Angola, and a state school in Mozambique. Since 1974, all Portuguese schools are part of the tertiary system. The schools in Lisbon and Porto have separated themselves from the Church, and the school in Coimbra has come under the jurisdiction of the Ministry of Education.

6.15.1. Training in Fachhochschulen and Universities

Since 1979, the above mentioned three schools have been converted to colleges for social services (*Instituto Superior de Serviço Social*). The four year course of study is set in the framework of a national curriculum. Between 86% and 96% of those enrolling are women and the final qualification is that of Diploma for Social services (*Diplomado em Serviço Social*). Following the law of 1985 relating to *Hochschulen*, all private colleges not connected with universities or other colleges, can award a licentiate (*Licenciatura*) and are entitled to set up post-graduate courses leading to an MSW (*Mestrado*). Those qualifying have the title *Assistente Social* or *Trabalhador Social*. In 1980 the first university course was initiated - a four year course for social work at the Institute for Social and Political Science at the state Technical College of Lisbon which leads to a Diploma in Social Policy. Since 1986 there has also been a course in 'social services' at the Portuguese Catholic University in Vizeu. Here for the first time it is possible to obtain all three qualifications: the licentiate, masters and a doctorate.

6.15.2. Developments and Perspectives

As yet there is no definite date for any further developments in training at colleges or universities. For the academic year 1998/9 the *Universidade de Tràs-os-Montes e Alto Douro* opened a five year basic social work course at Miranda do Douro leading to a licentiate in social work. This provides training in psychosocial counselling and therapy, administration, research and social planning. Thus on the usual criteria Portugal has in effect developed a training system that has become exclusively established at university level.

6.16. Italy

Italy has nothing like the tradition of state welfare (as, for example, Germany or England). From the time of the foundation of the state until the first half of the century, the personal social services were firmly in the hands of the Church and private institutions. State control was, at most, nominal. The state first became involved during the period of Fascism and created insurance institutions as a socio-political instrument (i.e. about 60 years later than Germany). In the postwar republican constitution the idea of the welfare state was taken up, but until now only rudimentarily realised. State kindergartens, for example, only made their first appearance in 1968, and it was not until the end of the seventies that community-based health and social centres (*Unità Sanitarie Locali* - USL; now after partial privatisation, *Azienda* - called ASL) were set up with a standardised structure and statutory guidelines. State involvement in youth policy is almost completely absent. Against this background the delayed professionalisation of social work is understandable. In Italy the term 'social service' is usual (only recently are the terms 'social work' or 'social pedagogy' in use). The first school of social work was founded in 1928. Most training courses for the social professions (which includes both social workers and pedagogues) were, however, created at the end of the sixties. Courses were (and still are today) mostly heterogeneous - as a rule training establishments are private, but there are also university colleges involved. At the same time there are regular courses at universities.

6.16.1. Training in Fachschulen

Up until 1987, social work training took place in 91 *Fachschulen* (79 private, 12 public) and seven schools which were affiliated to universities. *Fachhochschule* training as we (i.e. in Germany) understand it, does not exist in Italy. In 1987 with the introduction of specialised university schools (*scuole dirette a fini speziali*), 35 of these training establishments were transferred to the university sector. Pedagogues (*educatori professionali*) were to be trained in private schools maintained by the provinces or communes (about 10 altogether) and the ASLs (about 20). These are three year full time courses. Additionally both courses can be taken at universities.

Alongside this there is still a training for family and residential workers (*assistente domiciliare e dei servizi tutelari*) which is run by the regions and involves 600 hours of tuition. It is also worth mentioning training for 'animators' (*animatori*) which is unregulated and offered in various private institutions (involving from 200 to 1,200 hours).

6.16.2. Training in Universities

In 1993 after the introduction of the specialised university schools not a university qualification three year part time courses leading to a 'University Diploma in Social Service' were initiated. In the meantime there remains the possibility in several universities of a course in educational science (*corso di laurea in scienze dell' educazione*), in order to take account of out-of-school activities this has been renamed 'pedagogical science' (*corso di laurea in scienze della formazione*) so as to allow social pedagogues and related occupations the opportunity to specialise. The course lasts four years. It is comparable to the model of the German 'pedagogical science' (*Erziehungswissenschaft*) and leads to a doctorate (*laurea)*.

6.16.3. Developments and Perspectives

The fundamental reforms in the health and social areas began in 1978 with the establishment of the local centres (USL), which, particularly in the northern regions, have developed the integration social and health services (*Unità Socio Sanitarie Locali* USSL). The relevant legislation that was then intended, has not yet materialised. The reorganisation of the social and health structures is also still up in the air, and with it the degree of professionalisation, despite the step by step introduction of university courses for the social professions. As before there still exists an unsupervised juxtaposition of courses and qualifications of highly variable quality. Full time university courses in educational science with the possibility of specialising in social work/ social pedagogy have only been implemented in a few universities. Social pedagogy is hardly developed as a science, there is still a large gap between theory and practice. Efforts to introduce reforms in relating training to practice are overshadowed by socio-political circumstances: in Italy too the dismantling of the welfare state is in full swing. Public responsibility in social affairs, in any case underdeveloped, is gradually reverting to the private and commercial domain.

6.17. Greece

Unlike many other European countries in which modern social work came with industrialisation about 100 years ago, professional social work in Greece has a relatively recent tradition. The first 'Free School for Social Welfare' was founded in 1937, but further development was interrupted by the second world war. The first school of the post war era (the 'Pierce College - School for Social Welfare') was established in Athens in 1945 with American help (and until 1975 under American leadership). The (approximately 300) graduates of this school were crucial in the further development of social work in this period. Experts form the 'American Mission' also provided technical support in building up social services and in the training of personnel. A second school (the 'YWCA/IAKE - School of Social Work) followed in 1948, and in 1957 a third school was established by the diaconate of the Orthodox Church (until 1965 this school trained theologians to graduate level). Subsequently in 1960, there followed the opening of the 'Athens School for Youth Aid'. All of these schools were private institutions. The state only became involved in 1970 with the establishment in the tertiary sector of two departments of social work at Centres for Higher technical and Vocational education' (KATEE) in Heraklion and Patras. These two training courses were switched to 'Technical Educational Institutions' (TEI). This signalled the end of the private schools, when in 1984/85 departments of social work became established in the Schools of Health and Social Welfare of the TEI. Henceforward social work training was exclusively located in the TEI system. Greece is thus one of the few European countries with no more private training institutions.

6.17.1. Training in Fachhochschulen

The Greek *Hochschule* system makes a clear distinction between 'university' and 'non-university', even in tertiary sector education. Social work training at three TEIs is a three and a half year non-university training. The entrance qualification is the *Arbitur*, courses are free, organised according to a nationally binding curriculum and offer theoretical knowledge and practical competence. Practice constitutes 45% of the training. There are about 250 graduates a year of whom 95% are women. The qualification is a diploma (*Ptychion*) with subsequent recognition by the Ministry of National Education and Religion (MNE). This recognition is a prerequisite for the professional practice of social work.

6.17.2. Developments and Perspectives

The introduction of university basic courses in social work was announced as early as 1983, although as yet this has not materialised. Social work graduates can, however, go on to study chosen 'related' four year university courses e.g. in the subjects of political science, administration, pedagogy and medicine. Complementing the TEI training, there has, since 1966, been the possibility at one university of specialisation in social work leading to an MA within the subject of 'social administration' (p.21). Expansion of the long demanded opportunities for university education is imminent. Further training, university or non-university, is scarcely developed yet.

6.18. Turkey

The last century of the Ottoman Empire (1299–1923) was characterised by wars, poverty and social disintegration. The traditional religious welfare institutions were no longer able to respond adequately, so that when the first modern aid agency, the 'Red Crescent' was founded in 1868, this was followed by the establishment of the orphanages (*Darüssafaka*). After the foundation of the republic in 1923, a national child protection agency was created and in 1928 the 'Society for Philanthropy' was brought into being. Both organisations worked exclusively with volunteer helpers. Only in 1948 were state welfare responsibilities handed over to the Minister for Education, Health and Social welfare. From the outset, social work in Turkey has been closely linked with the health system. The first training institution, founded in 1961 by the Ministry for Health and Social Welfare was the Academy for Social Work (*Sosyal Hizmetler Akademisi*). The second was created in 1967 as the 'Department for Social Work and Social Services' in the Faculty of Social and Administrative Sciences at Hacettepe University in Ankarra. In 1985 there was the first 'specialists in social services' who were trained in the Faculty of Medicine at the University of Istanbul. In the first phase of social work training Turkey received international support (UNICEF, UNESCO etc.) and the curriculum was strongly influenced by American ideas.

6.18.1. Training in Universities

In 1982 during the era of the military regime and as a consequence of the 'High School Law' of November 1981, the Academy for Social Work and the Department for Social Work and Social Services were amalgamated in an independent 'College of Social Work' (*Sosyal Hizmetler Yüksekokulu*) at Hacettpe University in Ankara. Training is basic, more generic than specialised (as in German university courses), lasts eight semesters and includes a 30% practice component. There are an approximately equal number of men and women students. Study leads to a university diploma and, since 1984, the professional title is that of 'social worker' (*Sosyal Çalismaci*).

6.18.2. Developments and Perspectives

Since the mid eighties there has been the possibility at the College For social Work for post-graduate studies leading to an MA or PhD. Since the early nineties this has also been possible at two other universities. The current training opportunities can barely meet the growing demand in modern Turkish society for qualified professionals.

6.19. Central and Eastern Europe

Training for the social professions in the countries of the former 'Eastern Block' is bound up with the societal transformation that has taken place. Central to this transformation is the shift from the socialist planned economy to a capitalist free market. This has been accompanied by democratisation of the political system as well as changes in social structure and culture. Social change has been characterised by the concurrent need to deal with the collapse of the old authoritarian regime, the consequences of structural change which have not lead to a gradually implemented and social policy regulated capitalism, but to a liberal uncurbed 'turbo-capitalism'. Despite the social, economic and political differences between individual countries, these three factors have everywhere lead to a rapid increase of social problems, which have quickly approached the western European levels, and with regard to poverty and shortages have by far overtaken them. Training for the social professions in central, south eastern and eastern Europe can find itself subject to a certain tension. On the one hand, there is a need for trained professionals in the public services, and on the other hand the slowly emerging civil society has a need for socially and democratically motivated 'activists' who will set up organisations that are independent of the state and are involved at grass roots level. The tension between these two emphases is resolved differently in different training establishments: the state *Hochschulen* are more closely bound up with the public sector social services, and the independent/private schools cooperate more closely with the non-statutory sector. Training for the social professions is thus bound up with the character of the training institutions with their correspondingly different traditions. It may be that an unbroken tradition of social pedagogy at universities will result, or that the 'Schools of Social Work' of the twenties will be re-established. With regard to formal standards of the institutionalised courses, neither type is yet validated (supervision, supervised practice). On the other hand, there is the flexibility and a demand for setting up self initiated projects and initiatives - with all the opportunities for learning that they present. At the end of the 1990s, the process of rapid change in the countries of central and eastern European countries was not yet complete. In particular, the successor states of the former Yugoslavia and the Soviet Union are confronted with additional institution change, so that systems for training in the social professions are only occasionally seen and with an emphasis on high school study.

6.20. Hungary

Developments in Hungary exemplify education around three subject orientations. The course for social policy is geared towards the local or regional political level is, for example, particularly concerned with unemployment and job creation programmes. The social pedagogy course has been primarily developed in the pedagogical *Hochschulen* and is concerned with work with children, young people and their families. Social work courses can be placed somewhere between these two. The basis for these courses is the *Hochschule* law of 1993 which defines the duration of courses in universities (up to 5 years for an MA) and *Fachhochschulen* (4 years), and a decree of 1996 regarding establishment of the social professions. At the end of the nineties, there were courses in social policy at the universities of Budapest, Debrecen and Pecs. Budapest also has a university social work course.

6.21. Lithuania

Lithuania provides an example of the development of differentiated courses. After independence in 1990 a very rapid development took place, characterised by the adoption of western European and American concepts (as a result of finance from these countries). 1992 saw the first one year course for social work at the university of Vilnius. In the same year a master's programme was initiated simultaneously with a college based BA course. In 1998 there came a BA in social education at the University of Kaunas. At the end of the phase of innovation, and resulting from an evaluation by the 'Social Ministry' (social work) and the Education Ministry (responsible for social pedagogy), it was declared that social work and social pedagogy should stand neatly separate from each other. Social work was to be hierarchically structured in the 'medical colleges' up to the universities, while social pedagogy was only to be on offer at the universities. Qualifications were differentiated according to the American model (BA, MA, doctorate). The third model of study for social educators was to be developed at the University of Kaunas and to integrate at least programmatically the advantages of social work and social pedagogy.

6.22. The Czech Republic

In the Czech republic too, the development of social work has been prompted by the dynamics of the changes. The increase in social problems has meant that unqualified personnel have had to be employed in the social sector (over 60%). In the meantime eleven academies of social work offer a three year course. Likewise at three universities there is a three year BA course and a five year master's course. Curricula are modelled on courses from the USA, the Netherlands and also Great Britain.

6.23. Poland

Poland provides an example of the modernisation of the social work curriculum. After the establishment of the first Schools for Social Work in 1991, there began a nationally coordinated process of constructing a 'modern' training programme. In this, methodological, social and organisational qualifications were identified as needed for the preparation of social workers. These were to be gained on a five semester course with elements of social work as a discipline, social science (sociology, pedagogy, policy, medicine, psychology, law, management), social phenomena as well as methods of intervention. Courses also included practice, a project and specialised elective studies. This model, which was instituted in 15 *Fachhochschulen*, can be seen as a standardised programme that is valid world wide. To this extent, 'modernisation' signifies the adoption of global standards. The EU PHARE programme has played a significant role in this process which helped the implementation of the predominantly American social work models. The connection with the occasionally available Polish domestic tradition, e.g. social pedagogy, plays no part, these developments are not noticeable in the conceptual basis and interests of institutions (*Fachhochschulen*, universities).

6.24. Russia

Social work training in Russia takes place in 100 'Schools of Social Work'. They were established in 1991 and standardised in 1995. Here too, study is on a multi-disciplinary basis. On the one hand the demands on social work with regard to the rapidly growing poverty, unemployment and disorganisation (not only in the towns, but also in rural areas) are immense. On the other hand, the state's resources go back to meet the needs of social policy.

6.24.1. Prospects

Admittedly some institutions have been successful in surviving during the upheaval of the transformation process, and this includes the *Hochschulen* of central, south eastern and eastern Europe, but the current and future development of social work in these countries is not predictable. The situation of countries which are partly en route for the

European Union, partly in a state of confusion from mafia-like early capitalism is decidedly heterogeneous. Training is in a similar position. The reality is simply not consistent with the modernisation programme. Creative new developments are to be seen alongside the tradiiional authoritarian attitudes or social engineering of state intervention. The anti-state movement at the end of state socialism not only liberated democracy, but prepared the ground for unfettered capitalism that wealth on a few, and poverty for many. If no (renewed) counter movement of state social security emerges, then the fine songs about a civil society that were sung in central and eastern Europe, could well become a swan song. In this respect it is reasonable that the eastwards extension of EU-Europe should be a social one.

References

Kendall, K. 2000. *Social Work Education: Its Origins in Europe*. Alexandria, VA.: Council on Social Work Education.

Lorenz, W. 1994. *Social Work in a Changing Europe*. London, Routledge.

Seden J. 1999. *Counselling Skills in Social Work Practice,* Open University Press, Buckingham.

Shulman L. 1991. *Interactional Social Work Practice,* FE Peacock Publishers, Itasca.

Simpkin M. 1983, *Trapped Within Welfare: Surviving Social Work,* Macmillan, London.

Thompson N. 2001), *Anti-discriminatory Practice,* 3rd edn, Palgrave, Basingstoke.

Trevithick P. 2000), *Social Work Skills: A Practice Handbook,* Open University Press, Buckingham.

7

Learning Communication Skills for Social Work

Learning to communicate in a professional manner in a variety of contexts with people from a diverse range of backgrounds can be difficult, but it is a fundamental skill without which it is difficult to perform many other social work tasks or, perhaps, the social work role at all.

Communication not always, but sometimes, takes place in difficult and challenging contexts. Finding a way to engage with someone who avoids all contact with social care agencies is not easy; nor is explaining to someone that you have concerns about their parenting skills or to a carrer that their son is experiencing a mental health crisis and needs urgent admission to hospital. Communicating with people with different communication needs to yourself can also pose challenges if you do not speak the same language or know enough about their specific mode of communication or preferences.

For qualified or student social workers who are communicating with service users, carers or other professionals, or for students in simulated situations such as role play carried out in front of peers and teachers, these circumstances can conjure up a variety of uncomfortable emotions. Embarrassment, anxiety, fear and uncertainty are but a few of those emotions described.

7.1. Standards

Clear learning aims follow on from clear standards. Social care standards take account of the views of people who use services and their carers. The standards of communication skills expected of student social workers, laid down by Health Emergent International Services (HEIs) and Care Councils for Wales and Northern Ireland, will need to reflect this aim. Practice assessors should be as mindful of the views of people who use services and their carers in this as in any other aspect of their professional work.

What service users and carers value in their communication with social workers will help in developing standards locally.

— The Social Care Institute for Excellence (SCIE) practice review illustrates the standards of communication that service users and carers expect from social workers.

Other sources of information about the standards that service users and their carers expect from services and service providers can be found in the following publications:

— A lot to say: A guide for social workers, personal advisors and others working with disabled children and young people with communication impairments.

— The good practice guide for support workers and personal assistants working with disabled people with communication impairments (written by disabled people using Scope services in Essex and in partnership with consultants from the Essex Coalition of Disabled People).

7.2. Assessing Communication Skills

Building the confidence of students in communication skills was seen in the practice review as a key element in teaching and learning for beginning and qualifying level practice. Students described this as reaching a state of "feeling ordinary" and having "confidence" in communication skills.However, self-reporting on achieving a level of "feeling ordinary" or feeling "confident" is not enough. Some markers to help establish who is a confident practitioner, for example, being prepared, being reflective or, indeed, an overconfident practitioner, are probably helpful. Otherwise, these are difficult notions to capture without measures, particularly as the SCIE practice review noted discrepancies of perception between students and other stakeholders.

Service users, carers, HEIs and agencies expressed concerns about students' written skills whereas students did not.

There are a number of questions that arise from the SCIE practice review findings relating to assessment of communication skills, and which HEIs and their partner agencies could ask themselves:

— Is it better to assess communication skills separately or as part of other learning outcomes?
— Is it better to assess competence through written or observational methods?
— Should academics share their role of assessor with practice assessors?

The combined findings from practice and research are that evaluation tends to be concerned with satisfaction with the process and method of training, rather than individual and collective learning through learning aims and with outcome measurements. Shifts in thinking about practice learning, skills laboratories and learning resource centres offer the chance to try out new ways of teaching and learning, including evaluating outcomes.

7.3. Service User and Carer Involvement

One of the degree requirements is service user and carer involvement. While this is a moral imperative, it is also a pragmatic one, recognising involvement as a strong lever for improving social care. Although not the prime focus of this chapter, nevertheless, no respondents discussed the involvement of users in the planning of courses when asked what factors in planning might help improve teaching. SCIE has produced a companion resource guide to this, called Involving service users and carers in the social work degree. The benefits of this involvement include: the availability of more immediate feedback and a true sense of the impact on the recipient of the student's communication skills; material to reflect upon in supervision and academic assignments; a focus on individual learning objectives; and a contribution to the overall appraisal of the student's learning.

Students' emphasis on learning communication skills by putting them into practice strongly indicates that user and carer involvement should be part of practice settings as well as the classroom. Inviting users and carers to become part of the learning and assessment of student communication skills in practice settings has very obvious benefits. Service users and carers can give feedback on the range of communication modes used by the student, for example, written (including recordings on file), verbal, telephone, use of interpreters and so on. Feedback can be given directly to the student or via a third party, that is, the practice assessor in a situation acceptable to the service user/carer. The benefits of this involvement include: the availability of more immediate feedback and a true sense of the impact on the recipient of the student's communication skills; increased material to reflect upon in supervision and in academic assignments; a focus on individual learning objectives; and a contribution to the overall appraisal of the student's learning.

7.4. Practice and Academic Settings

The SCIE practice review identified a 'fault line' between practice settings and college, as noted above in the confusion about 'where, when and how' to teach communication skills. Some respondents understood the need for closer collaboration and expressed "goodwill and commitment" to achieving this. Putting goodwill and commitment into action will involve filling in the fault line with shared, explicit standards, aims and outcome measures that apply to both settings. Review findings demonstrate that teaching, learning and the assessment of communication skills needs to take place in the academic setting, in the agency and in the relationship between the two.

Students consider the practice placement as a place to get experience but not a place to learn: this observation from one academic illustrates the importance for HEIs and practice assessors in ensuring that students understand that the application of theoretical understanding to practice situations is equally important in both the classroom and practice setting.

7.4.1. Applying Theory

The research review found that the theoretical underpinning of teaching and learning of communication skills is underdeveloped, with little in the literature to assist educators to teach and students to learn effectively. The practice review found that there were few attributed teaching models mentioned in the review. Egan's SOLER model was the only one to be mentioned more than once, indicating a continued emphasis on the teaching of counselling skills as a basis to communication skills in social work.

7.4.2. Writing Skills

Writing skills were identified clearly as a concern by all stakeholders with the exception of students. Attention to writing skills particularly for a younger intake of students who it is anticipated may have a lower skills base could represent a resource implication for HEIs and agencies.

The Department of Health Requirements for social work training in England include a requirement on providers of social work education to ensure that "in addition to the university's own admission requirements for the degree, all entrants have achieved at least Key Skills level 2 in English and mathematics". Also, the requirement that providers must "satisfy themselves that all entrants can understand and make use of written material and are able to communicate clearly and accurately in spoken and written English". Therefore the new degree status of qualifying social work education may go some way in establishing that entrants to training will have the necessary written skills required to begin an academic course of this standard, regardless of their age.

However, the standard of written skills expected from students at all stages of recruitment and training should be explicit and measured to avoid confusion about what is acceptable practice, and to avoid negative resource implications.

7.4.3. Transferability

Effective professional communication with children, adults and those with particular communication needs requires the ability to transfer learning across a range of practice settings and from training to doing.

In their study of transfer of learning, Cree and colleagues suggest the following factors need to exist for transfer of learning to be able to take place:

— The original learning must be in place and understood;
— The learner must be able to see and understand the connections between the original learning and the new learning;
— There must be sufficient opportunity to try out this new learning in practice.

7.4.4. Learning From Other Professionals

Renewed interest in communication is in part related to the exposure that social work has received in the mass media in recent years. Independent inquiries into adult and child homicides raise crucial issues about lack of communication, both with services users and within and among different professional groups. It is imperative that educators ensure that teaching and learning includes the necessary communication skills needed to work across adult and childcare services.

Service users and carers emphasise the need for social workers to be able to communicate effectively, verbally and in writing, with other professional groups, in order to be able to access services that they need, and to avoid repetitive questioning from the various professionals involved in people's lives.

Evidence from the practice review suggests that social work programes prior to the degree were already paying attention to interprofessional education, with more opportunities planned for the new degree.

7.5. Changes in Social Work Training

Preparing and putting into place the new three-year degree programe in social work, at the same time as phasing out the current Diploma in Social Work qualification, posed an enormous challenge for those involved in the education of social workers.

It may be helpful for everyone involved in the new social work degree to be knowledgeable about the background to its introduction and, above all, its main purpose.

In England, the consultation paper on A quality strategy for social care (DH,) signalled the introduction of the changes. It included the modernisation of qualifying training for social workers in its proposals to support quality and continuous improvements in social care. The registration by the GSCC of all social workers and students under the 2000 Care Standards Act from 2003 is also part of this strategy. The thrust of all the new arrangements is that service users and carers get high quality social work services in terms of both processes and outcomes. Thus the changes, including service user and carer participation in training, are the means to the ends of improving experiences and outcomes rather than ends in themselves.

Issued under the 2000 Care Standards Act, the Requirements for social work training in England specify "what providers of social work training must do", covering the entry, teaching, learning and assessment requirements for the degree courses. The national occupational standards for social work (TOPSS,) and the Benchmark statement for social work (QAA,) form the basis for the assessment of competence at the end of the programe and the award of the degree. Taken together, the requirements, standards and benchmark statement comprise the prescribed curriculum for the degree. The emphasis is on practice with academic learning to support it. To this end, students will spend at least 200 days gaining experience and learning in practice settings.

Listed below are a number of key documents and web links that give detailed information about the changes in social work education and the initiatives that are being implemented to support this process:

1. A quality strategy for social care: the process of change in social work education began with this consultation paper and included the modernisation of qualifying training for social workers in its proposals to support quality and continuous improvement in social care.
2. 2000 Care Standards Act: the registration by the GSCC of all social workers and students under this Act is a component of the quality strategy for social care above.
3. The Department of Health have a dedicated website for social work education with updates and further information about requirements for training and assessments; entry requirements; and teaching, learning and assessment requirements.

4. The Practice Learning Taskforce was established in 2002 to work with statutory, voluntary, private, user and carer-led organisations and with HEIs to help secure sufficient quality, quantity and diversity of practice learning and assessment opportunities for social work students.
5. Performance indicator: the provision of social work practice learning will be a performance indicator for local authorities, which takes effect in 2004. Local authorities are being asked to provide the Department of Health with the number of practice learning days currently provided for Diploma in Social Work students, as part of the Performance Assessment Framework for social services departments. This information will be used to develop targets against which the Department of Health will monitor performance in local authorities. This new monitoring is an indication of the importance attached to the successful delivery of the new degree.

7.6. Teaching and Learning Communication Skills

The changes to social work education have direct implications for teaching and learning communication skills:

— The social work degree and the current recruitment drive to attract and inspire young people to enter social work both suggest a younger intake of students. HEIs anticipate an increased need to cover basic communication skills for younger, less experienced, students.

— An increased emphasis on practice learning will require more rigorous systems and standards for teaching, learning and assessment of communication skills within practice settings.

In particular, it consolidates the literature in three areas: theories of practice learning, methods of practice learning, and the use of e-learning strategies in conjunction with practice learning.

— The focus on practice learning opportunities, including the increased number of student days in practice settings, requires a shift in thinking about the types of opportunities and the range of practice assessors:

The centrality of practice learning to the creation of confident and relevant social work professionals is recognised within the degree. The need to reform the way practice learning takes place and its aims have also been part of the development of the new qualification.

The degree is committed to practice learning opportunities that include the primacy of users' experiences and an understanding and experience of collaborative working with other professions. Achieving these goals requires a shift in perception from individual assessors of individual students to a workplace where every social care worker sees practice learning as their business. The costs of students in the workplace can be set against the benefits of extending learning and raising standards across the workforce.

The new emphasis on teaching and learning through practice is closely linked to another of the degree requirements of 'learning from, about, and with other professionals'. Communication skills are likely to be a prominent part of such collaborative practice learning.

7.7. Supporting Initiatives

Two of the government initiatives to support practice learning are of particular relevance to teaching and learning communications skills through practice. They offer ways to strengthen the relationships between employers and programe providers, and to promote practice learning in practice agencies.

- Learning resource centres offer organisations the opportunity to develop practice learning for students and for the workforce.
- Skills laboratories are the responsibility of programe providers who have been provided with pump-priming funding for 2003/05 to enable programes to realign their present arrangements for delivering social work training to a more practical focus for the degree. The laboratories could draw on the expertise of service users and practitioners to offer rehearsal opportunities to students, particularly in communication skills. They provide an environment for the development and assessment of social work students' skills at each stage of the integration of learning between 'field' and classroom settings.

The Department of Health (England), Universities UK, the Health Professional Council (HPC), the General Medical Council (GMC) and the Nursing and Midwifery Council (NMC) have prepared a joint statement setting out guiding principles relating to the commissioning and provision of communication skills training, and the required support for healthcare students, at pre-registration and undergraduate level.

The NHS Plan for England (DH,) stated that by 2002 it will be a precondition of qualification to deliver patient care in the NHS that an individual has demonstrated competence in communication with patients. In addition, reports highlighting failures in health and social care systems, such as the Kennedy Report (The Bristol Royal Infirmary Inquiry, July), The Cancer Plan (DH, September), the Health Service Ombudsman's Report for England, and the report from the Victoria Climbié Enquiry (Lord Laming, January), reinforce the need for improved communication skills for all health and social care staff.

Ensuring that healthcare students are suitably prepared for their first post is only the foundation on which they will continue to build during their careers. Developments in specialist communication skills, improving the skills of existing staff and induction programes for all healthcare staff are being developed by the National Health Service University (NHSU) in partnership with experts, patients and local health communities. This will build on the work of others, including the regulatory and professional bodies.

Social workers who are good at communication:

— Are courteous
— Turn up on time
— Speak directly to service users, not carers or personal assistants
— Don't use jargon
— 'Open their ears' and 'think before they talk'
— listen and 'really hear' and accept what carers are saying
— Explain what is happening and why
— Do what they say they are going to do and don't over-promise say honestly when they can't help are patient and make enough time to communicate with disabled service users recognise the loss of dignity people experience when approaching social services for the first time the 'cost' in this and respond sensitively

— Don't assume anything about a user's abilities simply because of a disability
— Understand the importance of privacy peace and quiet and users' and carers' choice of meeting place
— Know that closed questions can be easier for service users with communication difficulties to answer
— Check out that they've been understood
— Find a mode of communication that works
— Remember that young people may prefer to talk while doing something else
— Build trust, empathy and warmth
— Work in organisations that help them to do all these things.

References

Morris, J. 2002 *A lot to say: A guide for social workers, personal advisors and others working with disabled children and young people with communication impairments*, London: Scope.

Essex Coalition of Disabled People and Scope. 2002. The *good practice guide for support workers and personal assistants working with disabled people with communication impairments*, London: Scope (www.scope.org.uk).

Harding. T. and Beresford, P. 1996. *The standards we expect: What service users and carers want from social services workers*, London: NISW.

GSCC (General Social Care Council). 2002. *Codes of practice for employers and social workers*, London: GSCC.

Levin, E. 2003. *Involving service users and carers in the social work degree*, London: SCIE.

Egan, G. 2002. *The skilled helper: A systematic approach to effective helping*, Pacific Grove, CA: Brookes/Cole.

DH (Departmant of Health). 2000. *A quality strategy for social care*, London: DH.

TOPSS. 2002. *The national occupational standards for social work*, Leeds: TOPSS.

8

Technology for Social Work Education

The development of technology in social-work education is set not only in the broader context of the use of technology in higher education generally, but also in the parallel context of the use of technology in social work practice. The latter is important for a subject area with two primary characteristics: the need to acquire not just academic knowledge but also professional expertise and understanding of the aims, methods and values of social work; a strong emphasis on practical preparation for work in social work agencies, which is expressed through the universal use of practice placements within agencies as a major component of social-work professional education and training.

Within contemporary social work practice, it is possible to identify several broad themes concerning the use of new technology: a low level of overall penetration into the work of social work agencies; a primary focus on developing basic client information systems; a preoccupation with the needs of managers and local and central government for financial and statistical data used for accountability and policy purposes.

As a consequence, there has until recently been little expectation by employers that those completing professional social-work training will be computer literate, although that situation is now changing. Those who do acquire such skills may experience frustration at the limited opportunities within agencies to develop and apply them in their work with clients.

8.1. Barriers for Social-work Education

For social work courses the issues are, then, primarily about how technology is used for educational purposes. However, for some educators there is a secondary objective of contributing to initiatives which may indirectly help to reshape social-work practice through diffusion, example and opportunity. The barriers for social-work education include many shared with other disciplines, but also some that are unique, or at least less common. Those that are familiar, applying across most or all disciplines, may be characterised as:

Structural: organisational resistance and/or antipathy towards new technology, arising from an unwillingness to contemplate organisational changes which the use of new technology requires.

Developmental: failure or unwillingness of course planners, managers and instructors to consider the potential of new technology in relation to curriculum needs and requirements; identifying the place of Computer-Assisted Learning (CAL) in the curriculum and developing the competence and confidence of teachers to use CAL and adapt teaching styles to a CAL environment.

Conceptual: confusion about the nature of the activity - whether CAL, Computer-Based Learning (CBL) or Computer-Assisted Instruction (CAI). The term CAL is used here with an emphasis on learning rather than instruction; and on computer assistance rather than the more fully entrenched role implicit in CBL.

Practical: availability of and access to required technology, quality software and appropriate computer teaching environments (including educational, technical and administrative supports); the second aspect depends on the extent to which software is designed to be used entirely by students working alone, or as part of a teaching and/or other shared learning experience.

Philosophical/ideological: individual resistance by staff, through apathy, anxiety or hostility, including the 'not invented here' syndrome; also, collective resistance by academic (and some professional) groupings to new technology having other than a minor, adjunctival role to play in education for human-service professions.

Personal: individual resistance by academics and practitioners to new technology in professional education and training, largely out of fear of job change, relocation or loss; these views are shared by some students who see the introduction of new technology as less attractive than conventional instruction, and which may require more effort on their part.

On the positive side, there is an international cooperative endeavour to contribute, primarily at an academic level, but also at a practitioner level, to change. This work finds its strongest collective expression though a series of international conferences known as HUSITA (Human Services Information Technology Applications), and through the work of the European Network for Information Technology in the Human Services (ENITH). These endeavours provide a means of meeting, sharing and networking, and the focus for publication of conference papers and other texts, such as international comparative studies.

The educational dimension to this work is an important one amongst other aspects that include concerns about the needs of social-work practitioners, service users and other citizens, combined with emphasis on ethical themes of empowerment, disability, discrimination and confidentiality. The educational dimension includes development of simulation software in the areas of child protection and discrimination, and information software in the areas of child protection, care management, social work literature (CareData from NISW) and social work and technology (Social Work and Information Technology from CHST).

Within the social work education dimension to this cooperative work there are, inevitably, both similarities and differences. The differences are exemplified by development within the Netherlands, Belgium and some other continental European countries of the concept of social informatics'. In these European contexts, the concept is dealt with as a taught course on the curriculum, rather than the more experiential introduction to using technology as an educational medium across all aspects of the curriculum, found in British and North American higher education.

8.2. CAL FOR SOCIAL WORK

In comparison with other forms of non-traditional instruction—print-based, video, audio etc.—CAL has yet to make much impact on social-work education delivery for reasons outlined earlier.

In order to challenge some of the criticisms which are made of CAL for social-work education, it is necessary first to understand something of the conventional practices of mainstream social-work education, and the values, attitudes and beliefs that underpin them. Based on a view that the nature of social work is contested and contestable, and that these complexities and ambiguities must be reflected in the curriculum, the main characteristics of contemporary educational practice in this field are that:

— Most learners already possess some relevant knowledge and skills;
— Teaching and learning must be, at least in part, experiential (real or simulated);
— Education and training methods should be learner-centred;
— Learners should be involved in identifying and managing their own learning needs;
— Instruction should include, wherever possible, elements of group-based learning;
— Staff should act primarily as facilitators and enablers of learning.

While not each and every class or study-session of a social work course will incorporate every aspect of the above, learners and staff will, overall, share a view of the education and training process to which this description closely corresponds. It is not difficult to see that a central tenet of contemporary social-work education is interaction, between teacher and learner, and amongst learners themselves.

Thus, any new instructional medium has not only to contend with the set of macro- and messo-level issues outlined at the beginning of this, but must then prove itself in relation to a set of micro-issues specifically concerned with the nature and experience of teaching and learning. Put at its simplest and most challenging new modes of education and training must be able not only to match the content of conventional offerings but also their process and outcomes.

This would be challenge enough to CAL if its use was to be simply adjunctival, complementing or supplementing mainstream methods of instruction. The literature of CAL's recent history in higher education generally, and specifically in social work, shows this is its primary function; staff recommend rather than require student use.

However, increasingly British higher-education funding support for "CAL development is linked with notions of 'greater efficiency', which translates into cost-savings, particularly of teacher-learner contact time.

Thus, CAL for social-work education and training must, if it wishes to be taken seriously as a mainstream method of instruction, be designed primarily as a replacement for, rather than a supplement to existing delivery. Put another way, to be acceptable to both educators and learners, CAL must offer and deliver learning experiences at least as effective as those currently in use.

In trying to respond to this challenge, the temptation is to look first for technological solutions, for example by designing CAL materials that are sophisticated, incorporating sound and graphics, possibly video, perhaps in CD-ROM format, in the belief that these will in some unspecified way compensate learners for the absence of more conventional features of teaching and learning, particularly that of engaging with the content of the material. Yet, most social work departments currently lack access to the computer hardware required to run such programs, or on such a small scale that use of CAL material could never be more than adjunctival.

While multimedia features play an increasingly important role in CAL, greater technological sophistication alone will not redeem a program which lacks a clear and coherent teaching and learning strategy. Effective software requires interactivity both at the level of design of how imaginatively users can access and be presented with material, and at the level of how they are helped to respond to the content. Thus the most appropriate and fruitful response to the challenge of developing CAL materials for social work lies initially in a deeper understanding of what constitutes effective teaching and learning, and how the content, structure and process of CAL materials can be designed to deliver it.

8.3. Developing the Interpersonal Skills

We turn now to the specific work within the ProCare project team of creating social work and nursing modules in the field of Interpersonal Skills (IPS) under the headings of Design and Structure, Content, Functioning and Implementation.

8.3.1. Design and Structure

Curriculum design within UK higher education has, in recent years, become an extremely complex task. Where once curriculum content and structure were the sole province of academics, a range of influences, some competing, now play a significant part in shaping the planning of courses and programes. Of most significance here are:

— The near-universal modular restructuring of higher-education courses;

— The shift from an input-driven to an outcomes-led curriculum model;

— Attempts to create interdisciplinary and interprofessional education.

The first of these led to an early decision that CAL materials would be designed to fit the modular course structures now commonly found in higher education throughout the UK. The decision called for materials to be designed within a context of prescribed module sizes, expressed in credit points, with indications of likely overall 'student effort hours' required for successful completion. This would assist social-work tutors who wished to consider the use of ProCare materials as part or whole replacement for existing teaching arrangements. The second factor was significant for program design in that it required CAL materials to state clearly and consistently the objectives of each module (and in turn, each unit and session), and how the learner would achieve them.

8.3.2. Interprofessionalism

Our early belief that it would be relatively easy to design materials for interprofessional use was challenged by educators and students alike. This led us to consider a choice between separate versions for Social Work and Nursing, or a combined program offering choices about specific Social Work or Nursing case examples. In practice, it proved necessary to develop separate versions for Interpersonal Skills, given the more fundamental differences involved between the two professions, allied to practical issues about developing and evaluating the source materials. For Research Methods, the differences between the professions were less critical and a single module approach was developed which allowed the user to choose at any stage between being offered social work or nursing case examples,

Specialism. Here, the central question for development concerned whether to meet needs of specific groups in and related to the two professions, such as staff working in residential settings; in special educational needs; in the fields of disability and psychiatry; or in voluntary and private-sector settings. A decision was made to provide materials of a generic nature, while earmarking them for future development once basic versions of the programs are stabilised.

8.3.3. Content

With the primary focus on content in mind, in seeking to create a framework for development, the following elements of curriculum philosophy and design were conceived of as central:

— What are the overall aims of the module?

— What are the objectives of the module, expressed as competencies to be achieved?

— What knowledge and skills must learners acquire in order to become competent?

— What knowledge and skills might learners already possess, and how can they be accessed?

— What might constitute an effective teaching and learning process?

Discussions of these issues amongst project staff resulted in a design for the IPS module consisting of eight units, which together cover the key phases of contact between social workers and their clients, *viz:*

— Communication and IPS

— Making Contact

— Assessment

— Planning

— Implementation

— Maintaining Contact

— Endings

— Evaluation

This structure is complemented by two key tools, described later, of a Notepad facility and a Skills Bank. Most of the eight units above consist of two CAL sessions; each session, following a short introduction and objective setting stage, includes the following elements, in a similar sequential format.

Context activity. These require learners to begin each session by identifying, through recall and review, past and/or current relevant knowledge and practice skills. This activity also helps orientate the learner towards the new information and other activities encountered within the session.

Teaching Content. Information is presented in the form of major theoretical perspectives, key concepts, critical issues, contrasting viewpoints, etc. Much as in conventional teaching, it seeks to engender a sense of enquiry; critical thinking, and a willingness to live with the ambiguities of professional practice.

8.3.4. Integration and Preparation Activity

Students are required to use the learning they have acquired during the session (and preceding ones) in preparation for real or simulated practice. Learners may be asked to undertake a range of tasks, including:

- Searching for evidence of specific interpersonal skills embedded in case dialogue;
- Planning for handling hypothetical interactions between workers and clients;
- Proposing alternative ways of dealing with complex interpersonal communications between clients and workers;
- Undertaking self-assessment of their own interpersonal skills, and identifying ways and means of improving them.

As the above illustrates, within the IPS module, structure and process are inextricably linked. Laying out the various elements of the curriculum strategy helps learners to develop a familiarity with the way in which the module works in educational terms, while also recognising that all effective learning involves a process and outcome. Students are also prepared for their use of the module by a User's Guide which explains, in a non-jargonistic way, how the modules were conceived, how they are intended to work, and how to obtain help if problems, either technical or educational, are encountered.

8.3.5. Functioning

The way that software functions is shaped by a variety of factors including the specification of computers available to users, the programming and design time and skills available, the program size planned, and the authoring system(s) and environment used. The first of these factors was discussed earlier as a significant limiting factor for implementation in most social-work educational settings. Other key aspects considered here are navigation, hypertext, special *tools and* authoring system(s).

Navigation. The requirements were that users have a clear overall view of the program, and their current position and progress, combined with freedom to move around the program at will rather than along preset paths. This presents dilemmas in that the knowledge incorporated in each program is incremental and cumulative so that 'naive' users need to understand earlier sections to gain from later ones. That the material has a logical progressive structure is, however, no reason to provide a straitjacket; just as books allow users to browse, flip, dip and peruse as well as to read through from start to finish, so should CAL.

Hypertext. Use of hypertext facilities provides definitions, explanations, answers to questions and reference information in the form of pop-up notes. It is also used for making links between different sections of the program so that users can move from one topic of interest to another in a non-linear fashion. Hypertext is one aspect of interactivity in which the user makes decisions and choices rather than just being a passive respondent.

8.3.6. Special Tools

The Notepad facility referred to earlier allows students to undertake written tasks, to make notes, and to copy key materials for use in assignments and seminars. It is context-sensitive with relevant text already included, and notes can be stored, printed or transferred to a word processor of choice. The Skills Bank is an index of interpersonal skills referred to in the program with a brief description of each.

Students are helped to understand that most skills are of a generic nature, with applicability in a variety of practice situations. Other interactive features include demonstrations of specific human-service tools and techniques, such as Ecomaps and Genograms.

8.3.7. Authoring Systems

Given that both modules are largely text-based and offer less scope that many other subjects for visual representation, easy handling of text and use of hypertext facilities were important criteria. This led to the choice of the Windows-based Guide program for the CAL authoring of Interpersonal Skills, with some Visual Basic add-ons for features requiring particular forms of representation or interactivity. For Research Methods, this was switched to use of a Visual Basic environment which accessed Guide text windows with the aim of achieving a more professionally designed product, a move from scrolling to paging, more integrated and systematic accessing of special features such as the Notebook, glossary and other add-ons, and a more promising development route for multimedia and extended graphics.

8.3.8. Implementation

Implementation has involved establishing test and trial sites within selected social-work courses for evaluating staff and student reactions to IPS. Other less formal feedback has been through demonstration at workshops and conferences. The programe for formal evaluation was initiated by a Training the Tutors event, at which social work educators proposing to introduce the module in their work with students were offered an intensive 24-hour orientation workshop. This proved invaluable in a number of respects in that it:

— Created a 'safe haven' for educators and ProCare staff to discuss the potential and limitations of IPS materials;

— Offered an opportunity for shared creative thinking on how to implement module-use in different settings and circumstances;

— Generated the basis of a tutor-use network for ongoing support and development.

Initial reactions to the IPS module have been encouraging, with important lessons learnt about content, structure, presentation, and how the program is used. Of particular interest have been the evaluation comments endorsing the project team's decision to provide a program requiring a low level of technology, and which appears to have been easy to install and maintain, both stand-alone and networked.

Currently, within test and trial sites, the primary focus has been on use of IPS as an additional learning resource rather than as a complete replacement for existing teaching. As TLTP materials are made available at no cost to UK higher-education institutions, this does not constitute a 'product acceptability' problem at this stage. However, it may become a critical issue if a move is made to offer ProCare materials on a more commercial basis; there, economic viability may well be determined, in large part, by its potential to replace rather than supplement teaching.

8.4. Social Work Education Through On-line Technologies

Social Work education has for some time laboured under the tag of being somewhat behind the times in relation to the use of e–learning, and at the University of Western Australia (UWA) this idea rings true. One reason for this is that pedagogies within Social Work tend to hold true to the people oriented nature of the discipline, and it has been difficult to see how technology can replicate this aspect of the field.

Nevertheless, the problem exists that Social Work students are very often lacking in some of the digital literacies that are increasingly becoming important in the workplace, and as in other discipline areas, it is incumbent upon educators in this area to provide their students with opportunities to develop such competencies.

The challenge, then, was twofold: find a way to introduce technologies that are of relevance to the discipline, *and* overcome the resistance Social Work students show toward such technologies in general. Blogging was trialled in an upper level Social Work unit at UWA which focused on the development of communities and community practice and, despite uniformly negative feedback from the students on the perceived "difficulty" of the technology, the blog entries and comments themselves showed clear evidence of the students having developed as a community of learners.

8.4.1. Role of Blogging

Of the many social networking trends and technologies that have made their way into education, blogging has been quite speedily adopted and has become a commonly used tool in the processes of both research and teaching and learning practices. Evaluations of, and research into, the effectiveness of using blogs, particularly in a tertiary education context, have been quite extensive and relatively unanimous in terms of general findings. Many researchers have pointed out that so-called "transmissive pedagogies" seem to have become the primary feature, and primary failing, of on-line learning, particularly with the widespread utilisation of what are now considered traditional On-line Learning Environments (OLEs) such as WebCT, Blackboard, etc.

In discussing the use of blogs in education, both James Farmer and Jean Burgess, for example, have stressed the need to "reconceptualise on-line learning," that is, to move away from the trends of simply delivering content through OLEs, or having learners produce static pieces of digital media. For both authors blogging is seen as one part of a solution for both of these problems. For example, Farmer sees the blog as providing a re-centring of knowledge communication within the *learner*, de-emphasising the learning *environment*, and similarly Burgess sees the blog as a means of contributing to the "reconceptualisation of students as critical, collaborative, creative participants in the social construction of knowledge."

Blogging has become as much an important part of the digital literacy of academics and other tertiary educators as it has of the literacy of digital age learners. The term "literacy," or "literacies," has itself been heavily worked over as offshoot terms such as "networked literacy," "digital literacy," and "new literacies" come to the fore. Warlick points out that blogging has a very distinct relationship with literacy, since it requires a reiterative process of reading, thinking, rereading, commenting, evaluating, reading more, and so on. Collectively these activities, brought together within the learning task of blogging, become the new literacy, or learning literacy, of Prensky's "digital natives." Warlick also contends that the teaching of literacy in a traditional sense can become more beneficial to these learners if it is redefined to include other contextual aspects such as "networked" literacy and the information overload that characterises the on-line landscape within which digital age learners come into contact with the world. Burgess seems to support this view, stating that blogs provide the means and the opportunity for the learner to develop literacies that are appropriate to the "networked, technologised" environments they encounter in various social contexts – school, work, community etc.

As a central component of these newly emerged literacies Burgess stresses the development of generic competencies as an inherent benefit of using blogs in education, and as a strong rationale for their introduction to courses. She characterises these competencies as critical technological literacy, creative literacy, and the previously mentioned network literacy. The first of these, critical literacy, she describes as the strong development of an informed understanding of on-line technologies and the social contexts that define them. Creative literacy is the competence, and confidence, to play with technology for the purpose of producing content that is appropriate to the on-line environment that houses it, and serves its social goals. Network literacy, arguably the most vital to learning literacy, is the ability to manipulate multiple technologies for the communication, collaborative construction, and sharing of knowledge.

8.4.2. Social Learning

A key point evident in Burgess' definition of network literacy is the social practice that both characterises and directs the learning process. These social practices are particularly evident in blogging activities which educators typically define as learning through conversation. In a tertiary context, particularly in the humanities and social sciences, learners have traditionally expressed their knowledge in the essentially private context of submission of written work to a lecturer/tutor. As such, conversation in this context is brief, non-reflective, and typically, on the tutor's side, consists in large part of a small amount of summative feedback.

The conversation conducted within a blog brings the learner into a new social realm, that is, a community of learning, and of learners. This community clusters learners together and brings them into a vastly expanded learning experience with elements of social participation that engages them in a conversation about their growing knowledge. Farmer, et al point out that as part of this "reconceptualising" of on-line learning we must acknowledge the limitations of other communication tools in comparison with blogs. Email, for example, offers very little in the way of management of knowledge, while wikis, although collaborative in nature, cannot generally be said to engage learners in a "conversation" around learning. Likewise Burgess highlights the conversational aspect of blogging in the communal, or networked context, with the emphasis on commenting, linking to external resources or even classmates' work, discussion of each other's work, and the integration of experience gained in other learning communities. Downes quotes Will Richardson, of *Weblogg-Ed*, as saying that blogging "offers students a chance to

i) reflect on what they are writing and thinking as they write and think it,
ii) carry on writing about a topic over a sustained period of time, maybe a lifetime, and
ii) engage readers and audience in a sustained conversation that then leads to further writing and thinking", thus encapsulating the cyclic process that many educators now accept as being central to the pedagogy of blog use.

In fact we might even extend this further to say that the student blog is a *dialogic* work, in Bakhtin's sense of the term, within which a conversation is sustained within this environment with other "works" and "authors."

With its capacity for the facilitation of higher order thinking and learner reflection, blogging as an educative practice seems to have been firmly placed within the realm of social constructivism.

Social constructivists Vygotsky, Ferdig and Trammell are often quoted for their 2004 proposal of four main pedagogical features of blogging:

i) Development of knowledge through reading, analysing and posting;
ii) Willing ownership of learning;
iii) Enculturation into a community of practice
iv) Opportunities for the exploration and expression of diverse perspectives.

This is consistent with Vygotsky's earlier stressing of the crucial role social interactions play in the accumulation of knowledge. The key then, is active participation in social activities while learning, and educational blogging, it is argued, not only fosters this active participation, but also feeds into the "social connectedness through technology" with which digital age learners are already familiar.

8.5. Digital Identity

A key element in any social interaction is projection of self and this can best be seen at work, in an educational context, in the face-to-face tutorial where interactions are immediate and received according to the elements of self that are expressed via various physical and verbal means. This is also where, for some learners, projection of self can be severely limited, or hindered, due to shyness, lack of confidence, or intimidation by stronger, more outspoken communicators. To a small degree discussion boards, being the primary means of communication in many traditional OLEs, have offered more introverted learners a safer environment within which to communicate their learning, but with limited capacity for development of an "effective social presence". This is largely due to the uncertainty associated with discussion boards as to whether posts will elicit a response, or even be read.

The greatest difference between a discussion board and a blog is arguably the extent to which an individual learner (or even a group of learners) can take ownership of not only the conversation they are conducting, but also the space within which it is being conducted. This ownership typically takes the form of creative manipulation of the on-line environment to personalise the learning space, and establish an individual (or group) social presence. Where discussion boards allow little more than the expression of ideas through basic text entries, the blog space allows manipulation of its physical appearance to suit the tastes of the user, as well as the inclusion of interactive rich media elements such as hyperlinks, images, sound files, videos and animations. The discussion board is static and generic, while the blog space is dynamic and personal. Thus the blog offers the learner much greater control of their means and mode of expression, and therefore greater opportunity, and motivation, for projection of self.

By means of these combined elements of personalised space, projection of self, dialogic expression, and of course an unlimited pool of potential participants in an open, on-line, conversation, the learner constructs an undeniable social presence - a digital identity.

The notion of the digital age learner, has had a huge impact on the field of research into Education and has gained particular currency at a tertiary level where it is often claimed that educators are not paying enough attention to the learning styles of this new breed of student. As Bennett represents it, one of the main claims made about digital natives is that they are "active experiential learners dependent on... communications technologies for accessing information and interacting with others," and that they are more proficient in their use of technology than their teachers. The most salient point for educators, therefore, is the argument that they have different learning preferences from previous generations of learners.

There are several reasons why Social Work teaching at UWA has been slow to embrace e-learning in general and more specifically a blog, despite there being several examples of its effective use to teach practice issues such as child welfare and advocacy; about controversial issues; subjects such as Social Work history; and general course materials. Some of the concerns for Social Work learning through web-based technologies ably identified by Waldman and Rafferty have also been concerns for Social Work at UWA, such as equity, hardware issues and lack of teaching staff expertise and confidence. As they note, Social Work has been the 'tortoise' versus the technology 'hare' in its recognition of the value of e-learning. But perhaps more significantly, Social Work remains a 'people' practice and pedagogies tend to try to replicate as far as possible the experiences of working directly with people rather than interfacing with technology.

Social Work students expect to be working directly with people who ask for or need their assistance to address the issues they face in leading productive and satisfactory lives. They will also be working directly with other professionals to provide necessary services and within organisations where there is a high degree of interpersonal interaction. They therefore expect teaching and learning to focus more on the interpersonal and do not consider technology to have a major place in their tuition.

The teaching and learning environment for Social Work has traditionally been the face-to-face, small group interaction in which interpersonal skills are learned and practiced. There is a great emphasis on being able to critically reflect on presenting issues and contributing environmental factors and one's own responses, to the extent that Social Work education is arguably at the forefront of producing graduates with higher order cognitive skills. This alone would make it a suitable candidate for e-learning where these skills are emphasised. However, technology to enhance learning has, in the main, consisted of video to record role-plays of interviews and other activities to be used for reviewing and reflection to develop skills.

Not only does Social Work teaching require a high level of educator involvement, it also requires a high degree of student involvement with the educators and their peers. Often it is interaction with peers in a collaborative setting that contributes to better learning. Social Work students differ little from other students in having family and other caring responsibilities, as well as the need to financially support themselves, but their ability to avail themselves of fully flexible learning at this University is circumscribed by a curriculum which values the learning of Social Work skills through interpersonal and collaborative work. This means, that in many cases, they must physically attend classes.

Nevertheless, it is also true that increasingly a great part of Social Work involves interaction with technology in the form of gaining and receiving information, or recording and disseminating information such as client details. This often takes student Social Workers by surprise, especially when they go on their first field placement and find themselves required to use possibly unfamiliar computer programmes quite extensively - far more than they engage with clients.

Despite Social Work's continuing desire to be recognised as a scientifically based profession it still relies on a constructivist theoretical framework to guide its practice and, by extension, its teaching. Consequently individuals make meaning of their experiences and situations and encourage clients to make meaning of their own circumstances to determine how to address them productively: so too in the preparation of new professionals meaning-making is a central activity using reflection and collaboration where students are both learners and teachers, contributing to others' learning. Pedagogical strategies to support such learning typically rely on critically reflective activities, such as journaling, and group projects requiring a collaborative effort.

The reluctance of Social Work education in the main to actively engage with web-based educational mechanisms also rests on the experience of its educators, who, for the most part, have learned their Social Work skills in a world in which technology had a minor role in the interactions between people. They are now having to learn new skills, however, with the exception of those educators who contributed to the special edition of Social Work Education in 2008 and a few others, this tends not to extend to actively embracing what appears to the outsider to be a never ending and rapidly changing technological environment. Social Work educators still engage the students face to face and assist them to learn interpersonal skills without the assistance of technology. Added to this is the paucity of Learning Objects suitable to digital teaching. Creativity in the classroom is impeded by the lack of resources and the time to develop materials.

Finally, there exists a real philosophical challenge to Social Work in on-line tuition which encourages the creation of digital identities. Social Work practice rests primarily on authenticity, which a creation of an on-line identity may compromise unless this forms part of the teaching and exploration with students as to how to maintain an authentic identity in the digital space created by the student.

In order to engage with the digital era, which will increasingly be the norm for Social Work students, not only must the educators be willing to be digital learners, but they must also reconceptualise the learning environment where students both form communities of learning and take charge of their own learning in a more facilitative process than in face to face classrooms. 'Electronic pedagogy' requires this reformulation.

The experience of using the blog in the Community Work unit in 2009 showed that there was indeed the creation of a communicative, collaborative digital space, of which the students took ownership, and shared their knowledge and experiences. The detailed postings and on-line interaction demonstrated this quite clearly. This was an objective of the course for community work students, but for it to be achieved on-line was a bonus, especially as the feedback throughout and at the end of the semester suggested resistance to the use of the blog. However, given the perceptions of the students, it is clear that attention needs to be paid to helping students recognise their progress and acquisition of these attributes throughout.

As mentioned previously, Social Work tuition focuses on developing reflective practitioners which is mainly addressed through the production of individual reflective journals, although some small group activities allow for reflective feedback and comment from the students to others. One of the blog requirements was for students to comment individually on others' work which was challenging in firstly having to publicly make their positions available for all to see and to provide critical feedback publicly. Without exception the 2009 class rose to this challenge with care and consideration as well as being able to provide sometimes confronting insights into beliefs or suggested strategies.

8.6. Social Work E-learning

These arguments for making teaching and learning practices more relevant to the skills and learning styles of digital age learners are especially prevalent in the consideration of blogging as an educational tool.

With the question of "good fit" between E-learning and student preference in mind, the argument for making the teaching practices more closely aligned with the learning preferences of the students is largely redundant if the students typically seem not to be "digital natives," despite being, for the most part, in the age group identified by Prensky. The greater argument, therefore, is that these non-natives need assistance with the development of the new literacies identified above, as well as needing to be provided with opportunities for social learning experiences, so that they may be better prepared for the workplace beyond university, where these literacies and experiences have become vital. From a new literacies point of view then, it was hoped that using a blog in an upper level Social Work unit would foster the development of skills qualitatively different to what a Social Work degree at UWA typically provides in the traditional face to face context, particularly the development of meta-cognitive skills in higher order thinking. From a social learning point of view it was hoped that the blogging activity would lead the students to experience the implications of public ownership of, and responsibility for, the provision of feedback on another person's or group's work. An equally important element was the fact that community development is a key aspect of Social Work, and so blogging would allow the students to engage in community development in a technological sphere.

8.6.1. Community Work Teaching

Community work teaching is one of the core areas for Social Work learning, taught often through interactive workshops with elements of simulated practice. Recently at UWA this teaching has incorporated practice learning from actual rather than simulated situations with student groups undertaking activities off campus. As another intensive educator-involved activity that requires a high level of student interaction with each other, this mode of teaching demands a great deal from students in time, collaboration and self-directed learning. The discipline of Social Work's first experience of E-learning was the use of on-line resources to assist in this process, both to the allow students to engage in the necessary collaborative interactions and to permit lecturer-student communication without students having to come onto campus for face-to-face group meetings or consultation with the lecturer. It was not intended initially to take the place of face-to-face interaction entirely, remaining mindful of the essence of community practice which, for many community work practitioners, is in the formation of relationships and the public work carried out together in a place.

One of the important aspects of learning in this unit is to learn from each other about different projects, which was only possible by devoting lecture time for all groups to tell each other what they were doing. While this was useful, students tended to treat it as a formal presentation, spending a great deal of time in preparation and wishing to be assessed on their work. This rather overtook the simple aim which was to learn from and teach others. Consequently, in following years students were asked to post to a blog on what they were doing, which resources they had found useful, to ask questions, and generally to engage with groups outside of their own. This too needed to form part of an assessed piece of work and encourage the use of the blog to communicate with each other. Hence the use of the blog developed into a more structured and more extensive set of activities, albeit replicating as far as possible the pedagogical strategies used in the classroom. The blog exercise now requires the students to post collaboratively as a group to a blog set up specifically for their group, and to post individually to a central Unit blog. In this case study, there were nine group blogs and one Unit blog.

The group blogs (one for each student group) were given a name and a structure of the group's own choosing, and allowed each group to present and reflect on their work, engage with the work of other groups, and to reflect on their own learning as a result of these engagements. The individual posts to the Unit blog required that each student give an evaluation of the project and work of one other group.

As a social learning experience the blogging activity held great potential for bringing the students into a social space with many layers of meaning. Within the context of a unit focusing on the development of communities in Social Work, this space was represented by the blogspace, which had a number of physical layers, as well as figurative layers which represented a variety of constructs. These figurative layers can be characterised as follows:

i) *Writing space:* The blog activity would require that the students post entries to their own group blog, giving expression to their group experience and their group project, as well as comment on the work of other groups.

ii) *Thinking space:* The students would be required to reflect on the style and content of the posts of other groups with a view to both learning from them and giving feedback on their work.

iii) *Owned space:* Each group having its own blog would allow them to have a learning space over which they had ownership and could therefore use to project a group identity through their labelling of the space and the material posted to it.

iv) *Sharing space:* Both the Unit Coordinator and the student groups could use the blog site to provide additional resources to be shared amongst the groups. These could be links to external sites, or each other's blogs, images, video etc.

v) *Collaboration space:* the posting and commenting aspect of a blog would allow for collaborative learning by the students being able to provide input into the projects of other student groups.

vi) *Support space:* Through the sense of community engendered by this activity the students could make, or ask for, *explicit* offers of support to each other through the dialogues going on within the blogs, or feel *implicit* support through the shared experience of the activity.

References

Bennett, S., Maton, K., & Kervin. L. 2008. The 'digital natives' debate: A critical review of the evidence. *British Journal of Educational Technology, 39*(5), 775-786.

Cauble, A., & Thurston, L. 2000. Effects of interactive multimedia training on knowledge, attitudes, and self-efficacy of Social Work students. *Research on Social Work Practice 10*(4), 428-437.

Cooper, L. 2001. Using online technology to teach controversial issues. *New Technclogy in the Human Services 13*(3 & 4), 11-21.

Faux, T., & Hughes, C. 2000. A comparison of using the Internet versus lectures to teach Social Work history. *Research on Social Work Practice 10*(4), 454-467.

9

Partnership in Social Work Education

The essence of partnership is sharing. It is marked by respect for one another, role divisions, rights to information, accountability, competence, and value accorded to individual input. In short, each partner is seen as having something to contribute, power is shared, decisions are made jointly and roles are not only respected but are also backed by legal and moral rights.

> ... the notion of partnership may be more of an aspirational value than a statement of the actual nature of relationships between social workers and service users.

Collaboration is an unnatural act between non-consenting adults. Invited in 1990 to write about her new vision of 'social work education in the year 2000' Phyllida Parsloe suggested that it should have three main concerns: partnership, poverty and peace. Her discussion focuses primarily on partnership, which she viewed as linked to an educational philosophy and structure that would support adult learning, including the opportunity to learn about partnership with others. She emphasised the importance of 'natural justice and openness', and clarity about where power and responsibility lay to assist students to experience a partnership with staff.

Parsloe suggested that partnership with service users challenges 'clientism', the devaluing of a group of people by those with power, and that if social workers are confident, clear of their role, know what they are meant to be doing, and are supported by their organisation, they are less likely to suffer the burnout that leads to clientism.

> Above all they [social workers] need to know how to keep for themselves the discretionary space in which to develop a relationship of partnership with users within the constraints and supports of bureaucracy.

She anticipated that partnership would become more likely with the development of user groups and yet paradoxically harder to achieve, as social workers are likely to feel threatened and withdraw into bureaucracy and professionalism.

Parsloe also anticipated that partnership with other professionals would be problematic because the theoretical base for this work is 'particularly meagre'.Social scientists have taught with a client focus and have failed to theorise partnership with other professionals.

9.1. Regulatory Context of Partnership

An analysis of the regulatory context that underpins the social work degrees introduced in England, Wales, Northern Ireland and Scotland between 2003-05 indicates the following requirements for the learning, teaching and assessment of 'partnership work'.

9.1.1. United Kingdom

Code of Practice for Social Care Workers: partnership is mentioned specifically in relation to: 'Working and respecting the roles and expertise of workers from other agencies and working in partnership with them' (6:7) and implied in terms of collaboration with service users and carers.

Quality Assurance Authority (QAA) Benchmark Statement for Social Work: partnership is related to requirements such as interdisciplinary and cross-professional collaboration and engagement with service users, carers and other stakeholders. It is referred to specifically in the context of effective interagency collaboration.

National Occupational Standards (NOS) for Social Work: the concept of partnership is embedded rather than used explicitly. It is implied in ideas about collaborative working with individuals, families, carers, groups and communities, in working to develop and maintain effective working relationships and working within multidisciplinary and multiorganisational teams.

9.1.2. England

Department of Health Requirements for Social Work Training: 'All social workers will learn and be assessed on partnership working.

9.1.3. Northern Ireland

Northern Ireland Framework Specification for the Degree in Social Work: NOS are adapted to respond to the Northern Ireland context. Partnership is mentioned both in relation to requirements during the degree and at the point of qualification. For example: knowledge of interprofessional working, working in partnership with colleagues and provider organisations and reviewing in partnership with service users. Partnership working can be inferred from other material throughout the Framework.

9.1.4. Scotland

The Framework for Social Work Education in Scotland, Standards in Social Work Education: partnership is specifically mentioned throughout the Framework in terms of underpinning knowledge, transferable skills and competence. For example, working in partnership with service users, carers, partner organisations and colleagues in other organisations. Students must understand factors leading to effective interprofessional working. The whole of Standard 6 involves working in partnership to help individuals achieve and maintain greater independence.

9.2. Importance of Partnership

In the context of social work education, as in practice, the concept of 'partnership' work is loosely defined, expressed through multiple terminologies, embodying different nuances, at one and the same time both contested and taken for granted. From the outset of the Review, this alone presented significant challenges in defining the boundaries for exploring our sources. Our aim here is to try to encapsulate the primary constructs used in the literature denoting what may broadly be considered to be 'partnership work' in social work education.

Noteworthy is the variety of discourses used to describe what we will call 'partnership work' in the content, processes or outcomes of social work education. 'Partnership' itself is a term fairly commonly used in the UK literature, much less so in North America and elsewhere. There is a plethora of other terms to be grappled with: participation and participatory action, involvement and collaboration, as well as interprofessional, interdisciplinary, multiprofessional, shared, or joint education/practice, to name but a few. Only a minority of papers explicitly attempt to define what they mean. On the positive side, this hybridity alone allows the space for many and varied initiatives in social work education. More negatively, however, neither the hybridity nor the potential tensions embedded within the concept of partnership itself receive much, if any, attention within the social work education literature. Noteworthy by its absence, for example, is any significant discussion of the complexities of working in partnership with service users for whom intervention is unwelcome and/or resisted.

9.3. Levels of Partnership

Ager and colleagues, discussing both the social work degree programe at the University of Dundee, and an earlier audit of eight social work programes in Scotland, draw on an adaptation by Mackay of Arnstein's 'ladder of participation'. The adaptation was designed with reference to user participation in practice, but may easily be applied to the education context. It identifies 'levels' of participation along the continuum: not involved, informed, consulted, attended working groups, influence on action, shared action, delegated function, controlled decisions and actions. While best not applied in too rigid or linear a fashion, the model can be illuminative in judging what is meant by partnership, in the content and the processes or outcomes of social work education.

Much of the literature describes partnership work that is effectively at the lower end of the continuum, including, typically, consultation with users and carers and their involvement in academic or practice-based curricula. Users and carers are, for example, invited to bring their own testimonies, share their experiences or act as trainers with students in the classroom, to engage with student learning in the community, or informally to provide feedback on student practice. In some contexts, however, the meaning of partnership is extended considerably further along Mackay's continuum, to embrace some degree of shared action and influence on outcomes. Among other writers articulating this approach, Curran has described the establishment of 'collective workshops' on the (old) Diploma in Social Work (DipSW) programe at the University of Bath. The workshops integrated users and carers with educators, practitioners and advocates, at all levels of planning, providing and reviewing teaching in mental health.

9.4. Collaborative Practice and Group Work

The hybridity of concepts related to 'partnership work' in the literature is partly accounted for by the range of underpinning theorisations of professional practice and role. Some authors frame their discussions in the language of teamwork and collaboration. Partnership in this sense is about the development of cooperative learning as team members, of communication, cooperation and coordination either between professionals or between practitioners and users. Alongside this is a particular focus on understandings and negotiations of professional roles, remits and identities, complementarities and differences.

A few authors draw on theories of group work underpinning partnership-oriented initiatives in social work education. Kacen provides an interesting example of an exercise in 'intergroup bridging', grounded in existentialist, gestalt and learning theories, to increase understandings and reduce potential tensions between the student, professional and user.

9.5. Partnership as Empowerment

For some writers, partnership is the expression of a core social work value, with concepts of rights, exclusion, discrimination and power central to the thrust of participatory practice. Discussing both the process and the content of social work education, Curran identifies four dimensions of power to be challenged: power in observable decision making, in non-observable decision making, in the construction and defining of concepts, and through the discursive practices linking power to knowledge. She contends that partnership must be embedded throughout social work education—'a whole-programe philosophy' with the lived experience of users, carers and students foregrounded, and the knowledge and status of 'experts' challenged at all times.

Not unrelated to this are some interesting debates about whether partnership denotes an ideal, an 'aspiration', or a reality. Trevillion and Bedford make the distinction between the objectives of 'pragmatism', whereby students learn how to work together with other professionals in the real external world, and 'utopianism', whereby they learn to become flexible, holistic practitioners—interprofessional selves, for a better future world. In contrast, Curran, discussing partnership with users and carers, rejects exactly such a distinction as a 'form of repressive power':

User empowerment was not promoted to deny reality, but as recognition of users' lived experiences.

9.6. Formidable Mandate

Ager et al express the view of many authors, that in the 21st century we have a 'formidable mandate' to involve users and carers in social work services, and that those involved in social work education have a responsibility to carry through this mandate. Ager et al describe user and carer involvement in social work education as a slowly emerging process, linked to social trends such as the consumerism of the 1980s, the development of social models of disability and disability rights movements, public unease about poverty and social exclusion, and the lack of accountability of welfare services. More recently, emancipatory legislation surrounding human rights, and user and carer rights in particular, 'has raised the question of why the consumers of social work services are not much more keenly involved in educating and assessing social workers'.

9.7. Policy and Practice Imperatives

A majority of writers arguing the education case either for partnership with users and carers or between professionals, locate their work within contemporary policy contexts. In the UK and elsewhere, they draw attention towards the requirements for, and moves towards, both 'joined-up' services across professional domains, and services that are inclusive of and responsive to the voices of users and carers. These imperatives demand not only organisational restructuring, but the realignment of professional orientation, understandings and skills. They define and shape the world of practice for which we are preparing social work students.

More specifically, the requirement for qualifying social work programmes to embrace partnership work has been formalised in education policy and guidance in both the UK and the US, providing an explicit rationale for addressing the issue. Humphris and Hean argue that the emphasis on interprofessional learning is driven by government policy to improve the quality of collaboration against a background of failures in interprofessional systems. In the UK context, Elliott et al are among the first to give a full account of the development of the new degree at the University of Plymouth, expressly designed to promote user and carer involvement in line with the government initiatives outlined in the Department of Health Quality Strategy for Social Care. Ager et al discuss similar developments in the Scottish context, at the University of Dundee.

9.8. Social Work Value base

For a distinct constituency of educators and authors, the commitment to partnership work in social work education is grounded not just in policy requirements, but in a philosophy and value base central to the core of social work. For Parsloe and Parsloe and Swift, educating for partnership work is about upholding standards of natural justice all too easily submerged under bureaucracy, and challenging the 'clientism' that devalues the powerless. Hendricks and Rudich make a different but related point, when championing the case for involving students in collaborative 'community building'. They cite social work's history of service to communities, by way of challenge to individualised and agency-specific intervention.

Probably the strongest value-based manifesto for partnership in social work education comes from those who place partnership and/or participation within the discourses of rights and power, with strong commitment to empowerment, often alongside antidiscriminatory or AOP.

Many papers make reference to the several partnership relationships commonly involved in education processes and organisation, curriculum content and associated practice competences. Russell and Hymans, for example, discussing an interprofessional community-based project, identify a content and practice competence focus on partnership between social work and nursing students, and between students and users. The process and organisation of this practice learning experience involved partnership between all of these stakeholders, as well as between nursing and social work educators, and between the educators and community organisations. Not least, such examples demonstrate the complexity of what was often involved.

Most reported interprofessional partnership education involves health-related professions—nursing primarily, as well as occupational therapy, speech therapy, midwifery and general practice, and, less commonly, law and education. The range of users and carers involved is wide, with, among others, examples from mental health social work, disability, child and family support and child protection. Interestingly, there appears to be no less attention paid to partnership with users and carers in areas of practice that may involve some degree of social control—such as mental health and child protection—than in others. As discussed earlier, the potential for partnership work with involuntary clients appears taken somewhat for granted, rather than problematised in itself as a topic for critical reflection in social work education. Notable by its absence is any significant discussion of working in partnership either with user and carer organisations or with other professional organisations, as opposed to their representatives. Many studies describe partnership arrangements made with professional agencies or user and carer groups in order to facilitate partnership education initiatives. Several emphasise the significance of understanding organisational cultures in order to achieve effective interprofessional work. However, few expressly discuss student learning to work with other organisations, rather than other people, as the focus of curriculum content or practice competence.

9.9. Partnership as Embedded in Social Work Education

One of the most salient issues for those planning social work education is the question of where and how partnership work sits, both within curricula, and within programe structures and processes. By far the majority of the initiatives reported to date concern discrete courses or practice learning projects, many of them demonstrating the 'creative and inclusive methods of promoting partnership' called for by Levin on behalf of SCIE. From these, there runs a continuum through more comprehensive partnership-oriented developments, to (more rarely) wholesale integration of partnership, in partnership.

The most far-reaching examples of embedded interprofessional partnership initiatives reported are those where a dual qualifying programe was established, training 'joint practitioners' or 'hybrid workers'. We found reports of three such programes in England. (It is worth noting that these were prior to the introduction of the new degree framework, which allows for shared learning but not dual qualification.) At London South Bank University students trained together for a joint social work and nursing degree in learning disabilities. The same specialism was involved in the former joint DipSW/DipHE (Nursing) programe at the Universities of Salford and Manchester. At Portsmouth in the mids nursing and social work students learned together, apparently to become 'twice the practitioner' in mental health (McCray,). In North America, we found two initiatives of this sort reported. The first was an early joint Masters programe in social work (MSW) and public health at the University of Minnesota; the second, a joint qualifying degree in law and social work, at McGill University in Canada. Echoing messages from the wide-ranging CAIPE systematic review of interprofessional education in health and social care, all five reports highlight the many complexities of providing joint programes. Unfortunately, none of these initiatives appears to have been evaluated systematically. This said, all of the authors are positive about their achievements and the potential for student learning.

The case for fundamental integration of partnership with users and carers into the structures and processes of social work education programes, and at a level that might equate with the middle or higher rungs of Mackay's ladder, has some strong protagonists. As Scheyett and Diehl assert:

> ... [in] a true partnership between clients and social workers in social work education.... Clients would have significant roles throughout

> the educational process, working together with educators in establishing goals for social work education, creating strategies to meet these goals, and implementing and evaluating these educational strategies in formal academic settings.

As yet, there are few, if any, manifestations of this ideal reported in the literature. Ager et al, discussing their 2004 audit of qualifying social work programes in Scotland, found (with some exception at the Open University) very little evidence of user and carer involvement in the governance of education programes. Closest perhaps comes the model of the Service User and Carer Group involved in the new social work degree at the University of Dundee. This stakeholder group, linked to a grassroots network of local user and carer groups, has formal representation within programe structures, meets regularly, and has been involved from the outset in strategic design, development, planning, delivery and ongoing review of the degree programe. The initiative is too young yet to have been evaluated. But as reported by Ager et al, it embodies for students and carers the ethos of partnership not just in content, but modelled and made real in processes embedded throughout the programe.

Some other initiatives demonstrate similar commitment to partnership work embedded in the structures of part, if not all, of the programes involved. There are many examples where social work students are given the opportunity to work together with other students on interprofessional modules, projects or workshops, albeit often elective rather than core. Structural barriers to these can be many; overcoming them requires clarity of purpose, commitment to cross-discipline collaboration and institutional support infrastructures.

A current example of partnership work with users and carers embedded in substantial parts (if not the whole) of the programe, is the establishment at the University of Plymouth of 'collective workshops'. These involve a consultative group of users, carers, academics and practitioners meeting regularly and working collaboratively to develop practice learning for the new degree. As with the Dundee example, the emphasis here is on rejecting tokenism, embedding and modelling partnership work within programe structures and processes, as well as teaching and learning about partnership work and how to do it, within the practice setting. By way of critique of the NOS and

General Social Care Council (GSCC) requirements for practice, the consultative group concluded that those 'would mean only tokenistic participation from users and carers due to their prescriptive nature'. They describe as a 'transforming moment ... the first step towards real and meaningful collaboration between professionals and users and carers' the decision to start instead from the question: 'what should a student social worker look like at each stage of practice?'.

9.10. Discrete Initiatives for Partnership Work

Far more prevalent are accounts of discrete teaching and learning initiatives within social work education programes. These focus on partnership with users and carers, between professions, or both, and take place within the classroom and practice learning arenas.

In the classroom setting, there are a good few examples of direct user and carer participation in teaching about partnership work, either, to use Manthorpe's distinction, as cotrainers, or as bearers of the testimony of their own experience. Boylan et al, for example, tell us of care leavers invited to discuss, on an equal footing with DipSW students, their perceptions of social workers, and the Citizens as Trainers Group et al report empowering young citizens as social work trainers. Likewise, mental health service users and/or carers have been involved in particular modules or workshops as consumer teachers, as have members of learning disability user groups. Occasionally, as with the Israeli 'intergroup bridging—dynamic circles exercise', users have also participated in structured exercises or role-play. In another instance, carers of children with long-term neurological developmental disabilities or illness have acted as teachers and advisors to students, using a solution-based approach in collaborative and interdisciplinary working.

Several authors have been careful to draw attention to key practicalities and points of principle in managing the process of user and carer participation in social work education. Among these are: fair and realistic remuneration for participants; physical access; the need for careful planning, preparation and support of trainers; attention to relational issues and power imbalances; agreements about confidentiality; and dangers of atypical representation and of labelling participants according to their user or carer status while sidelining their identity. The objectives of the classroom-based initiatives reported are, for the most part, to inform and develop students' understandings of users' and carers' experiences and views, to confound stereotypes, to learn skills in communication and inclusive behavior, and to question their own roles and status. For users and carers, the objectives most commonly reported are to allow their voices to be heard, to be valued and understood, to make a contribution to student learning and potentially to the improved quality of professional practice.

There are some particularly distinctive classroom-based initiatives worth noting. Independently, Scheyett and Diehl and Scheyett and Kim in the US, and Shor and Sykes in Israel, describe the use of 'structured dialogue' between mental health users and social work students. Structured opportunities are created for students to hear from users about their experiences of illness, of life and of the 'helping' professions. Facilitators guide the encounters, taking responsibility for introducing themes for discussion, ensuring that the conversation flows, and that all participants have a voice. Both initiatives are described as successful. The authors conclude that there is strong potential for the structured dialogue model to improve student attitudes towards, and learning about, people with mental illness, and to undermine the one-dimensional representations and preexistence stereotypes with which students may start out. Feedback from users and carers contributing to structured dialogue sessions indicated its validating and empowering potential for them. Less structured an approach is the 'user conversation' described by Elliot et al at the University of Plymouth. Here, users and carers meet individually with students to discuss 'what they think a good social worker should be like'. Students write an account of the conversation and users and carers give direct feedback on their interpersonal skills, the values and assumptions they display, the accuracy of their account and their ability to reflect on feedback. The process models a reversal of the usual power relationship, with users and carers also as informal assessors, judging students according to user/carer defined criteria.

There are reports of a range of classroom-based opportunities for learning about partnership work that do not involve the direct participation of users or carers, nor indeed of students from other disciplines. None is especially distinctive, and the learning methods and content themes involved fit broadly within the summary provided below.

9.11. Practice Learning Opportunities

Many of the practice learning opportunities privileging interprofessional partnership work that are reported in the literature take place in agency settings. Some are multidisciplinary, and most are primary health or other health-related. The focus commonly is on students' socialisation, their developing student understanding of other professions and intergroup relations, recognition of role distinctions, boundaries and complementarity, understanding of common and different core knowledge and value bases, and the development of collaborative, communication, networking and conflict resolution skills.

Several papers also give accounts of interesting community-based practice learning initiatives. The focus here is on student learning, in collaboration with community groups and outside of agency settings, about users' and carers' lives and lifestyles and their service needs. Bordelon, for example, describes a 'co-operative, participatory learning project', where students worked together with a local disability community action group, framing proposals to meet their service needs, and in doing so developing their knowledge, collaborative and interpersonal skills. Unfortunately no evaluative data as such are presented, but the author reflects that outcomes exceeded expectations, in terms of 'trusting relationships' established and active participation achieved. Other North American projects also have a distinctive community action or community development focus, encouraging students to work with and learn from users as community members and as resources, rather than as victims. Two papers focus on the teaching and learning of research practice as fertile ground for learning about partnership work. Julia and Kondrat's recent review of the teaching of participatory action research found it strikingly absent from MSW programes in the US. However, Pierpont et al describe an innovative 'empowerment research' project, with students learning from users as experts, about the impact of policy and practice on their lives.

9.12. Methods and Content Themes

The methods of learning and teaching deployed in social work education about partnership are many and varied. Whether or not the participants include stakeholders other than social work students and educators, there is a preponderance of adult learning methods described, involving interactive, experiential, enquiry and practice-based learning, rather than received learning.

The content of teaching and learning centres around several key themes. Primary among these is knowledge and understanding about the experiences, identities, perspectives and value bases of others, be they users and carers or others. Alongside these, more prominently in the context of interprofessional partnership work, is an emphasis on the understanding of professional roles, their complementarity and boundaries, the potential for role conflict and the need for role clarity. Teamwork and, less commonly, group work, may provide the conceptual framework for understanding both how professionals may work together, and how they may work with users and carers. Core skills provide another central focus, with the emphasis on collaboration, communication and networking, as well as interpersonal and advocacy skills.

9.13. Carer Assessment of Partnership Work

Several papers make the case for user involvement in the assessment of student practice, arguing that this can empower users and carers and provide a valuable source of feedback for students. Parsloe and Swift, in a brief workshop report of their research for the Department of Health, maintain that users bring to such assessment not only their unique experience of the student's practice, but also different criteria from educators for judging practice qualities. Likewise the early work of Wikler, more firmly grounded in empirical evidence, identified that while educators prioritised various aspects of student 'behavior', carers were more concerned with 'experiential' qualities, in particular the capacity to 'really listen'. A similar point was made by the collective workshops at the University of Plymouth, in rejecting NOS criteria, in favor of their own sense of 'what a student social worker should look like'.

As yet, there are few examples to be found of user and carer involvement in formal assessment of students' practice, let alone their written work; Higher Education Institutions are likely to be reluctant to allow this. Ager et al found in their audit that most of the user and carer feedback currently sought in Scottish social work programes is indirect and not formally required. Although 75% of the practice teachers asked said that they 'always' sought such feedback through informal conversations, direct observation or a questionnaire—the views sought were unlikely to be representative. The authors argue that there are significant possibilities for the creative development of the role of users and carers in assessing students, including, potentially, the assessment of project work and group presentations. However, we must be aware that this presents challenges too. It requires time and resources, attention to confidentiality and representation, avoidance of tokenism, and the ability to disaggregate service issues from student practice.

The Review did identify some innovative initiatives involving users and carers in student assessment. One such initiative involves the assessments of 'user conversations', which are incorporated into the formal evaluation of students' 'safety to practice', on the new degree programe at the University of Plymouth. Among the more notable initiatives in the US was the impressively early project reported by Wikler, in which parents of children with learning disabilities both observed and were interviewed by social work students, rated them on the basis of these encounters, and compared their own rating priorities with those of the educators.

9.14. Modelling Partnership

An interesting strand of practice and thinking about the 'what' and the 'how' of partnership in social work education addresses the principle expressed by Preston-Shoot, that students should be recognised:

> ... not as passive recipients but active determinants who share responsibility for defining clear goals and participating actively.

The point is taken up by other authors, arguing that if social work education about partnership work is to have meaning and integrity, it must accord with the reality of students' lived experience. Henderson, for example, albeit without empirical substantiation, draws a discomforting parallel between the 'symmetrical experiences of oppression' of students and users. Huff and Johnson propose that the empowerment of students provides a model for their subsequent empowerment of users in practice.

Two reports of specific initiatives to model a partnership-based approach in the educator–student relationships are both to be found in the US. Huff and Johnson base their own conclusions on experience with second semester qualifying graduate social work students at a large south eastern university. Students worked in partnership with teachers and with each other, using learning contracts to define the scope and goals of their work, and, to an extent, determining the nature and weight of their assessment. Meanwhile Bordelon describes how the participatory learning approach adopted in a community-based project engaged him as educator/facilitator with his students in a shared and, according to his account, mutually beneficial learning experience.

9.15. Timing of Partnership

There is little reported debate about when students should learn about and experience partnership work with users and carers. The literature describes such initiatives at many stages of student training. Where this work is embedded throughout programes or courses, the principle is that partnership with users and carers should be integral to all aspects of student learning, throughout.

The timing of interprofessional partnership learning is more contested, with the issue linked to concerns about the establishment and consolidation of professional identity and confidence. Glen outlines the arguments for early interprofessional learning, and those against. The findings of Pollard et al seem to suggest that interprofessional learning is best introduced before boundaries and stereotypes have become entrenched. Miller et al, by contrast, argue that students should learn about and develop confidence in their own roles before learning about, or with, others.

9.16. Benefits from Education about Partnership

Many papers argue the benefits of partnership education on grounds of attributed developments in students' fitness to practice, that is, their knowledge, attitudes, values and intentions, rather than the tangible demonstration of these in practice. Whether with users and carers or with other professionals, it is argued that partnership work encourages students to develop their capacities for self-reflection, and for critical reflection on practice. Several papers claim that students express increased appreciation of users and carers as individuals, improved understanding of their experiences and strengths, and reduced stereotyping and stigmatisation. Where interprofessional education is concerned, many authors similarly contend that students develop increased knowledge and understanding of their own and others' roles, identities and perspectives, knowledges and cultures, more positive attitudes towards other professionals, and greater recognition of the potential for complementarity as well as conflict. It is in the context of these discussions that several of the data extracted papers, exploring the assessment of, or changes in, student attitudes and understandings of other professions, are to be located.

Where reports do claim that the benefits of partnership learning are demonstrated in practice, this is largely in terms of practice skills. In the interprofessional partnership context, students are said to demonstrate improved collaborative, comm_nication, conflict resolution and networking skills. With users and carers, they improve their skills in listening, showing empathy and respect, acknowledging emotions and strengths, and behaving with openness and clarity. Only in the case of Scheyett and Kim has it been possible to subject these findings to more rigorous scrutiny.

There is also some debate, as yet without conclusive evidence, about the benefits or costs of interprofessional education to students' current or future professional identity. As Barr tells us, for some, the thrust towards interprofessional learning is seen as 'a thinly disguised threat to professional identity'. Barr and Waterton argue that it is only by developing and valuing role difference that effective interprofessional learning can be achieved. However, Torkington et al maintain that interprofessional learning leads not to the loss of professional identity, but to its adaptation. Trevillion and Bedford, for their part, argue that one of the strong objectives and benefits of interprofessional education is that students become flexible, holistic practitioners, reflective on internal as well as external process, and imbued with a new sense of interprofessional self.

9.16.1. Benefits for Users and Carers

According to Scheyett and Diehl:

> Consumer-partnered social work education is clearly grounded in social work values and principles, but there is a need to demonstrate that it makes a difference... that it results in social workers who are more responsive to, and effective with, consumers of... services than social workers provided a more traditional experience.

While many express this hope, rarely do authors claim to establish links between service outcomes for consumers, and student learning about partnership work. Exceptions are cases such as Bordelon, who considered that his students and community group partners achieved not only trusting relationships, but effective service plans far exceeding expectations. Few studies, however, are sufficiently outcome-focused let alone sufficiently rigorous to enable us to judge whether indeed partnership education 'makes a difference'.

Several papers do, however, claim to describe the positive impact on users and carers of the process of their involvement in partnership education. As service consumers, they report feeling empowered through the process of participation in social work education; they appreciate being listened to, feeling valued and recognised as individuals rather than victims. In one UK case, young service users have also received vocational course accreditation for their contributions. In their capacity as trainers or consultants, users and carers warn of the pitfalls of tokenism, and 'consultationitis', whereby they are invited to participate too late, too minimally to make an impact, or else not for long enough to see results. Where, however, these hasards are avoided, reports suggest that users and carers express genuine enthusiasm for contributing to social work education and making a difference to the practice of the future.

Conceptual confusion about partnership is rife in the social work educational research literature. The concept is undertheorised, simultaneously contested and taken for granted. There is no guarantee that greater clarity would lead to better practice.

Partnership with users and carers in social work education includes children and families, mental health, disability, child protection and other areas of practice; there seems no less attention paid to partnership in areas that may involve some degree of social control (such as mental health or child protection) than others. This said, the important question of how to think about, let alone address the particular challenges of working in partnership with those who do not want to participate is rarely raised in the education literature.

The majority of partnership education initiatives reviewed involve discrete modules, or projects, where, typically, students of different professions worked together towards shared goals, or users brought their own experiences to the classroom. Rarer were those initiatives reported where partnership work could be described as embedded throughout programe curricula, structures and processes. The most far-reaching such examples for interprofessional partnership work were integrated joint programes, with students from different professions learning together throughout. The complexities of providing such programes have been highlighted, but none has been rigorously evaluated.

There are a few impressive examples reported of partnership with users and carers in social work education, including the new degree programes at the Universities of Plymouth and Dundee. These developments need strong institutional support, motivation, establishment of strong grassroots networks, careful attention to practicalities and principals; they tend to rest firmly on a value-based commitment to partnership.

Many of the discrete partnership education initiatives reported demonstrate the type of 'creative and inclusive methods of promoting partnership' called for by Levin on behalf of SCIE. They focus on students developing understanding of other professions and intergroup relations, on distinctions and commonalities in core knowledges and value bases, and on the development of collaborative, communication, networking and conflict resolution skills.

There is an increasing number of examples in the literature of user and carer participation in teaching about partnership work, either, to use Manthorpe's distinction, as cotrainers, or as bearers of the testimony of their own experience. The emphasis here is on developing students' understandings, empathy and interpersonal skills, reducing stereotypes, and recognising users' and carers' strengths and identities. Two of the data extracted studies evaluated specific examples, one involving parents of children with disabilities and the other, users of mental health services. They suggest that a model of consumer-partnered social work education using structured dialogue, acknowledges the wisdom and experience of service users and enables them to become fully engaged in teaching, assessment, course review and curriculum committees that will shape future social workers.

Some studies suggest practice learning as a better opportunity for learning about partnership than taught modules. The process of setting up the placement itself was seen as an opportunity to model partnership between student, tutor and practice teacher, although students noted the power differentials that sometimes limited their involvement.

Several papers make the case for user involvement in the assessment of student practice, arguing that this empowers consumers and can provide a valuable source of feedback for students. This requires time and resources, attention to confidentiality and representation, avoidance of tokenism, and the ability to disaggregate service issues from student practice. There is scope for development in this area; as yet, despite some innovative initiatives, most user/carer assessment of students is indirect and informal.

Coverage of the implications of 'race', class, sexuality, religion, culture and language was not prominent. Jackson and Morris report that 'race' and language were better addressed than the other areas, in the education programes that they examined, but argue that if there is little explicit teaching in all these areas, an understanding of how oppression can create barriers to partnership working will not be grasped.

The timing of interprofessional partnership learning is contested, with the issue linked to concerns about the establishment and consolidation of professional identity and confidence. Glen advocates interprofessional learning before boundaries and stereotypes have become entrenched; however, she and others warn against the dilution of professional skills where an interprofessional priority is adopted early. Kane suggests that the key is to combine understandings but contribute separate talents, and many studies contest that the issue is less about when it happens and more about the tensions created to fit it all in.

9.17. From Rhetoric to Reality

There are no overall conclusive findings reported on whether partnership work in social work education is effective for students, nor which approaches to teaching and learning about partnership might be more effective than others. This is particularly so since only two of the studies reviewed indepth followed students through into subsequent practice, and one of these did so only three months after qualification. Where reports claim that partnership education has been effective, they focus mainly on student perspectives, attitudes and knowledge, not on demonstration of practice as such. Even here, there are mixed findings. The Pollard et al survey provides a large-scale study within which there are variable findings about perceptions of interprofessional work; likewise the other studies addressing effectiveness are characterised by mixed or indicative, rather than secure, results.

However, some messages do emerge about the factors that support partnership, such as making clear and reiterating the definition and expectations of partnership, making greater use of practice learning to promote partnership, developing more extensive and integrated user and carer participation, modelling partnership through interdisciplinary provider teams, establishing partnership-based relationships with students, and possibly (although this remains the subject of debate) introducing interprofessional experiences earlier into the social work education process. Studies rarely claim to tell us whether partnership education improves service outcomes for consumers. However, there seems good evidence that, if well managed, the process itself can be valuable for users and carers. Scheyett and Kim, for example, suggest that the 'structured dialogue' partnership model they describe honours service users' and carers' experience and wisdom by inviting them to participate in the education process. In this sense 'a school of social work can model for students true partnership with consumers in a strengths-based framework'.

Overall, the evidence predictably suggests rather greater commitment to education for partnership work with users and carers, and between professionals, than the outcome evidence from research can sustain at this time. However, this partly reflects the nature of the available evidence base rather than the state of education, the impacts of which remain largely undetected and unidentified. The implementation of partnership-focused education needs more research that evaluates longer-term effects and monitors changes for the same population over time using multiple sources or more carefully designed comparative studies.

9.18. Partnership Work in Practice Learning

In practice learning no examples of a defined 'partnership curriculum' were identified. The findings on partnership in practice learning are contradictory and frequently appear to depend on the commitment of individual organisations and practitioners. Some participants argue that practice is the 'driver' for partnership education since policy requires joint working and service user involvement. Others feel that the university curriculum is determining the quality of partnership learning and practice is following or even lagging behind.

Time itself was found to be an important aspect of developing effective partnership education. This includes both the time involved in developing and maintaining relationships and also the timing and staging of teaching and learning about partnership. In the literature, there is considerable debate about the timing of interprofessional learning, particularly in terms of the development of professional identity. There is no similar debate about the timing of service user involvement. There is agreement that this should happen as early as possible, both in course planning and delivery.

Programes are involved in micro-evaluations of partnership teaching and learning. More extensive evaluation, focused on some of the initiatives developed for the new degree, will be required to explore the relationships between identified aims and outcomes and the development of good practice.

References

Cheers B. 1998, *Welfare Bushed: Social Care in Rural Australia,* Ashgate, Aldershot.

Clark C. 2006. *Moral Character in Social Work*, Toronto.

Munn P & Munn T. 2003. Social work: Moving forward, *Rural Social Work,* 13 (1), 22-34.

Parker S, Fook J & Pease B. 1999, Empowerment: The modernist social work concept *par excellence,* In Pease B & Fook J (eds), *Transforming Social Work Practice: Postmodern Critical Perspectives,* Allen & Unwin, St Leonards, pp. 150-157.

10

Integrating Genetics into Social Work

Current and emerging advances in the science of genetics provide significant promise for enhanced health and well-being and an opportunity for social workers to make a major contribution. As rapid discoveries in genetics (the study of single genes and their effects) and genomics (the study of the functions and interaction of all the genes in the genome) continue to identify genetic components of common diseases such as Alzheimer's, diabetes, cancer, heart disease, mental illness, and even behavioral characteristics, virtually everyone will be affected. Knowledge of the genetic make-up of oneself or a family member may present significant dilemmas and may lead to a serious consideration of alternative life plans. A genetic test can alert people to advanced detection and management of some disorders, but currently the ability to test for a genetic disorder often exceeds science's ability to prevent or cure genetic disease. The social worker's role in encouraging clients to become their own advocates in bringing genetic issues to the forefront of quality health care is being defined in part by the completion of the Human Genome Project (HGP), the international effort to map and sequence all the genes in the human body.

A social worker is often the first to provide psychosocial services to individuals and families with genetic disorders. Therefore, it is imperative that social workers become more aware of the ethical, legal and psychosocial implications of a genetic diagnosis, genetic testing and genetic research in order to empower individuals and families to speak out for their rights as public citizens. In addition, the profession must continue to be active in shaping public policy as well as organisational policy as it relates to genetics and service delivery. Without specialised training, it is inappropriate for social workers to assume the role of genetic counselors, but they have important contributions to make within the social work scope of practice. Social workers can take an active part in ensuring that their clients are protected against genetic discrimination in areas such as health and life insurance, employment, and adoption. There are increasing opportunities for professional development of social workers in the field of genetics, and social workers should take the initiative to seek out those resources.

As critical issues are identified in the field of genetics, such as the benefits and risks of gene therapy, stem cell research, reproductive technology, and tissue cloning, social workers need to become more informed and sensitive to related ethical, legal, and psychosocial considerations to be helpful to their clients. It is also important that they become knowledgeable about genetic resources in the community.

The ongoing knowledge explosion in genetics and its positive and challenging sequelae present considerable opportunities for the social work profession. Increasingly social workers will be called on to develop as well as confront emerging policies related to genetic testing and treatment.

The National Association of Social Workers (NASW) recognises the need to integrate knowledge of genetics into social work practice in the context of the NASW Code of Ethics. The standards that are delineated in this brochure represent a foundation for introducing genetics into social work practice

10.1. Social Workers and Genetics

For more than years, social work as a profession has recognised the importance of genetic disorders in relation to social work practice and education. The Human Genome Education Model (HuGEM) project, funded by the National Institutes of Health and co-chaired by two social workers, offered workshops and training programs in genetics for social workers and other disciplines across the country from to. NASW was an active participant in this project, which served as a catalyst for increased involvement in the field. The National Coalition of Health Professionals in Genetic Education (NCHPEG) was formed in and included two social workers representing both NASW and the Council on Social Work Education (CSWE) on its steering committee. NCHPEG has developed core competencies in genetics for all health-care professionals; these competencies have been useful in the development of these practice standards for social workers.

In addition to the efforts to improve social work education in genetics, the social work practice community has worked to clarify the social work role in genetics. An NASW Social Work Practice Update in defined the role of social workers in genetics, emphasising practice, policy, and ethical issues. The NASW policy statement on Genetics provided a framework all social workers could use to understand ethical and practical issues in genetic testing and research. In these NASW documents, it was made clear that social workers in all fields need to understand the ethical and practical issues involved with genetic testing. These include informed consent, confidentiality, self-determination, equal access, and the implications of knowing one's genetic make-up. The Practice Update emphasised the importance of social workers assisting individuals and their families in weighing the positive and potentially deleterious aspects of genetic testing and treatment options. The Policy Statement included a commitment by NASW to continue work to establish the social work profession as a leader in the field of genetics, to support the development of programs, training, and information that provide social workers with current genetic information for use with clients, and to support policies that provide protection for clients from employment and insurance discrimination.

10.2. Goals of the Standards

These standards address genetics as an expanding field of knowledge for social workers and emphasise the need for clarification of, understanding of, and education about this specialised area.

The standards are designed to enhance social workers' awareness of the skills, knowledge, values, methods, and sensitivity needed to work effectively with clients, families, health care providers, and the community and to increase their understanding of the impact that the field of genetics has, and will have, on them. It is hoped that these standards will lead to the development of clear guidelines, goals, and objectives for expanding current and future areas of social work practice, research, and policy in genetics.

The specific objectives of the standards are

— To inform social workers about genetics as an expanding field of social work knowledge
— To improve the quality of social work services provided to clients with genetic disorders
— To provide a basis for the development of continuing education materials and programs in genetics
— To ensure that social work services to clients with genetic disorders are guided by the NASW Code of Ethics
— To advocate for clients' right to self-determination, confidentiality, access to genetic services and nondiscrimination
— To encourage social workers to participate in the formulation and refinement of public policy (at the state and federal levels) relevant to genetic research, services, and treatment of populations with genetically identified predispositions or conditions.

10.2.1. Standard 1: Ethics and Values

When integrating genetics and social work practice, social workers shall function in accordance with ethical principles and standards of the profession as articulated in the NASW Code of Ethics.

10.2.1.1. Interpretation

Social workers can make a significant contribution to the field of genetics by advancing a humane and ethical approach. Among the current ethical issues of relevance to the social work profession are

— Equitable access to genetic services, including testing and treatment and financial coverage for these procedures
— Privacy and confidentiality of individual genetic information, particularly in relation to the insurance industry and employers
— Self-determination, including allowing the client to select or refuse genetic testing and treatment in a noncoercive, unbiased

manner; allowing the client to exercise the right to know or to refuse to know genetic information

- Informed consent, including protecting the right of the client to make decisions with regard to genetic testing and research based on a clear understanding of the risks and benefits
- Voluntary genetic testing and treatment
- Appropriate authority for genetic decision making on behalf of children and impaired adults
- Protection of the rights of those living with genetically determined conditions.

With its historic commitment to serving and empowering populations at risk and promoting human rights and social justice, social work is well suited to address the ethical challenges that arise from new genetic knowledge. The NASW Code of Ethics provides a philosophical framework for ethical social work practice and a set of ethical standards intended to define acceptable professional behavior. Cultural competence is highlighted and practitioners are enjoined to provide culturally sensitive services. Although the genetic make-up of all individuals across the spectrum of racial and ethnic groups is remarkably similar, the NASW Code acknowledges that members of different cultures have unique norms, traditions, and coping strategies that must be understood and respected. The client's right to privacy and confidentiality, self-determination, nondiscrimination, and social justice are clearly articulated in the Code. Genetic services should be interdisciplinary to achieve a holistic approach to client care. In this context, these standards address mutually respectful relationships among colleagues. The Code also acknowledges the complexity of ethical dilemmas, which defy simple answers. The Code suggests that the resolution of seemingly contrary mandates is best approached through a reasoned, systematic process that incorporates ethical theory and appropriate peer and interdisciplinary consultation and supervision.

10.2.2. Standard 2: Genetics Knowledge

Social workers shall acquire a basic understanding about genetics as a science and a field of study, including its biological, psychosocial, ethical, and legal aspects.

10.2.2.1. Interpretation

Advances in the scientific understanding of the human genome leads to better comprehension of diseases, both common and rare, and ultimately leads to better diagnosis and treatment. Because of the rapid increase in genetic knowledge and because most social workers do not have a background in genetics, they need to gain a basic understanding of predisposition to common illness and inherited disease patterns. Social workers must continually update their understanding as new knowledge becomes available.

Social workers need to become familiar with general terminology used in human genetics and basic patterns of biological inheritance and with the role of genetic factors in maintaining health and preventing disease. Because many diseases are now understood to involve a combination of causative factors, including but not limited to genetics, social workers need to understand how social, behavioral, cultural, economic, and environmental factors interact with biological factors to influence health. It is important to include a relevant medical history in social work assessments in working with families. A family history is crucial in determining a genetic diagnosis and in predicting how various family members might be affected in the future. Social workers therefore have an important role to play in this area, particularly in knowing when to refer their families to genetic counselors and genetic clinics.

Although new information on genetics has increased the understanding of the etiology of physical and mental illness, prevention and treatment of genetic disorders are very limited. This creates difficult dilemmas for people who are now in a position to decide whether to get tested themselves or to have their children tested. People who are at risk of genetic disorders will have increased options to use the new information to guide their reproductive behavior. However, many of the possibilities (for example, prenatal diagnosis, elective termination of abnormal pregnancies, in-utero treatments, in-vitro fertilisation, trait selection combined with selective implantation) raise serious moral questions.

As the genetic basis of common diseases becomes better known, it is especially important for social workers to become knowledgeable about indications for genetic testing and referral resources for such testing. In cases where genetic testing is available, social workers need to understand the potential benefits and risks of genetic knowledge to individuals, families, and communities. Social workers involved in the adoption process need to be aware of the impact of genetic testing on all parties, and place the best interests of the newborns and children first. Psychosocial reactions to genetic testing, cognitive responses, and coping strategies are important areas of knowledge for social workers, as are family issues.

A genetic test may provide people with information that can inform both their reproductive decisions and health behaviors. Because environment affects genetic expression, a genetic test may also alert people to a need to change their physical and social environments—something social workers are particularly skilled in assisting people to do.

Genetic testing has an uneven history in the United States, and social workers need to be familiar with this and have an understanding of how genetic information can be beneficial or misused. Social workers should understand and advocate for legislation that prohibits genetic discrimination and protects against inappropriate disclosure. Social workers working with clients should make efforts to keep current with legislative and legal developments through continuing education and in-service training.

Social workers need to be able to locate genetic resources in their communities and elsewhere. They need adequate understanding of genetic counseling and how it differs from other types of counseling. This knowledge is helpful in explaining to clients what to expect from genetics professionals and what to expect from social workers. They need to know when referrals are needed and how insurance coverage applies to genetic services.

10.2.3. Standard 3: Practice Skills in Working with Individuals, Families, Groups, and Communities

Social workers shall use appropriate practice theories, skills, and interventions that reflect their understanding of genetic factors in their work with individuals, families, groups, and communities.

10.2.3.1. Interpretation

Basic social work skills can be used to provide genetic services to individuals, families, groups, and communities. A professional commitment to continuing education in genetics is necessary for the integration of current and emerging genetic information and technology into appropriate social work settings. The social workers' biopsychosocial perspective is ideal for their role as liaisons between health professionals and clients, client advocates, and providers of psychosocial support services. Social work interventions can facilitate the identification of individuals in need of medical referral or genetic counseling services, and should include initiating referrals. The social worker should serve as an advocate for these clients, assisting individuals and families in adjusting to chronic health conditions, creating and maintaining appropriate self-help groups, resolving bereavement issues, and taking action at the community level regarding genetic privacy and potential discrimination.

More specifically, social workers should develop skills to

— Gather relevant genetic family history information, including a multigenerational family history that includes parents, children, siblings, grandparents, aunts/uncles, cousins

— Identify clients who might benefit from a referral for genetic services

— Properly communicate to clients the purpose of genetic services and the role of various genetic professionals

— Provide culturally sensitive services to clients with or at risk of genetic conditions

— Seek assistance from and refer to appropriate genetics experts and peer support resources

— Explore with clients the possible range of emotional effects they and family members may experience as a result of receiving or refusing genetic information

— Assist clients and their families in the genetic decision-making process, and in adapting to genetic information throughout the life cycle

— Discuss costs of genetic services and insurance benefits

— Discuss potential risks of discrimination in insurance, employment, adoption, and other areas
— Safeguard privacy and confidentiality of genetic information of clients to the extent possible
— Facilitate the creation and maintenance of support resources for genetic service clients
— Obtain current genetic information from reliable sources, for self, clients, and colleagues
— Educate clients, professionals and the community about policy issues regarding genetics
— Advocate for client-focused public policy in genetics.
— Assist clients in the understanding of the limitations and benefits of participating in genetics research and the importance of informed consent.

10.2.4. Standard 4: Client/Practitioner Collaborative Practice Model

Social workers shall be able to work with their clients with genetic concerns in a partnership that includes mutual respect, shared information, and effective communication.

10.2.4.1. Interpretation

Individuals and families who have genetic concerns and those serving them have a shared commitment to quality services for everyone. Clients have expert knowledge of themselves and their family situations. Social workers should build partnerships with clients who are affected by genetic diagnoses to create new genetic resources, fight genetic discrimination, and ensure that the needs of individuals and families with genetic concerns are met.

Social workers can be helpful to individuals and families in understanding the information they receive about their genetic makeup. Clients need to have a role in the collaborative team when choices regarding health care and other genetic services are being considered. Social workers should be aware of the psychological dynamics that individuals and families experience when making genetic decisions. In addition, social workers and their clients with genetic conditions should pool their knowledge, skills, and experience to advocate for needed programs and services.

10.2.5. Standard 5: Interdisciplinary Practice

Social workers shall participate in multidisciplinary teams that deliver comprehensive genetics services.

10.2.5.1. Interpretation

The complexity of genetic conditions requires a holistic approach to intervention. Individuals and families with genetic disorders, or at risk of them, need to receive services from a variety of health professionals working collaboratively to ensure optimal benefit. Multidisciplinary teamwork is central to the new, dynamic science of genetics. More effective services are provided when an interdisciplinary team shares its expertise with individuals and families with genetic disorders.

By virtue of their education and training, social work professionals are well suited to working as part of a multidisciplinary team. Social workers have expertise in identifying and coordinating services and in bridging gaps in professional communication among service providers.

A common goal for all disciplines is to provide quality services to the population of affected persons and their families. In particular, all disciplines must be attuned to the emotional and social needs of individuals with genetic conditions. Healthcare professionals such as social workers, psychiatrists, psychologists, and nurses who provide psychosocial services to individuals and families can include genetic issues in these services. Other health professionals such as audiologists, speech and language pathologists, nutritionists, occupational therapists, physical therapists, and special educators also provide important services to people with genetic disorders. They have much to learn from one another in helping their clients or patients who must cope with these disorders.

Social workers, with a team approach, can establish bridges between clients and health professionals such as genetic counselors, medical geneticists, and primary care physicians. In addition, the support group/professional partnership is essential in empowering individuals and families living with genetic disorders.

10.2.6. Standard 6: Self-Awareness

Social workers shall have and continue to develop an understanding of their own personal, cultural and spiritual values and beliefs pertaining to genetics and genetic therapies.

10.2.6.1. Interpretation

Genetic knowledge and practices may conflict with basic beliefs, not only in clients, but in social workers themselves. To be able to effectively assist clients, social workers must continually examine their own backgrounds and identify their assumptions, values and beliefs related to human reproduction, medical intervention and the value of life with major disabilities. Social workers must recognise the fact that clients come from a wide variety of religious and cultural backgrounds that may differ from those of the social worker.

Becoming a self-aware and self-reflective practitioner involves the examination of one's own bias about groups with views different from one's own. Social workers need to work to develop an understanding of different views, and to avoid judging clients with different values. They also must understand how a practitioner can subtly influence clients with different beliefs through choice of words and nonverbal expressions and reactions and must learn the skills to avoid doing so in their practice. There may be situations in which social workers will find themselves unable to empathise or remain objective. Self-awareness means taking responsibility for identifying such situations and working on one's issues so that they do not interfere with the client's decision-making. In instances where the social worker is unable to accomplish this, referral should be made to a social worker who can be neutral while assisting clients in this highly sensitive work.

10.2.7. Standard 7: Genetics and Cross-Cultural Knowledge

Social workers shall have and continue to develop specialised knowledge and understanding about the history, traditions, values, and family systems of client groups as they relate to genetics.

10.2.7.1. Interpretation

Social workers need to possess specialised knowledge regarding the influences of their clients' ethnicity, culture, values, religious and health beliefs, and economic situations to understand their client's use of genetic information and services. In providing clinical services, social workers can obtain the sociocultural knowledge through exploration with the client, starting with a family history, or health concern. The social worker will need to assess the meaning the client is placing on this concern. This process of cultural exploration is needed to assist in decision making regarding the pursuit of genetic information and later the results of that decision on the individual, the family, the community and the wider social context. NASW has developed NASW Standards for Cultural Competence in Social Work Practice that establish guidelines for practice.

There are many sociocultural barriers to genetic services. Social workers should use and promote the use of appropriate language and literacy levels when discussing genetic information with clients and their families. When taking a genetic family history, they should be culturally sensitive and aware of language and underlying emotional content. The social worker should be alert to cultural factors in working with individuals and families regarding their understanding of genetic information and issues in genetic decision making. As a client advocate, the social worker must address genetic privacy and confidentiality of genetic information with an awareness of possible cultural meaning and social stigma for an individual or a group.

In summary, social workers may assist in overcoming cultural barriers to genetic services by

- Using and promoting the use of appropriate language and literacy levels when communicating with clients and their families in regard to genetic information
- Being culturally sensitive in obtaining a genetic family history
- Being aware of cultural factors in working with individuals and families regarding the genetic decision making process and in adapting to genetic information
- Addressing genetic privacy and confidentiality of genetic information with an awareness of possible cultural meaning and

social stigma for an individual or a group

— Advocating for cultural competence in service delivery and throughout the health system

10.2.8. Standard 8: Research

Social workers shall contribute to, support, and be cognisant of the development of research-based and practice-relevant knowledge of the psychosocial, cultural, economic, and ethical implications of genetics on individuals, families and society.

10.2.8.1. Interpretation

Much remains to be learned about how to promote the well-being of individuals, families and society in the context of the genetic revolution. Research is needed on how individuals and families react to learning about their genetic risk status, how they make decisions based on that knowledge, and how society can ensure that genetic information is used for the common good. Research can inform the understanding of how genetic information may differentially affect the diverse cultural and ethnic groups within the society, and how to be culturally sensitive to these differences. The NASW Code of Ethics states that social workers should "contribute to the knowledge base" of the profession, and "promote and facilitate evaluation and research to contribute to the development of knowledge". Moreover, the Code states that "when generally recognised standards do not exist with respect to an emerging area of practice, social workers should...take responsible steps (including appropriate education, research) to ensure the competence of their work and to protect clients from harm".

Social work's "person-in-environment" perspective can make a unique contribution to the understanding of the impact of genetic information on the society. Social workers are ideally suited to observe the impact of genetic information on individuals, families, and society; draw preliminary generalisations; and form theories that may be tested in research studies to enhance social work practice. They can initiate surveys among client populations, and document potential problems created by genetic testing, such as discrimination in insurance and employment.

Social work research must be guided by basic ethical and cultural principles, as defined by the Code of Ethics of the National Association of Social Workers. Promotion of the well-being of the client is the primary responsibility of the social worker. Informed consent, the equitable selection of subjects, privacy and confidentiality, the right to withdraw from studies, and avoidance of harm are among the standards that are essential for ethical research studies (National Bioethics Advisory Commission,). The consequences of research must be considered, and appropriate institutional review boards consulted in the early stages of project development. Social workers must also keep current with emerging research by other professionals, and should collaborate in multi-disciplinary research with other interested professions, such as medicine, nursing, genetic counseling, psychology, and law.

10.2.9. Standard 9: Advocacy

Social workers shall safeguard the privacy and confidentiality of genetic information of their clients and advocate for and with clients when appropriate to ensure fair social policies and access to quality genetic services.

10.2.9.1. Interpretation

Social workers are keenly aware of the importance of maintaining their clients' privacy with regard to genetic information, as well as the potential for discrimination based on that information and the need for social advocacy and social action to better empower clients and communities.

To protect clients, social workers must be aware that there are limitations to the confidentiality of genetic test information. Insurance companies, employers, the criminal justice system, and other government agencies have enormous financial incentives to gain access to people's genetic information. Federal and state policies may not adequately protect people from the use of genetic tests for purposes of discrimination in underwriting and employment. Of particular concern to social workers is the potential for labelling individuals and withholding services from those with genetic conditions.

The right to confidentiality extends to both the decision whether to be tested and the decision of who is allowed access to the test results. Social workers should inform clients about the possible disclosure of confidential information and the potential consequences before the disclosure is made.

As public policy is developed to define access and funding for genetic services, social workers must be active participants to the process. Social workers should also keep current with federal and state legislation pertaining to genetics and encourage their clients to do the same.

References

Germain, C., & Gitterman, A. 1995. Ecological perspective. In R. L. Edwards (Ed.-in-Chief), *Encyclopedia of social work* (19th ed., Vol. 1, pp. 816–824). Washington, DC: NASW Press.

Guttmacher, A., & Collins, F. S. 2002. Genomic medicine: A primer. *New England Journal of Medicine, 347,* 1512–1513.

Jenkins, J., et al. 2001. Recommendations of core competencies in genetics essential for all health professionals. *Genetics in Medicine, 3,* 155–159.

Lapham, E. V., Kosma, C., Weiss, J. O., Benkendorf, J. L., & Wilson, M. A. 2000. The gap between practice and genetics education of health professionals: HuGEM survey results. *Genetics in Medicine, 2,* 226–231.

National Association of Social Workers. 1999. *Code of ethics of the National Association of Social Workers*. Washington, DC: Author

National Association of Social Workers. 2003. Genetics. In *Social work speaks: National Association of Social Workers Policy Statements, 2003–2006* (6th ed., pp. 161–166). Washington, DC: Author.

Weiss, J. O., Bernhardt, B. A., & Paul, N. W. (Eds.). 1984. *Genetic disorders and birth defects in families and society: Toward interdisciplinary understanding* (Birth Defect Original Article Series, Vol. 20, No. 4). New York: March of Dimes.

11

International Social Work Organizations

Organizing into associations is one of the hallmarks of the professions. Although his use of the term is outdated, Abraham Flexner pointed out in a 1915 speech to the U.S. National Conference of Charities and Correction that a profession is a "brotherhood" and tends to self organize. Within just a few decades of the first offerings of social work education in Europe and North America, social workers and others interested in social welfare came together for professional meetings and began to organize what are today the three major international organizations in the field of social work and social welfare. This chapter will describe the International Federation of Social Workers, the International Association of Schools of Social Work and the International Council on Social Welfare.

There is no firm date to mark the beginning of social work. Better documented are the beginnings of social work education and here it is known that by the very late 19th century, social work courses had been offered in England, the United States and the Netherlands, with Germany following in the early years of the 20th century. Social workers were active in important international movements of the early 20th century, especially movements for peace, women's rights, and improved labour conditions. As leaders in social welfare from various countries met each other, the benefits of exchanges of ideas became evident. This led to a proposal for an international conference on social work and social welfare, an idea that originated when European and Japanese social workers participated in the U.S. National Conference of Social Work in 1919. The official proposal for a conference was made in a letter from Dr. Rene Sand of Belgium to Julia Lathrop of the U.S. in 1923. Endorsement by national associations and by the League of Red Cross Societies followed.

In 1926, an organizing committee met in Paris; the Committee was comprised of representatives from 17 countries in Europe, Asia and North America and from a number of important international organizations. Among these were the League of Nations, the International Labor Organization, the League of Red Cross Societies, the International Migration Service, and the Save the Children Fund. Leading the way were Dr. Alice Masarykova of Prague as President and Dr. Rene Sand as Secretary General of the conference. Plans grew until the final event spanned two weeks and included international meetings of a number of organizations. The first International Conference of Social Work was held from July 8-13 1928 in Paris and was attended by 2,481 delegates from 42 countries . It is remarkable that so many travelled great distances almost 80 years ago. Yet, one of the conference speakers applauded the ease of travel in the day:

> *"In the last hundred years, the technical application of human invention has wrought nothing short of a revolution in international relations. The high seas— obstacles for so long to the free interchange of goods and ideas—have become a great medium for the exchange of both... Ships, railways, aeroplanes, telephones, wireless telegraphy, broadcasting—all these have made the world smaller, have brought us into close contact with one another"*

The Conference was only the first of what became the international social work and social welfare conferences. Two more were held before World War II interrupted international collaboration: 1932 in Frankfurt and 1936 in London. A planned conference for 1940 was never held; a planning meeting in Paris in 1946 and much less grandiose conference in 1948 in Atlantic City, New Jersey in the U.S. began the effort to rebuild the international social work/social welfare movement.

Particularly significant is that the 1928 conference "gave birth" to the three international organizations that are the topic of this chapter. Although they have been slightly renamed, both the IASSW and the ICSW have been in continuous existence since the 1928 meeting.

11.1. International Federation of Social Workers

11.1.1. Mission

The International Federation of Social Workers (IFSW) is a global organization striving for social justice, human rights and social development through the development of social work, best practices and international cooperation between social workers and their professional organizations. Association members work together through the international organization towards developing the common goals of the profession and in working on issues of concern to social workers globally. IFSW tries to achieve this international identity by:

1) Encouraging co-operation between social workers of all countries;
2) Providing means for discussion and the exchange of ideas and experience through meetings, study visits, research projects, exchanges, publications and other methods of communication;
3) Establishing and maintaining relationships with social work organizations and their members and representing them to international bodies relevant to social development and welfare;
4) Sponsoring biennial international symposia and conferences;
5) Developing and publishing policy statements to guide social work practice worldwide;
6) Advocating for the protection of human rights of practicing social workers; and
7) Providing consultation to the United Nations on issues of human development and human rights.

11.1.2. History and Activities

The IFSW celebrated its 50th jubilee in Munich in 2006, having grown from just 12 member organizations in 1956, to over 80 today. However, as noted above, the heritage of the modern IFSW stretches back to the First International Conference on Social Work held in Paris in July 1928, where it was agreed that an international association of social workers be formed. At the 1932 Second International Conference on Social Work held in Frankfurt, provisional statutes of the International Permanent Secretariat of Social Workers (IPSSW) were agreed. The IPSSW operated from Berlin, Geneva and Prague until 1956 when the International Federation of Social Workers was formed in Munich with 12 national member organizations and a new Secretariat was established in New York, sharing office with the National Association of Social Workers.

Of major concern to the new organization was the question of ethics and in 1957 work began on the establishment of what has become today 'Ethics of Social Work – Statement of Principles' (IFSW 2006). The President and Executive promoted the voice of social work at the United Nations and its bodies so much that by 1959, just three years after re-establishment, the IFSW was approved for consultative status with the United Nations Economic and Social Council (ECOSOC), with a special relationship later extended by UNICEF and the International Labor Organization (ILO). Teams of representatives are in action at the United Nations in Geneva, Nairobi, New York and Vienna. IFSW now also has formal partnerships with Amnesty International, CONGO (Conference of Non-Governmental Organizations in Consultative Relationship with the UN), Council of Europe; European Union, Habitat, IASSW and ICSW.

Encouraging a discourse of international social work was greatly strengthened by the decision to launch the Journal of *International Social Work*. IFSW joined its partner organizations, ICSW and IASSW in sponsoring the journal in 1959. The Journal remains one of the most significant refereed journals on international social work available today. While early conferences were held jointly, by the mid 1960's it became apparent that for various reasons the three foundation organizations, IFSW, IASSW and ICSW, had begun to move in their own directions; since then, some of the conferences have been held separately and some together.

Regional IFSW seminars and conferences have been a strong feature, particularly of the European region, and have extended with differing levels of success across all IFSW regions. The IFSW Executive Committee decided to establish a permanent and paid secretariat in 1972 in Basel, Switzerland, appointing Catherine Chuard (1972-1974), followed by Andrew (Andy) Mouravieff-Apostol as the Secretary General (1975-1992), assisted in his work by his wife Ellen.

Both enjoyed extensive networks within the United Nations system and Ellen remains today as the IFSW Main Representative to the UN Geneva.

From 1975 to 1992 Andy was IFSW Secretary General, and was elected lifelong Honorary President when he retired in 1992. For IFSW, Andy was the cornerstone. He communicated with social workers of all countries with warmth, knowledge and diplomacy and became like a father for the international social work community. His lifetime spanned close to a century and his history and background reflect the international character of the profession. Born in France in1913 of Russian/Ukrainian parents, his family were abroad when the 1917 revolution in Russia broke out it was impossible for the aristocratic family to return home; Andy was only able to return to Russia at the time of perestroika in the late 1980s. Working first as a journalist and then as a foreign correspondent in England before and during World War II, he also served in the Free French military forces. After the war Andy left journalism and took up a position with the World Council of Churches and later with the United Nations High Commissioner for Refugees. He served in many countries, but mainly in South America, where he met his future wife Ellen. The couple settled in Geneva, where Andy until his death worked as a professional interpreter at the United Nations and other international bodies.

The strengthening of the secretariat also heralded an era of increased activity in membership levels and by IFSW through its representative status with various organizations. The secretariat later moved to Oslo, Norway in 1992 and then in 1999 to Berne, Switzerland, where it is located today, with Tom Johannesen as the Secretary-General.

The 1980's were particularly active years for the IFSW in the area of human rights and social justice. By this time the IFSW had well established representative teams to the United Nations in New York, Geneva and Vienna. This focus of concern led the Federation to a strong engagement in the UN International Year of Peace 1986, recognized by the UN officially declaring IFSW a 'Peace Messenger'. Eight years later the United Nations designated IFSW as 'Patron of the International Year of the Family' for exemplary support of the UN program. Many outstanding social workers have contributed over the years to IFSW and its development. Among these are Jane Hoey whose major contribution to social work was in the establishment and enforcement of standards in public welfare administration in the United States, and in whose name a fund has been established to promote social work in developing regions of the world. Another is Chauncey Alexander who served as the first US President of IFSW 1980-1982, developing the concept of global policy papers, the international code of ethics, and mentoring and promoting other social work associations.

Social work grew out of humanitarian and democratic ideals, and its values are based on respect for the equality, worth, and dignity of all people. Human rights and social justice serve as the motivation and justification for social work action. IFSW promotes human rights by publishing statements on human rights issues and related matters and by raising awareness within the profession about the profession's commitment to its human rights heritage. IFSW has adopted an International Policy on Human Rights describing its commitment and giving guidance to social workers and social work organizations on human rights policy matters. To implement the human rights agenda of IFSW a special commission has been set up – the Human Rights Commission. Apart from its work on behalf of imprisoned and persecuted social workers around the world, the Commission has successfully developed two landmark publications with international partners, on human rights and social work and social work and the rights of the child.

IFSW and its member Associations have also produced other academic publications from time to time. *Social Work and Globalization* was produced as a special issue on the occasion of the IFSW and IASSW joint Conference in Montreal, 2000. Other publications include a series of edited books on social work in different countries, *Social Work Around the World*, which is now on its fourth issue. Regional newsletters and journals are also published wherever possible. A series of international policy papers has been developed and are regularly revised. Current policy papers cover Displaced Persons, Globalization and the Environment, Health, HIV/AIDS, Indigenous Peoples, Women, Migration, Older Persons, Peace and Social Justice, Protection of Personal Information, Conditions in Rural Communities, Refugees and Youth.

A highlight in the 1990's was IFSW's strong involvement in the World Summit for Social Development in Copenhagen in 1995. A special issue of the *IFSW Newsletter* was presented to a broader audience focusing on social work contributions to a new world order for social development in the areas of poverty eradication, unemployment, social integration and transition in Eastern Europe. Also the Fourth UN World Conference on Women in Beijing the same year had a strong IFSW presence.

The start of the new century brought with it a significant range of challenges for the social work professions. A worldwide shift in political orientation towards conservative and in some instances ultraconservative governments has meant that working to develop social services has been particularly difficult in more developed countries. Issues concerning the alleviation of poverty, human rights and HIV/AIDS continue to be major concerns. IFSW has responded to some of the major international issues experiences in recent years such as the Asian tsunami, serious human rights violations in the Sudan and the challenges faced by orphans and vulnerable children in Africa, through projects initiated by its regional bodies and in cooperation with partner organizations.

11.1.3. Membership

IFSW is the international organization representing professional social workers, although membership is through national social work organizations, not individual status. Only one national professional organization in each country may become a member of the Federation. Such an organization may be a national organization or a coordinating body representing two or more national organizations. Each member association or coordinating body must observe the IFSW Constitution and should require from its members regular professional training based upon an organized sequence of social work education incorporating ethical standards of practice and a body of knowledge compatible with social work principles. At present, there are national organizations in 84 countries in membership, representing just under 500,000 social workers across the world. Association members collaborate together through IFSW towards developing the common goals of the profession and in working on issues of concern to social workers internationally.

IFSW is divided into the five geographical regions of Africa; Asia-Pacific; Europe; Latin America and the Caribbean; and North America, each of which is represented by a regional president. An international elected executive committee steers the work of the Federation with a global President and Secretary General heading the body. The general executive meets every two years at the same time as an international Conference, at times held jointly with IASSW and ICSW.

IFSW also has a very successful program called 'Friends of IFSW,' providing affiliating social workers, social work students and organizations a link to international social work.

11.1.4. Challenges

IFSW has faced significant challenges at various times in its history, often due to political and ideological differences among its many members. However the international executive committee and the General Meeting of the member associations has made every effort to work in as harmonious a way as possible and to reconcile and overcome these issues. Serious problems have ranged from conflicts in places as varied as the Middle East, Sri Lanka and Zimbabwe. However the contentious issue of South Africa was one of the most significant, when by 1963 the attention of the world began to focus on South Africa and its Apartheid policy. The South African European Social Workers organization was a member of IFSW at that time and despite continued work on their part to establish a coordinating body of European and non-European social workers, due to government policies in that country, such an organization could not be established. The principles of non-discrimination are foundation principles for social work and after many years of agonized debate and attempts to resolve this very difficult and delicate situation South Africa was expelled from membership in 1970 and was not eligible to re-enter membership again until 1998. In fact, South Africa has yet to achieve membership of IFSW due to the persistent problem of being able to form a coordinating body between the white, colored and black South African social work associations.

There are various future priorities and challenges that face IFSW, including:

1) A core concern is to ensure that key policy statements are up-to-date and relevant. In this context both IFSW and IASSW have agreed a four-year process for the review of the international definition of social work and the international statement of ethical principles, leading to the 2010 joint conference in Hong Kong. Thereafter these core statements will be reviewed every 10 years.
2) Social work practice is becoming increasingly international with the migration of social workers from many countries in the developing world to the developed. A challenge for IFSW is to link with other organizations that are trying to improve conditions in the originating countries and stem this migration as far as this is possible.
3) Conflicts and consequent human rights abuses have intensified throughout many regions of the world in recent years and this challenges IFSW to take an even higher profile in defence of human rights. IFSW already issues statements of concern where violations of peoples' rights occurs, such as in Darfur, but the challenge for IFSW is to ensure that these words are translated into actions.
4) A similar challenge for IFSW is to respond as effectively as it can to natural disasters such as the Asian tsunami of December 2004.
5) The IFSW's engagement with debates on poverty, ways to achieve the Millennium Development Goals and tackle the consequences of HIV/AIDS remain important areas of concern for the organization.

An enormous commitment by many volunteers and a small but dedicated secretariat has over 50 years given rise to a significant organization with good reason to celebrate its achievements. Through a number of world and regional conferences, the development of core international documents to guide social work concepts and practices, and ongoing representation at the United Nations and other international bodies, IFSW is today a key global voice of international social work practice.

11.2. International Association of Schools of Social Work

The International Association of Schools of Social Work is the main organization representing social work education and educators around the world; in 2008, it will celebrate its 80th anniversary.

11.2.1. Mission

The primary mission of the IASSW is to strengthen social work education around the world. This has remained constant since the founding. The most recent formal review of the mission statement took place in 2000 and resulted in the following mission statement:

"The International Association of Schools of Social Work is an international association of institutions of social work education, organizations supporting social work education and social work educators. Its mission is:

1) To develop and promote excellence in social work education, research and scholarship globally in order to enhance human well-being;
2) To create and maintain a dynamic community of social work educators and their programs;
3) To support and facilitate participation in mutual exchanges of information and expertise;
4) To represent social work education at the international level."

The statement also commits IASSW to adhere to UN human rights declarations and conventions and to pursue social justice and social development.

11.2.2. History and Activities

A special section of the 1928 conference focused on social work education and was led by Alice Salomon of Germany. The delegates at the conference decided to *"write to all the training schools of social work asking them whether they would be prepared to become members of an International Association of Schools"*.. In addition to Alice Salomon, the founders of the International Committee of Schools of Social Work, as it was originally called, consisted of representatives from the Netherlands, Belgium, and Switzerland, soon joined by the United States, France, England, and Poland. Of the 111 schools of social work identified at the time, 46 schools from 10 countries agreed to become founding members of the new association. By 1939, membership had grown to 75 schools from 18 countries; by then, however, all German schools had withdrawn from membership.

In the early years, the International Committee sponsored seminars to exchange knowledge and strengthen social work education, including "summer schools"— seminars that intensively explored significant topics for social work. The organization continued to be led by Alice Salomon as President. She was pressured by her colleagues in Germany to resign after the Nazis came to power; Salomon was suspect for many reasons, including Jewish ancestry and her commitment to peace and internationalism. She resigned several times as President, but each time, her IASSW colleagues renamed her President. Just before she was expelled from Germany, Salomon completed the first world survey of social work education, published by the ICSSW in 1937. She produced an in-depth sociological and comparative analysis of social work education in 32 countries.

The International Committee established working relationships with the ILO and with the Commission on Social Questions of the League of Nations. A particularly important achievement was that the ILO set up a Center of Documentation for schools of social work in 1929.

> *"For the next ten years the ILO attempted, with moderate success, to collect and index the statutes, programmes of study, annual reports, publications, research and seminar reports, and lists of theses or other student reports from more than 100 schools of social work"*

As was true for each of the 3 organizations, World War II had a devastating effect. Not only were communications disrupted for the war period, but many teachers and students died and educational facilities destroyed. The plight of the school at Warsaw is recorded in early letters of the IASSW:

> *"I appeal most warmly in the name of the Board...to make their members send all they possibly can collect, books, papers, reports, etc. regarding social work to Mrs. Helena Radlinska, one of the founders of our Committee, professor of the State University of Lodz (Poland). Mrs. Radlinska had the great misfortune to see destroyed besides her private house, the School of Social Work, founded by her at the University of Warsaw as well as the University itself, and to lose by death two-thirds of the teaching staff. In spite of this great*

misfortune starting anew at the age of 75 years Mrs. Radlinska does what she can to rebuild a School of Social Work at the University of Lodz"

Kendall labelled the years 1945-1954 the "Restoration Years". A small conference was held in Atlantic City in the U.S. in 1948 and Rene Sand had agreed in 1946 to take on the Presidency of the International Committee of Schools of Social Work. Ironically, although devastation was significant, Kendall reports that the war and its aftermath created a new demand for social workers and thus, "by 1948, 359 schools were counted in 41 countries" in a report issued by the new United Nations. Social work as a profession and social work educational institutions began to disappear in the Communist countries, but grew substantially in the newly independent countries in Asia and Africa.

In the 1950's and 1960's, IASSW extended its outreach to programs in developing countries. The Congress was held in Madras, India in 1952, marking the first time the conference was held outside of Europe or North America. By 1956, the board of directors included members from Australia, Guatemala, Japan and India. The name of the organization was officially changed to the International Association of Schools of Social Work, although many member units are not independent schools but programs within larger institutions.

A major, but sadly temporary, milestone was the establishment of a Secretariat in 1971 with a paid Secretary General. Katherine Kendall served as the first paid Secretary General from 1971-1978. Originally in New York, the Secretariat moved to Vienna in 1978. Kendall was succeeded by Margarite Mathieu of Canada and then Vera Mehta of India. In the early 1990's, the organization experienced financial difficulties caused by the increased expenses of maintaining the Vienna office. A decision was taken by the Board to return to a volunteer-run organization and the Secretariat was closed in 1992. While finances have since permitted the hiring of an Administrative Assistant based in the office of the President, from 1993 IASSW has functioned without a professional executive officer.

As is true for ICSW and IFSW, IASSW holds a biennial world conference. These have been held regularly since 1928 except for the war years. At various times, the conferences have been held jointly with IFSW or with both IFSW and ICSW; in 2006 and 2008, the 3 organizations held/will hold separate conferences before joining in 3-way collaboration in 2010.It might be argued that the Biennial world conference with its call for papers and the co-sponsorship of the journal, *International Social Work,* are particularly important to the mission of the IASSW as both address the purpose of advancing scholarship and research in social work and social work education. IASSW played a lead role in the establishment of the journal and guided it in its early years. To further this objective of encouraging scholarship and research, IASSW has recently expanded its publication activity and has launched a book series through Venture Press. IASSW also assisted the Caribbean sub-regional group to launch *The Caribbean Journal of Social Work* in 2002.

In the 1970's IASSW secured significant funding to pursue a 6 year multi-country project on family planning and social work education. The project was implemented in 20 countries—as diverse as Iran, the Philippines, Kenya, and Jamaica. Curricula, field placements, project reports and a number of important publications resulted from the effort. The family planning project put IASSW on the forefront of a cutting edge issue and reflected sound working relationships with major governmental and private funding bodies.

While no initiative of this scale has been implemented since then, IASSW was active in the 1980's and 1990's to promote and assist the development of social work education in Eastern Europe, Russia and China. Consultations and seminars were sponsored to help countries establish or re-establish social work. Through recent efforts to strengthen the regional association of schools of social work in Africa and assistance in the establishment of sub-regional organizations in the Caribbean in the 1990s and in Southeast Europe in 2006, promotion of the growth and development of social work education continues to be a program priority of the IASSW.

In an effort to promote international exchange and innovation, IASSW began a program of small projects in 2004. A consortium of at least 3 schools in two or more countries with different cultures or social work educational systems may apply for funding for a project that advances social work education internationally. The projects must enhance international and cross-cultural collaboration. To date, among the projects that have been funded are one to develop a website on field education for Chinese schools of social work; a collaboration of schools in Kenya, the Philippines and England to develop a module on disaster management; a project sponsored by 18 schools in 9 different countries on indigenous social work education and practice; and a 10 country project on international social work and political conflict resolution that is setting up a network to enhance social work education and research in conflict and post-conflict situations.

IASSW led the effort to develop *Global Standards for Social Work Education and Training,* adopted by both IFSW and IASSW in 2004. This comprehensive document is the first set of standards for social work education at the global level. Although compliance with the standards is voluntary, they have been hailed by schools of social work—especially in the developing world—as helpful targets that will contribute to upgrading of social work

11.2.3. Membership and Organizational Structure

There are two categories of membership in the IASSW: school members and individual members. Social Work educational programs at the tertiary level are eligible to join as school members. Individual educators may also join, but individual member votes count as 1/10 of a school vote. Currently, there are member schools in more than 70 countries spread across Africa, Asia and the Pacific, Europe, Latin America, and North American and the Caribbean. Schools are also organized into regional associations. Although the regions differ greatly in their degree of formality and organization, each regional President serves on the IASSW Board and Executive Committee as a Vice-President. The Board of Directors is large and includes the elected officers of President, Secretary and Treasurer; 4 elected at-large members; regional representatives, including the Vice-Presidents; and national representatives. Chairs of task forces and committees also attend board meetings where they have a voice, but not a vote. Current committees and task forces include the International Exchange Task Force, the Nominating Committee, an award committee, the World Census Committee, the Women's Caucus, Publications, Human Rights, tne Projects Committee, and the UN representatives team.

11.2.4. Challenges

IASSW has faced several challenges over its almost 80 years of existence. Among them were the devastation and disruption caused by World War II and the financial difficulties of the early 1990's that led to the loss of Secretariat. In the 1980's, the organization faced a different kind of struggle over the membership of South African schools. The world's attention on the evils of the South African apartheid system intensified during the late 1970's and 1980's. A major initiative was to isolate the South African government by expelling South African organizations from participation in world bodies and events (although South Africa continued to be a member of the United Nations). The issue extended to social work education. Throughout the 1980's there was extensive work to assess the degree to which the South African schools were working to oppose apartheid and to ensure multiracial social work education. When the IASSW leadership decided to work with the reform-oriented South African schools and allow the JUC to retain membership, the schools in the Nordic region withdrew. Although reconciliation and re-entry of the Nordic schools occurred after the end of apartheid, the struggle over South Africa had a long-lasting effect on the organization.

Future challenges include pressures arising from changes in the educational sector, where mergers of social work programs into larger departments with other disciplines are becoming more common. When social work has less autonomy and less visibility, there is diminished allegiance to the profession and schools are less likely to maintain membership in social work organizations such as the IASSW.

While the *Global Standards* are a major advance, they are voluntary and some are concerned that free trade regulations will lead to externally-imposed criteria for social work education. IASSW needs to carefully monitor such developments and be prepared to respond. The process of developing the standards also gave renewed attention to the continuing challenge to achieve some universality—definition of what is essential and core education for professional social work— while encouraging diversity and indigenization of curricula.

11.3. The International Council On Social Welfare (ICSW)

The International Council on Social Welfare differs from the IFSW and IASSW because it is interdisciplinary and includes lay as well as professional members. The ICSW is,

> "a global non-governmental organization which represents a wide range of national and international member organizations that seek to advance social welfare, social justice and social development"

11.3.1. Mission

ICSW describes its mission as:

> *"to promote forms of social and economic development which aim to reduce poverty, hardship and vulnerability throughout the world, especially amongst disadvantaged people"*. The statement continues: *"It strives for recognition and protection of fundamental rights to food, shelter, education, health care and security. It believes that these rights are an essential foundation for freedom, justice and peace. It seeks also to advance equality of opportunity, freedom of self-expression and access to human services"*

11.3.2. History and Activities/Programs

The ICSW, under the earlier name of the International Conference on Social Work, was formed in 1928 out of the Paris conference with Rene Sand, a chief organizer of the 1928 meetings, as its founder and Alice Masarykova as first president. Sand soon succeeded Masarykova as President in 1932. Organized to promote the interests of the social welfare sector and to ensure international exchange of information and views, the ICSW held international conferences in 1932 and 1936, resuming in the post-World War II years. Records of the planning for a 1940 conference and all records of the early ICSW were destroyed in the bombing of London. Rene Sand's own story illustrates the disruption of organizational activities during the war years. He was taken prisoner in 1940 when the Nazi army invaded Belgium and was held in Tyrol, Austria until he was liberated in May of

1945. He resumed his active presidency of ICSW until 1948 when he encouraged younger leaders to take over.

ICSW regrouped after the war, focusing initially on relief for war-torn areas. A special meeting was held in 1947 in Holland on the theme: "Urgent Social Problems in the War Stricken Areas of Europe". The ICSW was one of the first NGOs to gain consultative status with the United Nations. Conference locations marked progress of the ICSW in the postwar years. The 1952 conference in Madras, India, was the first held outside the West. In 1956, the conference was held in Munich with participants from 55 countries. As Katzki observed, support for the conference in Germany showed that *"participants recognized in ICSW a force that could help heal wounds and contribute to a better understanding amongst peoples"* (p. 15). Geographic reach was extended through the 1962 conference in Brazil and the 1974 conference in Nairobi, Kenya.

It is worth noting that ICSW gave early recognition to human rights. The 1968 conference theme "Social Welfare and Human Rights" supported the United Nations International Year of Human Rights. The papers delivered at the conference contain messages relevant to this day. The human rights theme was echoed in 1976 in Puerto Rico: "The Struggle for Equal Opportunity-Strategies for Social Welfare."

The organization sought ways to expand its activities beyond the biennial conferences. In 1966, the name of the organization was changed to the International Council on Social Welfare to more accurately convey that membership and scope of activity are not limited to social work. Katzki records that by 1968, ICSW had almost 50 national committees in membership and that many of these were in developing countries. Efforts continued to strengthen national committees and build regional networks.

A particularly important area of activity is consultation at the United Nations. ICSW has the highest level of NGO consultative status with the United Nations and relates to the Economic and Social Council (ECOSOC), as well as to the ILO, UNICEF, UNESCO, WHO and other bodies. The Category I consultative status allows ICSW to attend ECOSOC meetings, circulate written statements to members, address a council committee, and submit items for ECOSOC consideration.

For at least 25 years, ICSW has emphasized social development. In 1982, ICSW officially described itself as: International Council on Social Welfare: A World Organization Promoting Social Development. The emphasis on social development intensified in preparations for and participation in the 1995 United Nations World Summit on Social Development held in Copenhagen. ICSW participated in the preparatory meetings for the Summit and organized a global NGO preparatory meeting. More than 60 NGO leaders attended this meeting in Helsinki in 1994.Over several years prior to and during the Summit, ICSW distributed copies of its policy papers on poverty and other Summit issues, monitored the official deliberations, and worked collaboratively with other NGOs. The Chair of the ICSW Summit Working Group, Julian Disney, reported success:

> *"ICSW widely circulated about a dozen policy papers and proposals for inclusion in the Summit agreements and we are pleased that many of our recommendations are reflected in the final documents"*

After the Summit, the organization has continued to participate in the activities of the Commission on Social Development and to monitor progress on the commitments agreed at the Summit. In 1997, ICSW signed a Memorandum of Understanding with UNDP to ensure closer cooperation on matters related to civil society, poverty eradication and social development. ICSW has continued to represent issues of social welfare and social development at numerous international meetings, including the World Economic Forum, the International Labor Conference, WHO, and the UN Commission for Social Development.

More recently, ICSW has been critical of the narrow definition of poverty expressed in the Millennium Development Goals (MDGs) and called for inclusion of the ideas expressed in the Summit Commitments. ICSW identifies employment as an important component of the fight against poverty, yet employment is neglected in the MDGs. The emphasis of the 2007 Social Development Commission UN meeting is on decent work for all, a theme actively supported by the ICSW.

ICSW makes its contribution through research and dissemination of information, exchange through conferences, and development of policy recommendations based on its research and linkages with local and national organizations.

ICSW experienced leadership difficulties early in the 21st century, when the elected President was harassed and jailed in his home country of Bangladesh. This coincided with a time when the organization was also without a permanentExecutive Director. Nonetheless, programs have continued. Global conferences were held in Malaysia in 2004 and in Brazil in 2006, with more than 1000 participants from 44 countries. A four-year plan for ongoing programs was adopted in 2004.

Regional activities have intensified as ICSW carries out its goal of "strengthening civil society in all parts of the world" (p. 2). Initiatives included efforts in Central and West Africa and the Black Sea area. In Europe, work at the European Regional Conference emphasized a "European Social Model" to promote balanced social and economic progress, equal rights, and solidarity.

11.3.3. Membership

There are several different membership categories. National Committees of ICSW are country level bodies that represent non-governmental organizations in the social welfare/social development field. There are currently national committees in 32 countries that are members. In addition, ICSW has International Member Organizations—global and/or regional organizations that support ICSW goals; and a number of members classified as Other Organizations who can affiliate within regions; and finally, Government Associates.

11.3.4. Challenges

The disruption caused by the arrest of the President of the ICSW in 2000 was described above and obviously posed a serious challenge to the organization. But, the ICSW has recovered and is actively pursuing an ambitious program. In 2004, ICSW adopted a 4-year global program with seven areas of work. These are: social welfare and social development; networking; communicating with stakeholders; global advocacy on "socially responsible global governance"; regional co-operation; North-South partnerships; and South-South policy dialogue.

A challenge is the lack of strong national committees in some countries. According to the Executive Director,

> *"the emphasis of ICSW's current global programme is to strengthen national umbrella organizations in the South. This is fundamental to achieving our goal of influencing governments to take seriously the road to reducing poverty in their countries and their regions"*

While establishing strong and sustainable national civil society organizations in the Global South may be particularly difficult, the problem also exists in industrialized countries. The United States, for example, no longer has a strong national committee and its participation in the ICSW has diminished.

11.4. Areas of Conflict and Collaboration

The three organizations have many common areas of interest and activity. All hold conferences, support the journal *International Social Work,* maintain consultative status at the UN and aim to represent social work and social welfare at a number of NGO committees and activities. All emphasize the value of international exchange and communication and all have continued to seek ways to strengthen their organizational activities and contributions between and beyond conferences. IFSW and IASSW have successfully collaborated in and sponsored an annual Social Work Day at the UN in New York. In 2007, a World Social Work Day has been launched by the IFSW and creates additional opportunities for collaborative efforts.

At some points in history, there have been conflicts within and between the organizations, especially over the status of apartheid South Africa. At other times, disagreements or barriers to collaboration have been more mundane—disputes over conference locations, expenditures, or hurt feelings over failure to give due credit to contributions of the collaborating partners. While mundane, these can be difficult to resolve and can pose obstacles to successfully speaking with a unified voice on the international scene.

Perhaps more distressing have been the consequences caused when the organizations and their leaders have been persecuted for their advocacy work. Over the course of history, each organization has suffered. In the 1930's, the President of IASSW was pressured by her own German colleagues to resign as she was deemed unfit by the Nazis. More recently, the elected President of the ICSW. Qazi Faruque Ahmed of Bangladesh, was unable to fulfill his duties as he and his local organization were persecuted by the government of the country. While pressure from ICSW members and others resulted in his release from jail, Dr. Ahmed was unable to serve as President due to this situation. Oppression and conflict have taken their toll many times, including the early 1990's when the head of the IFSW's Kuwait Association of Social Workers was captured and later killed by the Iraqi invaders. As a profession concerned with social justice and human rights, social work is seen as highly political and therefore as a threat to oppressive governments. This continues to put social work organizations and their leaders in danger.

The commonality of goals and program priorities suggest that the organizations can share successful strategies and lessons learned. All three organizations are working to strengthen the regions, identify and encourage growth of membership in Africa, Asia and Latin America, and promote increased communication and networking. Now that the organizations have agreed to co-host their world conferences, more emphasis on sharing information and successes can begin.

11.5. Future Considerations

Collaboration is important, but often challenging. IFSW, IASSW and ICSW have agreed that future world conferences will be jointly planned and held. There is a danger that a large and commonly planned conference will result in loss of important elements of each organization's needs and program. It is interesting to note that in a 1996 analysis of the contributions of the journal *International Social Work,* John Lawrence called for ICSW to discontinue its co-sponsorship to allow social work to strengthen and unify its voice. In a combined effort, care must be taken to ensure that attention to both education and practice is ensured and that participants who are not social workers are not overwhelmed by professional considerations.

In spite of dangers, collaboration is more important than ever. There is a compelling need to speak with a unified voice in order to represent social work and social welfare concerns more forcefully on the world scene. The impacts of neoliberalism and globalization have only intensified the need for progress on issues of poverty and human rights.

References

Statham, Daphne (2004). *Managing Front Line Practice in Social Work*. New York, NY: Jessica Kingsley Publishers.

The IMF's Approach to Promoting Good Governance and Combating Corruption — A Guide. International Monetary Fund. 20 June 2005.

Thyer, Bruce A. and John S. Wodarski. 2007. *Social Work in Mental Health: An Evidence-Based Approach*. Hoboken, NJ: John Wiley.

Turner, Francis J. 2005. *Canadian Encyclopedia of Social Work*. Waterloo, ON: Wilfrid Laurier University Press.

Wittenberg, Renee. 2003. *Opportunities in Social Work Careers* (Revised ed.). Chicago, IL: VGM Career Books.

12

Code of Ethics for Social Work

More than any other career, social work is committed to enabling people to cope with the challenges they face, and bringing some security and reassurance into their lives. Good intentions are the starting point. But as a social worker you back this up with professional expertise and knowledge acquired through intensive education and training, and practical experience.

Your focus is on improving people's well-being. They may be parents and children who are struggling in the face of deprivation, disability or abusive behaviour. Young adults who find it hard to handle the pressures of living independently. Clients of mental health services or people coping with disabilities. Those with drugs or alcohol problems, or managing with HIV/AIDS. Older people whose independence is waning, or refugees and homeless people. Your job will be, as far as possible, to support your clients in taking control of their lives. Success isn't guaranteed but when it happens the job satisfaction is considerable.

There are many other plus points. You'll have a professional qualification in a sector that's continuing to grow, offering the chance to work in a range of different settings. There will be scope to manage your own time and make your own decisions, whilst receiving professional support and training to develop your skills. Your career prospects will depend on what you want to achieve, as well as your dedication and capabilities. Good pension and other benefits are attached to most positions.

But it always comes back to people. If you're interested in people this is a career that you will always find stimulating.

12.1. Duties of Social Workers

You form partnerships with people, helping them to assess and interpret the problems they face and support them in finding solutions.

Sometimes you provide the service yourself – as advocate, guide, hand-holder, or critical friend. In other cases you will co-ordinate carefully planned 'packages of care' that involve doctors, nurses, lawyers, police, court officials and probation workers among others. Whatever the situation, you need to know how the law works, what services are available and how to use them to best advantage on behalf of your client.

You will also have certain legal powers and duties to protect people who cannot protect themselves, for example clients of mental health services who may be a danger to themselves or to others, or a child who is at risk of abuse.

This is a job carrying real responsibility. It requires initiative and commitment, as well as professional knowledge. You have to be quick-thinking, thorough, persuasive, non-discriminatory, non-judgemental -above all, committed to seeing things through. You will also need to develop skills to manage resources and budgets.

It sounds demanding and it can be, but you do not work in isolation. Mostly, you work in a team and have close support.

During your career you are likely to work with two broad client groups:

i) Children, families and young people

ii) Adults

As with children and young people, working with adults could take you into a wide variety of situations. You may be supporting someone though a period of temporary difficulty, or care may be needed over a much longer term.

Many cases will throw up complex problems requiring close co-ordination with other services. This is known as care management and would involve a formal assessment and written care plan agreed by everyone involved. In other cases, you may be the direct provider of support – in effect you are the service. Some cases involve both approaches.

There are many specialist areas. For example, residential care work enables clients of mental health services or people with a learning disability to live more independent lives in homes or hostels within the community. You help residents with their personal and social skills, and provide practical guidance on budgeting and benefits. You might also be looking at service provision, ensuring that what is offered to people from different ethnic backgrounds reflects their cultural or religious needs.

12.2. Mission of Social Work Profession

The primary mission of the social work profession is to enhance human well-being and help meet the basic human needs of all people, with particular attention to the needs and empowerment of people who are vulnerable, oppressed, and living in poverty. A historic and defining feature of social work is the profession's focus on individual well-being in a social context and the well-being of society. Fundamental to social work is attention to the environmental forces that create, contribute to, and address problems in living.

Social workers promote social justice and social change with and on behalf of clients. 'Clients' is used inclusively to refer to individuals, families, groups, organisations, and communities. Social workers are sensitive to cultural and ethnic diversity and strive to end discrimination, oppression, poverty, and other forms of social injustice.

These activities may be in the form of direct practice, community organising, supervision, consultation, administration, advocacy, social and political action, policy development and implementation, education, and research and evaluation. Social workers seek to enhance the capacity of people to address their own needs. Social workers also seek to promote the responsiveness of organisations, communities, and other social institutions to individuals' needs and social problems.

The mission of the social work profession is rooted in a set of core values. These core values, embraced by social workers throughout the profession's history, are the foundation of social work's unique purpose and perspective:

— Service
— Social justice
— Dignity and worth of the person
— Importance of human relationships
— Integrity
— Competence

This constellation of core values reflects what is unique to the social work profession. Core values, and the principles that flow from them, must be balanced within the context and complexity of the human experience.

12.3. Purpose of NASW's Ethics

Professional ethics are at the core of social work. The profession has an obligation to articulate its basic values, ethical principles, and ethical standards. The *National Association of Social Workers* (NASW) Code of Ethics sets forth these values, principles, and standards to guide social workers' conduct. The Code is relevant to all social workers and social work students, regardless of their professional functions, the settings in which they work, or the populations they serve.

The NASW Code of Ethics serves six purposes:

— The Code identifies core values on which social work's mission is based.
— The Code summarises broad ethical principles that reflect the professions' core values and establishes a set of specific ethical standards that should be used to guide social work practice.
— The Code is designed to help social workers identify relevant considerations when professional obligations conflict or ethical uncertainties arise.
— The Code provides ethical standards to which tne general public can hold the social work profession accountable.
— The Code socialises practitioners new to the field to social work's mission, values, ethical principles, and ethical standards.

— The Code articulates standards that the social work profession itself can use to assess whether social workers have engaged in unethical conduct. NASW has formal procedures to adjudicate ethics complaints filed against its members. In subscribing to this Code, social workers are required to cooperate in its implementation, participate in NASW adjudication proceedings, and abide by any NASW disciplinary rulings or sanctions based on it.

The Code offers a set of values, principles, and standards to guide decision making and conduct when ethical issues arise. It does not provide a set of rules that prescribe how social workers should act in all situations. Specific applications of the Code must take into account the context in which it is being considered and the possibility of conflicts among the Code's values, principles, and standards. Ethical responsibilities flow from all human relationships, from the personal and familial to the social and professional.

Further, the NASW Code of Ethics does not specify which values, principles, and standards are most important and ought to outweigh others in instances when they conflict. Reasonable differences of opinion can and do exist among social workers with respect to the ways in which values, ethical principles, and ethical standards should be rank ordered when they conflict. Ethical decision making in a given situation must apply the informed judgment of the individual social worker and should also consider how the issues would be judged in a peer review process where the ethical standards of the profession would be applied.

Ethical decision making is a process. There are many instances in social work where simple answers are not available to resolve complex ethical issues. Social workers should take into consideration all the values, principles, and standards in this Code that are relevant to any situation in which ethical judgment is warranted. Social workers' decisions and actions should be consistent with the spirit as well as the letter of this Code.

In addition to this Code, there are many other sources of information about ethical thinking that may be useful. Social workers should consider ethical theory and principles generally, social work theory and research, laws, regulations, agency policies, and other relevant codes of ethics, recognising that among codes of ethics social workers should consider the NASW Code of Ethics as their primary source. Social workers also should be aware of the impact on ethical decision making of their clients' and their own personal values and cultural and religious beliefs and practices. They should be aware of any conflicts between personal and professional values and deal with them responsibly. For additional guidance social workers should consult the relevant literature on professional ethics and ethical decision making and seek appropriate consultation when faced with ethical dilemmas. This may involve consultation with an agency based or social work organisation's ethics committee, a regulatory body, knowledgeable colleagues, supervisors, or legal counsel.

Instances may arise when social workers' ethical obligations conflict with agency policies or relevant laws or regulations. When such conflicts occur, social workers must make a responsible effort to resolve the conflict in a manner that is consistent with the values, principles, and standards expressed in this Code. If a reasonable resolution of the conflict does not appear possible, social workers should seek proper consultation before making a decision.

The NASW Code of Ethics is to be used by NASW and by individuals, agencies, organisations, and bodies (such as licensing and regulatory boards, professional liability insurance providers, courts of law, agency boards of directors, government agencies, and other professional groups) that choose to adopt it or use it as a frame of reference. Violation of standards in this Code does not automatically imply legal liability or violation of the law. Such determination can only be made in the context of legal and judicial proceedings. Alleged violations of the Code would be subject to a peer review process. Such processes are generally separate from legal or administrative procedures and insulated from legal review or proceedings to allow the profession to counsel and discipline its own members.

A code of ethics cannot guarantee ethical behavior. Moreover, a code of ethics cannot resolve all ethical issues or disputes or capture the richness and complexity involved in striving to make responsible choices within a moral community. Rather, a code of ethics sets forth values, ethical principles, and ethical standards to which professionals aspire and by which their actions can be judged. Social workers' ethical behavior should result from their personal commitment to engage in ethical practice. The NASW Code of Ethics reflects the commitment of all social workers to uphold the profession's values and to act ethically. Principles and standards must be applied by individuals of good character who discern moral questions and, in good faith, seek to make reliable ethical judgments.

12.4. Ethical Principles

The following broad ethical principles are based on social work's core values of service, social justice, dignity and worth of the person, importance of human relationships, integrity, and competence. These principles set forth ideals to which all social workers should aspire:

1. Service
2. Social Justice
3. Dignity and Worth of the Person
4. Importance of Human Relationships
5. Integrity
6. Competence

12.4.1. Service

Social Workers' Primary Goal is to Help People in Need and to Address Social Problems: Social workers elevate service to others above self-interest. Social workers draw on their knowledge, values, and skills to help people in need and to address social problems. Social workers are encouraged to volunteer some portion of their professional skills with no expectation of significant financial return (pro bono service).

12.4.2. Social Justice

Social Workers Challenge Social Injustice. Social workers pursue social change, particularly with and on behalf of vulnerable and oppressed individuals and groups of people. Social workers' social change efforts are focused primarily on issues of poverty, unemployment, discrimination, and other forms of social injustice. These activities seek to promote sensitivity to and knowledge about oppression and cultural and ethnic diversity. Social workers strive to ensure access to needed information, services, and resources; equality of opportunity; and meaningful participation in decision making for all people.

12.4.3. Dignity and Worth of the Person

Social workers respect the inherent dignity and worth of the person. Social workers treat each person in a caring and respectful fashion, mindful of individual differences and cultural and ethnic diversity. Social workers promote clients' socially responsible self-determination. Social workers seek to enhance clients' capacity and opportunity to change and to address their own needs. Social workers are cognisant of their dual responsibility to clients and to the broader society. They seek to resolve conflicts between clients' interests and the broader society's interests in a socially responsible manner consistent with the values, ethical principles, and ethical standards of the profession.

12.4.4. Importance of Human Relationships

Social Workers Recognise the Central Importance of Human Relationships. Social workers understand that relationships between and among people are an important vehicle for change. Social workers engage people as partners in the helping process. Social workers seek to strengthen relationships among people in a purposeful effort to promote, restore, maintain, and enhance the well-being of individuals, families, social groups, organisations, and communities.

12.4.5. Integrity

Social Workers Behave in a Trustworthy Manner. Social workers are continually aware of the profession's mission, values, ethical principles, and ethical standards and practice in a manner consistent with them. Social workers act honestly and responsibly and promote ethical practices on the part of the organisations with which they are affiliated.

12.4.6. Competence

Social Workers Practice within their Areas of Competence and

Develop and Enhance their Professional Expertise. Social workers continually strive to increase their professional knowledge and skills and to apply them in practice. Social workers should aspire to contribute to the knowledge base of the profession.

12.5. Ethical Standards

The following ethical standards are relevant to the professional activities of all social workers. These standards concern:

1. Social workers' ethical responsibilities to clients,
    - 1.1 Commitment to Clients
    - 1.2 Self-Determination
    - 1.3 Informed Consent
    - 1.4 Competence
    - 1.5 Cultural Competence and Social Diversity
    - 1.6 Conflicts of Interest
    - 1.7 Privacy and Confidentiality: Clients
    - 1.8 Access to Records
    - 1.9 Sexual Relationships
    - 1.10 Physical Contact
    - 1.11 Sexual Harassment
    - 1.12 Derogatory Language
    - 1.13 Payment for Services
    - 1.14 Clients Who Lack Decision-Making Capacity
    - 1.15 Interruption of Services
    - 1.16 Termination of Services
2. Social workers' ethical responsibilities to colleagues,
    - 2.1 Respect
    - 2.2 Confidentiality: Colleagues
    - 2.3 Interdisciplinary Collaboration
    - 2.4 Disputes Involving Colleagues
    - 2.5 Consultation
    - 2.6 Referral for Services

- 2.7 Sexual Relationships
- 2.8 Sexual Harassment
- 2.9 Impairment of Colleagues
- 2.10 Incompetence of Colleagues
- 2.11 Unethical Conduct of Colleagues

3. Social workers' ethical responsibilities in practice settings,
   - 3.1 Supervision and Consultation
   - 3.2 Education and Training
   - 3.3 Performance Evaluation
   - 3.4 Client Records
   - 3.5 Billing
   - 3.6 Client Transfer
   - 3.7 Administration
   - 3.8 Continuing Education and Staff Development
   - 3.9 Commitments to Employers
   - 3.10 Labor-Management Disputes
4. Social workers' ethical responsibilities as professionals,
   - 4.1 Competence
   - 4.2 Discrimination
   - 4.3 Private Conduct
   - 4.4 Dishonesty, Fraud, and Deception
   - 4.5 Impairment
   - 4.6 Misrepresentation
   - 4.7 Solicitations
   - 4.8 Acknowledging Credit
5. Social workers' ethical responsibilities to the social work profession,
   - 5.1 Integrity of the Profession
   - 5.2 Evaluation and Research
6. Social workers' ethical responsibilities to the broader society.
   - 6.1 Social Welfare

6.2 Public Participation

6.3 Public Emergencies

6.4 Social and Political Action

Some of the standards that follow are enforceable guidelines for professional conduct, and some are aspirational. The extent to which each standard is enforceable is a matter of professional judgment to be exercised by those responsible for reviewing alleged violations of ethical standards.

12.6. Social Workers' Ethical Responsibilities to Clients

1 Commitment to Clients
2 Self-Determination
3 Informed Consent
4 Competence
5 Cultural Competence and Social Diversity
6 Conflicts of Interest
7 Privacy and Confidentiality: Clients
8 Access to Records
9 Sexual Relationships
10 Physical Contact
11 Sexual Harassment
12 Derogatory Language
13 Payment for Services
14 Clients Who Lack Decision-Making Capacity
15 Interruption of Services
16 Termination of Services

12.6.1. Commitment to Clients

Social workers' primary responsibility is to promote the well-being of clients. In general, clients' interests are primary. However, social workers' responsibility to the larger society or specific legal obligations may on limited occasions supersede the loyalty owed clients, and clients should be so advised. (Examples include when a social worker is required by law to report that a client has abused a child or has threatened to harm self or others.)

12.6.2. Self-Determination

Social workers respect and promote the right of clients to self-determination and assist clients in their efforts to identify and clarify their goals. Social workers may limit clients' right to self-determination when, in the social workers' professional judgment, clients' actions or potential actions pose a serious, foreseeable, and imminent risk to themselves or others.

12.6.3. Informed Consent

(a) Social workers should provide services to clients only in the context of a professional relationship based, when appropriate, on valid informed consent. Social workers should use clear and understandable language to inform clients of the purpose of the services, risks related to the services, limits to services because of the requirements of a third-party payer, relevant costs, reasonable alternatives, clients' right to refuse or withdraw consent, and the time frame covered by the consent. Social workers should provide clients with an opportunity to ask questions.

(b) In instances when clients are not literate or have difficulty understanding the primary language used in the practice setting, social workers should take steps to ensure clients' comprehension. This may include providing clients with a detailed verbal explanation or arranging for a qualified interpreter or translator whenever possible.

(c) In instances when clients lack the capacity to provide informed consent, social workers should protect clients' interests by seeking permission from an appropriate third party, informing clients consistent with the clients' level of understanding. In such instances social workers should seek to ensure that the third party acts in a manner consistent with clients' wishes and interests. Social workers should take reasonable steps to enhance such clients' ability to give informed consent.

(d) In instances when clients are receiving services involuntarily, social workers should provide information about the nature and extent of services and about the extent of clients' right to refuse service.

(e) Social workers who provide services via electronic media (such as computer, telephone, radio, and television) should inform recipients of the limitations and risks associated with such services.

(f) Social workers should obtain clients' informed consent before audiotaping or videotaping clients or permitting observation of services to clients by a third party.

12.6.4. Competence

(a) Social workers should provide services and represent themselves as competent only within the boundaries of their education, training, license, certification, consultation received, supervised experience, or other relevant professional experience.

(b) Social workers should provide services in substantive areas or use intervention techniques or approaches that are new to them only after engaging in appropriate study, training, consultation, and supervision from people who are competent in those interventions or techniques.

(c) When generally recognised standards do not exist with respect to an emerging area of practice, social workers should exercise careful judgment and take responsible steps (including appropriate education, research, training, consultation, and supervision) to ensure the competence of their work and to protect clients from harm.

12.6.5. Cultural Competence and Social Diversity

(a) Social workers should understand culture and its function in human behavior and society, recognising the strengths that exist in all cultures.

(b) Social workers should have a knowledge base of their clients' cultures and be able to demonstrate competence in the provision of services that are sensitive to clients' culture and to differences among people and cultural groups.

(c) Social workers should obtain education about and seek to understand the nature of social diversity and oppression with respect to race, ethnicity, national origin, color, sex, sexual orientation, age, marital status, political belief, religion and mental or physical disability.

12.6.6. Conflicts of Interest

(a) Social workers should be alert to and avoid conflicts of interest that interfere with the exercise of professional discretion and impartial judgment. Social workers should inform clients when a real or potential conflict of interest arises and take reasonable steps to resolve the issue in a manner that makes the clients' interests primary and protects clients' interests to the greatest extent possible. Occasionally, protecting clients' interests may require termination of the professional relationship with proper referral of the client.

(b) Social workers should not take unfair advantage of any professional relationship or exploit others to further their personal, political or business interests.

(c) Social workers should not engage in dual or multiple relationships with clients or former clients in which there is a risk of exploitation or potential harm to the client. In instances when dual or multiple relationships are unavoidable, social workers should take steps to protect clients and are responsible for setting clear, appropriate, and culturally sensitive boundaries. (Dual or multiple relationships occur when social workers relate to clients in more than one relationship, whether professional, social, or business. Dual or multiple relationships can occur simultaneously or consecutively.)

(d) When social workers provide services to two or more people who have a relationship with each other (for example, couples, family members), social workers should clarify with all parties which individuals will be considered clients and the nature of social workers' professional obligations to the various individuals who are receiving services. Social workers who anticipate a conflict of interest among the individuals receiving services or who anticipate having to perform in potentially conflicting roles (for example, when a social worker is asked to testify in a child custody dispute or divorce proceedings involving clients) should clarify their role with the parties involved and take appropriate action to minimise any conflict of interest.

12.6.7. Privacy and Confidentiality

(a) Social workers should respect clients' right to privacy. Social workers should not solicit private information from clients unless it is essential to providing service or conducting social work evaluation or research. Once private information is shared, standards of confidentiality apply.

(b) Social workers may disclose confidential information when appropriate with a valid consent from a client, or a person legally authorised to consent on behalf of a client.

(c) Social workers should protect the confidentiality of all information obtained in the course of professional service, except for compelling professional reasons. The general expectation that social workers will keep information confidential does not apply when disclosure is necessary to prevent serious, foreseeable, and imminent harm to a client or other identifiable person or when laws or regulations require disclosure without a client's consent. In all instances, social workers should disclose the least amount of confidential information necessary to achieve the desired purpose; only information that is directly relevant to the purpose for which the disclosure is made should be revealed.

(d) Social workers should inform clients, to the extent possible, about the disclosure of confidential information and, when feasible, before the disclosure is made. This applies whether social workers disclose confidential information as a result of a legal requirement or based on client consent.

(e) Social workers should discuss with clients and other interested parties the nature of confidentiality and limitations of clients' right to confidentiality. Social workers should review with clients circumstances where confidential information may be requested and where disclosure of confidential information may be legally required. This discussion should occur as soon as possible in the social worker-client relationship and as needed throughout the course of the relationship.

(f) When social workers provide counselling services to families, couples, or groups, individual's right to confidentiality and obligation to preserve the confidentiality of information shared by others. Social workers should inform participants in family, couples, or group counselling that

(a) Social workers cannot guarantee that all participants will honour such agreements social workers should seek agreement among the parties involved concerning each.

(g) Social workers should inform clients involved in family, couples, marital, or group counselling of the social worker's, employer's, and agency's policy concerning the social worker's disclosure of confidential information among the parties involved in the counselling.

(h) Social workers should not disclose confidential information to third-party payers unless clients have authorised such disclosure.

(i) Social workers should not discuss confidential information in any setting unless privacy can be ensured. Social workers should not discuss confidential information in public or semipublic areas such as hallways, waiting rooms, elevators, and restaurants.

(j) Social workers should protect the confidentiality of clients during legal proceedings to the extent permitted by law. When a court of law or other legally authorised body orders social workers to disclose confidential or privileged information without a client's consent and such disclosure could cause harm to the client, social workers should request that the court withdraw the order or limit the order as narrowly as possible or maintain the records under seal, unavailable for public inspection.

(k) Social workers should protect the confidentiality of clients when responding to requests from members of the media.

(l) Social workers should protect the confidentiality of clients' written and electronic records and other sensitive information. Social workers should take reasonable steps to ensure that clients' records are stored in a secure location and that clients' records are not available to others who are not authorised to have access.

(m) Social workers should take precautions to ensure and maintain the confidentiality of information transmitted to other parties through the use of computers, electronic mail, facsimile machines, telephones and telephone answering machines, and other electronic or computer technology. Disclosure of identifying information should be avoided whenever possible.

(n) Social workers should transfer or dispose of clients' records in a manner that protects clients' confidentiality and is consistent with state statutes governing records and social work licensure.

(o) Social workers should take reasonable precautions to protect client confidentiality in the event of the social worker's termination of practice, incapacitation, or death.

(p) Social workers should not disclose identifying information when discussing clients for teaching or training purposes unless the client has consented to disclosure of confidential information.

(q) Social workers should not disclose identifying information when discussing clients with consultants unless the client has consented to disclosure of confidential information or there is a compelling need for such disclosure.

(r) Social workers should protect the confidentiality of deceased clients consistent with the preceding standards.

12.6.8. Access to Records

(a) Social workers should provide clients with reasonable access to records concerning the clients. Social workers who are concerned that clients' access to their records could cause serious misunderstanding or harm to the client should provide assistance in interpreting the records and consultation with the client regarding the records. Social workers should limit clients' access to their records, or portions of their records, only in exceptional circumstances when there is compelling evidence that such access would cause serious harm to the client. Both clients' requests and the rationale for withholding some or all of the record should be documented in clients' files.

(b) When providing clients with access to their records, social workers should take steps to protect the confidentiality of other individuals identified or discussed in such records.

12.6.9. Sexual Relationships

(a) Social workers should under no circumstances engage in sexual activities or sexual contact with current clients, whether such contact is consensual or forced.

(b) Social workers should not engage in sexual activities or sexual contact with clients' relatives or other individuals with whom clients maintain a close personal relationship when there is a risk of exploitation or potential harm to the client. Sexual activity or sexual contact with clients' relatives or other individuals with whom clients maintain a personal relationship has the potential to be harmful to the client and may make it difficult for the social worker and client to maintain appropriate professional boundaries. Social workers — not their clients, their clients' relatives, or other individuals with whom the client maintains a personal relationship — assume the full burden for setting clear, appropriate, and culturally sensitive boundaries.

(c) Social workers should not engage in sexual activities or sexual contact with former clients because of the potential for harm to the client. If social workers engage in conduct contrary to this prohibition or claim that an exception to this prohibition is warranted because of extraordinary circumstances, it is social workers — not their clients — who assume the full burden of demonstrating that the former client has not been exploited, coerced, or manipulated, intentionally or unintentionally.

(d) Social workers should not provide clinical services to individuals with whom they have had a prior sexual relationship. Providing clinical services to a former sexual partner has the potential to be harmful to the individual and is likely to make it difficult for the social worker and individual to maintain appropriate professional boundaries.

12.6.10. Physical Contact

Social workers should not engage in physical contact with clients when there is a possibility of psychological harm to the client as a result of the contact (such as cradling or caressing clients). Social workers who engage in appropriate physical contact with clients are responsible for setting clear, appropriate, and culturally sensitive boundaries that govern such physical contact.

12.6.11. Sexual Harassment

Social workers should not sexually harass clients. Sexual harassment includes advances, sexual solicitation, requests for sexual favors, and other verbal or physical conduct of a sexual nature.

12.6.12. Derogatory Language

Social workers should not use derogatory language in their written or verbal communications to or about clients. Social workers should use accurate and respectful language in all communications to and about clients.

12.6.13. Payment for Services

(a) When setting fees, social workers should ensure that the fees are fair, reasonable, and commensurate with the service performed. Consideration should be given to the client's ability to pay.

(b) Social workers should avoid accepting goods or services from clients as payment for professional services. Bartering arrangements, particularly involving services, create the potential for conflicts of interest, exploitation, and inappropriate boundaries in social workers' relationships with clients. Social workers should explore and may participate in bartering only in very limited circumstances when it can be demonstrated that such arrangements are an accepted practice among professionals in the local community, considered to be essential for the provision of services, negotiated without coercion, and entered into at the client's initiative and with the client's informed consent. Social workers who accept goods or services from clients as payment for professional services assume the full burden of demonstrating that this arrangement will not be detrimental to the client or the professional relationship.

(c) Social workers should not solicit a private fee or other remuneration for providing services to clients who are entitled to such available services through the social workers' employer or agency.

12.6.14. Clients Who Lack Decision-Making Capacity

When social workers act on behalf of clients who lack the capacity to make informed decisions, social workers should take reasonable steps to safeguard the interests and rights of those clients.

12.6.15. Interruption of Services

Social workers should make reasonable efforts to ensure continuity of services in the event that services are interrupted by factors such as unavailability, relocation, illness, disability, or death.

12.6.16. Termination of Services

(a) Social workers should terminate services to clients, and professional relationships with them, when such services and relationships are no longer required or no longer serve the clients' needs or interests.

(b) Social workers should take reasonable steps to avoid abandoning clients who are still in need of services. Social workers should withdraw services precipitously only under unusual circumstances, giving careful consideration to all factors in the situation and taking care to minimise possible adverse effects. Social workers should assist in making appropriate arrangements for continuation of services when necessary.

(c) Social workers in fee-for-service settings may terminate services to clients who are not paying an overdue balance if the financial contractual arrangements have been made clear to the client, if the client does not pose an imminent danger to self or others, and if the clinical and other consequences of the current nonpayment have been addressed and discussed with the client.

(d) Social workers should not terminate services to pursue a social, financial, or sexual relationship with a client.

(e) Social workers who anticipate the termination or interruption of services to clients should notify clients promptly and seek the transfer, referral, or continuation of services in relation to the clients' needs and preferences.

(f) Social workers who are leaving an employment setting should inform clients of all available options for the continuation of service and their benefits and risks.

12.7. Social Workers' Ethical Responsibilities to Colleagues

1 Respect
2 Confidentiality: Colleagues
3 Interdisciplinary Collaboration
4 Disputes Involving Colleagues
5 Consultation
6 Referral for Services
7 Sexual Relationships
8 Sexual Harassment
9 Impairment of Colleagues
10 Incompetence of Colleagues
11 Unethical Conduct of Colleagues

12.7.1. Respect

(a) Social workers should treat colleagues with respect and represent accurately and fairly the qualifications, views, and obligations of colleagues.

(b) Social workers should avoid unwarranted negative criticism of colleagues with clients or with other professionals. Unwarranted negative criticism may include demeaning comments that refer to colleagues' level of competence or to individuals' attributes such as race, ethnicity, national origin, color, age, religion, sex, sexual orientation, marital status, political belief, mental or physical disability, or any other preference, personal characteristic, or status.

(c) Social workers should cooperate with social work colleagues and with colleagues of other professions when it serves the well-being of clients.

12.7.2. Confidentiality with Colleagues

Social workers should respect confidential information shared by colleagues in the course of their professional relationships and transactions. Social workers should ensure that such colleagues understand social workers' obligation to respect confidentiality and any exceptions related to it.

12.7.3. Interdisciplinary Collaboration

(a) Social workers who are members of an interdisciplinary team should participate in and contribute to decisions that affect the well-being of clients by drawing on the perspectives, values, and experiences of the social work profession. Professional and ethical obligations of the interdisciplinary team as a whole and of its individual members should be clearly established.

(b) Social workers for whom a team decision raises ethical concerns should attempt to resolve the disagreement through appropriate channels. If the disagreement cannot be resolved social workers should pursue other avenues to address their concerns, consistent with client well-being.

12.7.4. Disputes Involving Colleagues

(a) Social workers should not take advantage of a dispute between a colleague and employer to obtain a position or otherwise advance the social workers own interests.

(b) Social workers should not exploit clients in disputes with colleagues or engage clients in any inappropriate discussion of conflicts between social workers and their colleagues.

12.7.5. Consultation

(a) Social workers should seek advice and counsel of colleagues whenever such consultation is in the best interests of clients.

(b) Social workers should keep informed of colleagues' areas of expertise and competencies. Social workers should seek consultation only from colleagues who have demonstrated knowledge, and competence related to the subject of the consultation.

(c) When consulting with colleagues about clients, social workers should disclose the least amount of information to achieve the purposes of the consultation.

12.7.6. Referral for Services

(a) Social workers should refer clients to other professionals when other professionals' specialised knowledge or expertise is needed to serve clients fully, or when social workers believe they are not being effective or making reasonable progress with clients and additional service is required.

(b) Social workers who refer clients to other professionals should take appropriate steps to facilitate an orderly transfer of responsibility. Social workers who refer clients to other professionals should disclose, with clients' consent, all pertinent information to the new service providers.

(c) Social workers are prohibited from giving or receiving payment for a referral when no professional service is provided by the referring social worker.

12.7.7. Sexual Relationships

(a) Social workers who function as supervisors or educators should not engage in sexual activities or contact with current supervisees, students, trainees, or other colleagues over whom they exercise professional authority.

(b) Social workers should avoid engaging in sexual relationships with colleagues where there is potential for a conflict of interest. Social workers who become involved in, or anticipate becoming involved in, a sexual relationship with a colleague have a duty to transfer professional responsibilities, when necessary, in order to avoid a conflict of interest.

12.7.8. Sexual Harassment

Social workers should not engage in any sexual harassment of supervisees, students, trainees, or colleagues. Sexual harassment includes sexual advances, sexual solicitation, requests for sexual favors, and other verbal or physical conduct of a sexual nature.

12.7.9. Impairment of Colleagues

(a) Social workers who have direct knowledge of a social work colleague's impairment which is due to personal problems, psychosocial distress, substance abuse, or mental health difficulties, and which interferes with practice effectiveness, should consult with that colleague and assist the colleague in taking remedial action.

(b) Social workers who believe that a social work colleague's impairment interferes with practice effectiveness and that the colleague has not taken adequate steps to address the impairment should take action through appropriate channels established by employers, agencies, NASW, licensing and regulatory bodies, and other professional organisations.

12.7.10. Incompetence of Colleagues

(a) Social workers who have direct knowledge of a social work colleague's incompetence should consult with that colleague when feasible and assist the colleague in taking remedial action.

(b) Social workers who believe that a social work colleague is incompetent and has not taken adequate steps to address the incompetence should take action through appropriate channels established by employers, agencies, NASW, licensing and regulatory bodies, and other professional organisations.

12.7.11. Unethical Conduct of Colleagues

(a) Social workers should take adequate measures to discourage, prevent, expose, and correct the unethical conduct of colleagues.

(b) Social workers should be knowledgeable about established policies and procedures for handling concerns about colleagues' unethical behavior. Social workers should be familiar with national, state, and local procedures for handling ethics complaints. These include policies and procedures created by NASW, licensing and regulatory bodies, employers, agencies, and other professional organisations.

(c) Social workers who believe that a colleague has acted unethically should seek resolution by discussing their concerns with the colleague when feasible and when such discussion is likely to be productive.

(d) When necessary, social workers who believe that a colleague has acted unethically should take action through appropriate formal channels (such as contacting a state licensing board or regulatory body, an NASW committee on inquiry, or other professional ethics committees).

(e) Social workers should defend and assist colleagues who are unjustly charged with unethical conduct.

12.8. Social Workers' Ethical Responsibilities in Practice Settings

1 Supervision and Consultation
2 Education and Training
3 Performance Evaluation
4 Client Records
5 Billing
6 Client Transfer
7 Administration
8 Continuing Education and Staff Development
9 Commitments to Employers
10 Labor-Management Disputes

12.8.1. Supervision and Consultation

(a) Social workers who provide supervision or consultation should have the necessary knowledge and skill to supervise or consult appropriately and should do so only within their areas of knowledge and competence.

(b) Social workers who provide supervision or consultation are responsible for setting clear, appropriate, and culturally sensitive boundaries.

(c) Social workers should not engage in any dual or multiple relationships with supervisees in which there is a risk of exploitation of or potential harm to the supervisee.

(d) Social workers who provide supervision should evaluate supervisees' performance in a manner that is fair and respectful.

12.8.2. Education and Training

(a) Social workers who function as educators, field instructors for students, or trainers should provide instruction only within their areas of knowledge and competence and should provide instruction based on the most current information and knowledge available in the profession.

(b) Social workers who function as educators or field instructors for students should evaluate students' performance in a manner that is fair and respectful.

(c) Social workers who function as educators or field instructors for students should take reasonable steps to ensure that clients are routinely informed when services are being provided by students.

(d) Social workers who function as educators or field instructors for students should not engage in any dual or multiple relationships with students in which there is a risk of exploitation or potential harm to the student. Social work educators and field instructors are responsible for setting clear, appropriate, and culturally sensitive boundaries.

12.8.3. Performance Evaluation

Social workers who have responsibility for evaluating the performance of others should fulfil such responsibility in a fair and considerate manner and on the basis of clearly stated criteria.

12.8.4. Client Records

(a) Social workers should take reasonable steps to ensure that documentation in records is accurate and reflects the services provided.

(b) Social workers should include sufficient and timely documentation in records to facilitate the delivery of services and to ensure continuity of services provided to clients in the future.

(c) Social workers' documentation should protect clients' privacy to the extent that is possible and appropriate and should include only information that is directly relevant to the delivery of services.

(d) Social workers should store records following the termination of service to ensure reasonable future access. Records should be maintained for the number of years required by state statutes or relevant contracts.

12.8.5. Billing

Social workers should establish and maintain billing practices that accurately reflect the nature and extent of services provided, and specifically by whom the service was provided in the practice setting.

12.8.6. Client Transfer

(a) When an individual who is receiving services from another agency or colleague contacts a social worker for services, the social worker should carefully consider the client's needs before agreeing to provide services. In order to minimise possible confusion and conflict, social workers should discuss with potential clients the nature of their current relationship with other service providers and the implications, including possible benefits or risks, of entering into a relationship with a new service provider.

(b) If a new client has been served by another agency or colleague, social workers should discuss whether consultation with the previous service provider is in the client's best interest.

12.8.7. Administration

(a) Social work administrators should advocate within and outside their agencies for adequate resources to meet clients' needs.

(b) Social workers should advocate for resource allocation procedures that are open and fair. When not all clients' needs can be met, an allocation procedure should be developed that is nondiscriminatory and based on appropriate and consistently applied principles.

(c) Social workers who are administrators should take reasonable steps to ensure that adequate agency or organisational resources are available to provide appropriate staff supervision.

(d) Social work administrators should take reasonable steps to ensure that the working environment for which they are responsible is consistent with and encourages compliance with the NASW Code of Ethics. Social work administrators should take reasonable steps to eliminate any conditions in their organisations that violate, interfere with, or discourage compliance with the Code.

12.8.9. Continuing Education and Staff Development

Social work administrators and supervisors should take reasonable steps to provide or arrange for continuing education and staff development for all staff for whom they are responsible. Continuing education and staff development should address current knowledge and emerging developments related to social work practice and ethics.

12.8.10. Commitments to Employers

(a) Social workers generally should adhere to commitments made to employers and employing organisations.

(b) Social workers should work to improve employing agencies' policies and procedures, and the efficiency and effectiveness of their services.

(c) Social workers should take reasonable steps to ensure that employers are aware of social workers' ethical obligations as set forth in the NASW Code of Ethics and of the implications of those obligations for social work practice.

(d) Social workers should not allow an employing organisation's policies, procedures, regulations, or administrative orders to interfere with their ethical practice of social work. Social workers should take reasonable steps to ensure that their employing organisations' practices are consistent with the NASW Code of Ethics.

(e) Social workers should act to prevent and eliminate discrimination in the employing organisation's work assignments and in its employment policies and practices.

(f) Social workers should accept employment or arrange student field placements only in organisations that exercise fair personnel practices.

(g) Social workers should be diligent stewards of the resources of their employing organisations, wisely conserving funds where appropriate and never misappropriating funds for unintended purposes.

12.8.11. Labor-Management Disputes

(a) Social workers may engage in organised action, including the formation of and participation in labor unions, to improve services to clients and working conditions.

(b) The actions of social workers who are involved in labor-management disputes, job actions, or labor strikes should be guided by the profession's values, ethical principles, and ethical standards. Reasonable differences of opinion exist among social workers concerning their primary obligation as professionals during an actual or threatened labor strike or job action. Social workers should carefully examine relevant issues and their possible impact on clients before deciding on a course of action.

12.8.12. Social Workers' Ethical Responsibilities as Professionals

1 Competence
2 Discrimination
3 Private Conduct
4 Dishonesty, Fraud, and Deception
5 Impairment
6 Misrepresentation
7 Solicitations
8 Acknowledging Credit

12.8.13. Competence

(a) Social workers should accept responsibility or employment only on the basis of existing competence or the intention to acquire the necessary competence.

(b) Social workers should strive to become and remain proficient in professional practice and the performance of professional functions. Social workers should critically examine, and keep current with, emerging knowledge relevant to social work. Social workers should routinely review professional literature and participate in continuing education relevant to social work practice and social work ethics.

(c) Social workers should base practice on recognised knowledge, including empirically based knowledge, relevant to social work and social work ethics.

12.8.14. Discrimination

Social workers should not practice, condone, facilitate, or collaborate with any form of discrimination on the basis of race, ethnicity, national origin, color, age, religion, sex, sexual orientation, marital status, political belief, or mental or physical disability.

12.8.15. Private Conduct

Social workers should not permit their private conduct to interfere with their ability to fulfil their professional responsibilities.

12.8.16. Dishonesty, Fraud, and Deception

Social workers should not participate in, condone, or be associated with dishonesty, fraud, or deception.

12.8.17. Impairment

(a) Social workers should not allow their own personal problems, psychosocial distress, legal problems, substance abuse, or mental health difficulties to interfere with their professional judgment and performance or to jeopardise the best interests of people for whom they have a professional responsibility.

(b) Social workers whose personal problems, psychosocial distress, legal problems, substance abuse, or mental health difficulties interfere with their professional judgment and performance should immediately seek consultation and take appropriate remedial action by seeking professional help, making adjustments in workload, terminating practice, or taking any other steps necessary to protect clients and others.

12.8.18. Misrepresentation

(a) Social workers should make clear distinctions between statements made and actions engaged in as a private individual and as a representative of the social work profession, a professional social work organisation, or of the social worker's employing agency.

(b) Social workers who speak on behalf of professional social work organisations should accurately represent the official and authorised positions of the organisation.

(c) Social workers should ensure that their representations to clients, agencies, and the public of professional qualifications, credentials, education, competence, affiliations, services provided, or results to be achieved are accurate. Social workers should claim only those relevant professional credentials they actually possess and take steps to correct any inaccuracies or misrepresentations of their credentials by others.

12.8.19. Solicitations

(a) Social workers should not engage in uninvited solicitation of potential clients who, because of their circumstances, are vulnerable to undue influence, manipulation or coercion.

(b) Social workers should not engage in solicitation of testimonial endorsements (including solicitation of consent to use a client's prior statement as a testimonial endorsement) from current clients or other persons who, because of their particular circumstances are vulnerable to undue influence.

12.8.20. Acknowledging Credit

(a) Social workers should take responsibility and credit, including authorship credit, only for work they have actually performed and to which they have contributed.

(b) Social workers should honestly acknowledge the work of and the contributions made by others.

12.9. Social Workers' Ethical Responsibilities to the Social Work Profession

1 Integrity of the Profession

2 Evaluation and Research

12.9.1. Integrity of the Profession

(a) Social workers should work toward the maintenance and promotion of high standards of practice.

(b) Social workers should uphold and advance the values, ethics, knowledge, and mission of the profession. Social workers should protect, enhance, and improve the integrity of the profession through appropriate study and research, active discussion, and responsible criticism of the profession.

(c) Social workers should contribute time and professional expertise to activities that promote respect for the value, integrity, and competence of the social work profession. These activities may include teaching, research, consultations, service, legislative testimony, presentations in the community and participation in their professional organisations.

(d) Social workers should contribute to the knowledge base of social work and share with colleagues their knowledge related to practice, research, and ethics. Social workers should seek to contribute to the profession's literature and to share their knowledge at professional meetings and conferences.

(e) Social workers should act to prevent the unauthorised and unqualified practice of social work.

12.9.2. Evaluation and Research

(a) Social workers should monitor and evaluate policies, the implementation of programs, and practice interventions.

(b) Social workers should promote and facilitate evaluation and research in order to contribute to the development of knowledge.

(c) Social workers should critically examine and keep current with emerging knowledge relevant to social work and fully utilise evaluation and research evidence in their professional practice.

(d) Social workers engaged in evaluation or research should consider carefully possible consequences and should follow guidelines developed for the protection of evaluation and research participants. Appropriate institutional review boards should be consulted.

(e) Social workers engaged in evaluation or research should obtain voluntary and written informed consent from participants, when appropriate, without any implied or actual deprivation or penalty for refusal to participate; without undue inducement to participate; and with due regard for participants' well-being, privacy, and dignity. Informed consent should include information about the nature, extent, and duration of the participation requested and disclosure of the risks and benefits of participation in the research.

(f) When evaluation or research participants are incapable of giving informed consent, social workers should provide an appropriate explanation to the participants, obtain the participants' assent to the extent they are able, and obtain written consent from an appropriate proxy.

(g) Social workers should never design or conduct evaluation or research that does not use consent procedures, such as certain forms of naturalistic observation and archival research, unless rigorous and responsible review of the research has found it to be justified because of its prospective scientific, educational, or applied value and unless equally effective alternative procedures that do not involve waiver of consent are not feasible.

(h) Social workers should inform participants of their right to withdraw from evaluation and research at any time without penalty.

(i) Social workers should take appropriate steps to ensure that participants in evaluation and research have access to appropriate supportive services.

(j) Social workers engaged in evaluation or research should protect participants from unwarranted physical or mental distress, harm, danger, or deprivation.

(k) Social workers engaged in the evaluation of services should discuss collected information only for professional purposes and only with people professionally concerned with this information.

(l) Social workers engaged in evaluation or research should ensure the anonymity or confidentiality of participants and of the data obtained from them. Social workers should inform participants of any limits of confidentiality, the measures that will be taken to ensure confidentiality, and when any records containing research data will be destroyed.

(m) Social workers who report evaluation and research results should protect participants' confidentiality by omitting identifying information unless proper consent has been obtained authorising disclosure.

(n) Social workers should report evaluation and research findings accurately. They should not fabricate or falsify results and should take steps to correct any errors later found in published data using standard publication methods.

(o) Social workers engaged in evaluation or research should be alert to and avoid conflicts of interest and dual relationships with participants, should inform participants when a real or potential conflict of interest arises, and should take steps to resolve the issue in a manner that makes participants' interests primary.

(p) Social workers should educate themselves, their students, and their colleagues about responsible research practices.

12.10. Social Workers' Ethical Responsibilities to the Broader Society

1 Social Welfare

2 Public Participation

3 Public Emergencies

4 Social and Political Action

12.10.1. Social Welfare

Social workers should promote the general welfare of society, from local to global levels, and the development of people, their communities, and their environments. Social workers should advocate for living conditions conducive to the fulfillment of basic human needs and should promote social, economic, political, and cultural values and institutions that are compatible with the realisation of social justice.

12.10.2. Public Participation

Social workers should facilitate informed participation by the public in shaping social policies and institutions.

12.10.3. Public Emergencies

Social workers should provide appropriate professional services in public emergencies, to the greatest extent possible.

12.10.4. Social and Political Action

(a) Social workers should engage in social and political action that seeks to ensure that all people have equal access to the resources, employment, services, and opportunities they require to meet their basic human needs and to develop fully. Social workers should be aware of the impact of the political arena on practice and should advocate for changes in policy and legislation to improve social conditions in order to meet basic human needs and promote social justice.

(b) Social workers should act to expand choice and opportunity for all persons, with special regard for vulnerable, disadvantaged, oppressed, and exploited persons and groups.

(c) Social workers should promote conditions that encourage respect for cultural and social diversity within the United States and globally. Social workers should promote policies and practices that demonstrate respect for difference, support the expansion of cultural knowledge and resources, advocate for programs and institutions that demonstrate cultural competence, and promote policies that safeguard the rights of and confirm equity and social justice for all people.

(d) Social workers should act to prevent and eliminate domination of, exploitation of, and discrimination against any person, group, or class on the basis of race, ethnicity, national origin, color, sex, sexual orientation, age, marital status, political belief, religion, or mental or physical disability.

12.11. Texas State Board of Social Worker Examiners Code of Ethics

(a) A social worker must observe and comply with the code of conduct and standards of practice set forth in this subchapter. Any violation of the code of conduct or standards of practice will constitute unethical conduct or conduct that discredits or tends to discredit the profession of social work and is grounds for disciplinary action.

(1) A social worker shall not refuse to do or refuse to perform any act or service for which the person is licensed solely on the basis of a client's age, gender, race, color, religion, national origin, disability, sexual orientation, or political affiliation.

(2) A social worker shall truthfully report or present her or his services, professional credentials and qualifications to clients or potential clients.

(3) A social worker shall only offer those services that are within his or her professional competency.

(4) A social worker shall strive to maintain and improve her or his professional knowledge, skills and abilities.

(5) A social worker shall base all services on an assessment, evaluation or diagnosis of the client.

(6) A social worker shall provide the client with a clear description of services, schedules, fees and billing at the initiation of services.

(7) A social worker shall safeguard the client's rights to confidentiality within the limits of the law.

(8) A social worker shall be responsible for setting and maintaining professional boundaries.

(9) A social worker shall not have sexual contact with a client or a person who has been a client.

(10) A social worker shall refrain from providing service while impaired due to the social worker's physical or mental health or the use of medication, drugs or alcohol.

(11) A social worker shall not exploit his or her position of trust with a client or former client.

(12) A social worker shall evaluate a client's progress on a continuing basis to guide service delivery and will make use of supervision and consultation as indicated by the client's needs.

(13) A social worker shall refer a client for those services that the social worker is unable to meet and terminate service to a client when continued service is no longer in the client's best interest.

References

Butler, Ian and Gwenda Roberts 2004. *Social Work with Children and Families: Getting into Practice* (2nd ed.). London, England; New York, NY: Jessica Kingsley Publishers.

Davies, Martin. 2002. *The Blackwell Companion of Social Work* (2nd ed.). Oxford, UK; Malden, MA: Blackwell.

Greene, Roberta R. 2008. *Social Work with the Aged and their Families* (3rd ed.). New Brunswick, NJ: Transaction Publishers.

Grinnell, Richard M. and Yvonne A Unrau . 2008. *Social Work Research and Evaluation: Foundations of Evidence-Based Practice* (8th ed.). Oxford, UK; New York, NY: Oxford University Press.

Mizrahi, Terry and Larry E. Davis . 2008. *Encyclopedia of Social Work* (20th ed.). Washington, DC; Oxford, UK; New York, NY: NASW Press and Oxford University Press.

Paugam, Serge. 1998. "Poverty and Social Exclusion: A Sociological View." Pp. 41–62 in *The Future of European Welfare*, edited by Martin Rhodes and Yves Meny.

Bibliography

Alba, R. D., and V. Nee. 2003. *Remaking the American mainstream: Assimilation and contemporary immigration.* Cambridge, Mass.: Harvard University Press.

Bailey R & Brake M (eds). 1975. *Radical Social Work,* Edward Arnold, London.

Banks, C. A. M. 2004. *Improving multicultural education: Lessons from the intergroup education movement.* New York: Teachers College Press.

Bennett, S., Maton, K., & Kervin. L. 2008. The 'digital natives' debate: A critical review of the evidence. *British Journal of Educational Technology, 39*(5), 775-786.

Brill N. 1995. *Working with People: The Helping Process,* 5th edn, Longman, White Plains.

Burlington, VT, Ashgate. Dominelli L, Bernard WT, eds. 2003. *Broadening horizons: international exchanges in social work.* Burlington, VT, Ashgate.

Butler, Ian and Gwenda Roberts 2004. *Social Work with Children and Families: Getting into Practice* (2nd ed.). London, England; New York, NY: Jessica Kingsley Publishers.

Camilleri P. 1999. Social work and its search for meaning: Theories, narratives and practices, In Pease B & Fook J (eds), *Transforming Social Work Practice,* Allen & Unwin, Sydney, pp. 25-39.

Cauble, A., & Thurston, L. 2000. Effects of interactive multimedia training on knowledge, attitudes, and self-efficacy of Social Work students. *Research on Social Work Practice 10*(4), 428-437.

Center for Multicultural Education, University of Washington. Castles, S. 2004. Migration, citizenship, and education. In *Diversity and citizenship education: Global perspectives*, ed. J. A.

Cheers B. 1998, *Welfare Bushed: Social Care in Rural Australia,* Ashgate, Aldershot.

Clark C. 2006. *Moral Character in Social Work,* Toronto.

Cooper, L. 2001. Using online technology to teach controversial issues. *New Technology in the Human Services 13*(3 & 4), 11-21.

Davies, Martin. 2002. *The Blackwell Companion of Social Work* (2nd ed.). Oxford, UK; Malden, MA: Blackwell.

Dean R . 2001. The myth of cross cultural competence. *Families in Society* 82(6): 623–630.

DH (Departmant of Health). 2000. *A quality strategy for social care*, London: DH.

Dominelli L, Bernard WT, eds. *Broadening horisons: international exchanges in social work.*

Dominelli, L. 2000. 'International Comparisons in Social Work', in: Pierce, R and Weinstein, J (eds.): *Innovative Education and Training for Care Professionals.* London, Jessica Kingsley.

Dominelli, L. 2002. *Anti-Oppressive Social Work Theory and Practice.* London, Palgrave.

Egan, G. 2002. *The skilled helper: A systematic approach to effective helping,* Pacific Grove, CA: Brookes/Cole.

Essex Coalition of Disabled People and Scope. 2002. The *good practice guide for support workers and personal assistants working with disabled people with communication impairments*, London: Scope (www.scope.org.uk).

Faux, T., & Hughes, C. 2000. A comparison of using the Internet versus lectures to teach Social Work history. *Research on Social Work Practice 10*(4), 454-467.

Germain, C., & Gitterman, A. 1995. Ecological perspective. In R. L. Edwards (Ed.-in-Chief), *Encyclopedia of social work* (19th ed., Vol. 1, pp. 816–824). Washington, DC: NASW Press.

Gillborn, D. 1990. *Race, ethnicity, and education: Teaching and learning in multi-ethnic schools.* London: Unwin Hyman/Routledge.

Goldstein H. 1986. Education for social work practice: a cognitive, cross-cultural approach. *International Social Work* 29(2): 149–164.

Gordon, M. M. 1964. *Assimilation in American life: The role of race, religion, and national origins.* New York: Oxford University Press.

Greene, Roberta R. 2008. *Social Work with the Aged and their Families* (3rd ed.). New Brunswick, NJ: Transaction Publishers.

Grinnell, Richard M. and Yvonne A Unrau . 2008. *Social Work Research and Evaluation: Foundations of Evidence-Based Practice* (8th ed.). Oxford, UK; New York, NY: Oxford University Press.

GSCC (General Social Care Council). 2002. *Codes of practice for employers and social workers*, London: GSCC.

Gutmann, A. 1987. *Democratic education.* Princeton, N.J.: Princeton University Press.

Guttmacher, A., & Collins, F. S. 2002. Genomic medicine: A primer. *New England Journal of Medicine, 347,* 1512–1513.

Harding. T. and Beresford, P. 1996. *The standards we expect: What service users and carers want from social services workers*, London: NISW.

Healy LM. 2001. *International social work: professional action in an interdependent world.* New York, Oxford University Press.

Jenkins, J., et al. 2001. Recommendations of core competencies in genetics essential for all health professionals. *Genetics in Medicine, 3,* 155–159.

Kendall, K. 2000. *Social Work Education: Its Origins in Europe*. Alexandria, VA.: Council on Social Work Education.

Lapham, E. V., Kosma, C., Weiss, J. O., Benkendorf, J. L., & Wilson, M. A. 2000. The gap between practice and genetics education of health professionals: HuGEM survey results. *Genetics in Medicine, 2,* 226–231.

Levin, E. 2003. *Involving service users and carers in the social work degree*, London: SCIE.

Lorenz, W. 1994. *Social Work in a Changing Europe*. London, Routledge.

Lyons, K. 1999. *International Social Work.* Aldershot, Ashgate.

Mizrahi, Terry and Larry E. Davis . 2008. *Encyclopedia of Social Work* (20th ed.). Washington, DC; Oxford, UK; New York, NY: NASW Press and Oxford University Press.

Morris, J. 2002 *A lot to say: A guide for social workers, personal advisors and others working with disabled children and young people with communication impairments*, London: Scope.

Munn P & Munn T. 2003. Social work: Moving forward, *Rural Social Work,* 13 (1), 22-34.

NASW Press. Coates J. 2003. *Ecology and social work: toward a new paradigm*. Halifax, Fernwood Press.

National Association of Social Workers. 1999. *Code of ethics of the National Association of Social Workers*. Washington, DC: Author

National Association of Social Workers. 2003. Genetics. In *Social work speaks: National Association of Social Workers Policy Statements, 2003–2006* (6th ed., pp. 161–166). Washington, DC: Author.

Parker S, Fook J & Pease B. 1999, Empowerment: The modernist social work concept *par excellence,* In Pease B & Fook J (eds), *Transforming Social Work Practice: Postmodern Critical Perspectives,* Allen & Unwin, St Leonards, pp. 150-157.

Paugam, Serge. 1998. "Poverty and Social Exclusion: A Sociological View." Pp. 41–62 in *The Future of European Welfare*, edited by Martin Rhodes and Yves Meny.

Razak, N. 2003. *Perils and Possibilities: Complicating the Understandings of Racism, Imperialism and Nationalism in International Socicl Work.* PhD-Thesis. Adelaide, Australia, Flinders University.

Razak, N. 2003. *Perils and Possibilities: Complicating the Understandings of Racism, Imperialism and Nationalism in International Social Work.* PhD-Thesis. Adelaide, Australia, Flinders University.

Rojek C, Peacock G & Collins S. 1998, *Social Work and Received Ideas,* Routledge, London.

Rosenthal H. 2005, The deprofessionalisation of social workers, *AASW National Bulletin,* 16 (1), 15.

Schon D. 1983, *The Reflective Practitioner: How Professionals Think in Action,* Basic Books, New York.

Seden J. 1999. *Counselling Skills in Social Work Practice,* Open University Press, Buckingham.

Shulman L. 1991. *Interactional Social Work Practice,* FE Peacock Publishers, Itasca.

Simpkin M. 1983, *Trapped Within Welfare: Surviving Social Work,* Macmillan, London.

Statham, Daphne (2004). *Managing Front Line Practice in Social Work.* New York, NY: Jessica Kingsley Publishers.

The IMF's Approach to Promoting Good Governance and Combating Corruption — A Guide. International Monetary Fund. 20 June 2005.

Thompson N. 2001), *Anti-discriminatory Practice,* 3rd edn. Palgrave, Basingstoke.

Thyer, Bruce A. and John S. Wodarski. 2007. *Social Work in Mental Health: An Evidence-Based Approach.* Hoboken, NJ: John Wiley.

TOPSS. 2002. *The national occupational standards for social work,* Leeds: TOPSS.

Trevithick P. 2000), *Social Work Skills: A Practice Handbook,* Open University Press, Buckingham.

Turner, Francis J. 2005. *Canadian Encyclopedia of Social Work.* Waterloo, ON: Wilfrid Laurier University Press.

Weiss, J. O., Bernhardt, B. A., & Paul, N. W. (Eds.). 1984. *Genetic disorders and birth defects in families and society: Toward interdisciplinary understanding* (Birth Defect Original Article Series, Vol. 20, No. 4). New York: March of Dimes.

Wittenberg, Renee. 2003. *Opportunities in Social Work Careers* (Revised ed.). Chicago, IL: VGM Career Books.

Zeitlinger. Freire, P. 1997. *Pedagogy of the oppressed*, 20th anniv. ed., trans. M. B. Ramos. New York: Continuum.

Index